MANAGING
SALES
for
BUSINESS
GROWTH

MANAGING SALES for BUSINESS GROWTH

Robert J. Calvin

amacom
American Management Association

This publication is designed to provide accurate and authoritative information in regard to the subject matter covered. It is sold with the understanding that the publisher is not engaged in rendering legal, accounting, or other professional service. If legal advice or other expert assistance is required, the services of a competent professional person should be sought.

Library of Congress Cataloging-in-Publication Data

Calvin, Robert J.
    Managing sales for business growth / Robert J. Calvin.
        p.   cm.
    Includes index.
    ISBN 0-8144-5021-0
    1. Sales management. I. Title.
    HF5438.4.C338   1991   91-53050
    658.8'1—dc20   CIP

Printing number

10 9 8 7 6 5 4 3 2 1

In memory of my father:
Joseph K. Calvin

To my wife and in-house editor,
Jane,
for her support and assistance.

Contents

Preface

Good sales management properly applied is the least expensive, most accessible means for you to beat your competition, increase your profits, and grow. A smaller business may not have the financial resources of its larger competitors, but it does have equal access to the same sales management techniques. As this book shows, it costs little if anything more to properly hire, train, compensate, motivate, and evaluate salespeople. Effective time and territory management, forecasting, planning, budgeting, and good communication and control need cost no more than performing these same functions poorly. *Managing Sales for Business Growth* explains how—through the proper application of these techniques plus the use of computers for sales force automation and a well organized export program—you can maximize your company's revenues.

Since your success depends on the success of your salespeople, hiring the right people is of the greatest importance. Chapter 1 describes proven sources to use in your search for good people and presents essential interviewing skills for identifying top producers. You will learn about inexpensive techniques for effectively training and testing salespeople in product, customer, and competitor knowledge and selling skills in Chapter 2, which also discusses the do's and don'ts of field training.

If your compensation program does not reward positive action and produce superior results, you'll want to refer to Chapter 3; it shows you how to use various combinations of salary, commission, and bonus to accomplish these goals. Chapter 4 presents easy-to-understand programs for realigning territory boundaries and increasing the percent of a salesperson's time actually spent with customers. A constant concern for every sales manager is the unmotivated sales force. In Chapter 5 you will encounter nonmonetary motivational techniques, including sales contests, that not only satisfy salespeople's need for recognition, achievement, usefulness, and belonging, but also improve their results. You will learn how to deal with both the superstar with the super-ego and the ex-star who has hit the complacency plateau.

Chapters 6 and 7 zero in on various aspects of communication: how to make sales meetings more productive and why we often communicate better with customers than our salespeople. You will learn how to use sales forecasts, budgets, and sales plans in Chapter 8. The effective use of performance appraisals in motivating, controlling, and communicating with your sales force is covered in Chapter 9. In Chapter 10 I stress the importance of using computers to automate your sales and sales management functions; in the 1990s it may very well be the only way you can compete. And, finally, the benefits of exporting, and the operational aspects of beginning or refining an export program, are covered in Chapter 11.

Managing Sales for Business Growth blends sales management theory and practice into an action-oriented guide for success. I've made an attempt to fill chapters with useful, concrete information and real-life examples that emphasize a smaller business' most important resource, people. You will find step-by-step detail on practical, inexpensive, and proven techniques for solving your sales management problems. The book focuses on organizations where one person performs most sales management tasks.

I have spent the last twenty years dividing my time between buying, managing, building, and selling smaller businesses, doing consulting work for larger companies, and teaching. I have learned from my mistakes as a small-business owner, from the successful experiences of my larger clients, and from the input of my students. This book represents the best ideas from all these worlds.

I wish to acknowledge the contributions made to this book by a number of other individuals: Richard J. Thain, Associate Dean Graduate School of Business, University of Chicago, who helped organize the subject matter; Andrea Pedolsky, my editor, who gave the book focus; my daughters, Amy and Susan, who displayed great understanding; and my parents, Joseph and Pauline Calvin, whose encouragement never faltered.

1

Hiring Salespeople

Hiring effective salespeople is your most important responsibility as the sales manager of a small but growing business. Training, compensation, motivation, and supervision applied to weak salespeople produces mediocre results at best. In a small but growing business your most valuable resources are not machines but people. Because a small business employs a small sales force, each person's performance has crucial importance.

In spite of this, most small-business sales managers possess minimal knowledge, experience, or aptitude for hiring effective salespeople. Cast the play correctly, and directing it becomes much simpler. There is no actor-proof play; there is no salesperson-proof product/service. This chapter suggests inexpensive techniques for successfully hiring salespeople, regardless of the product or service your company offers. Basically, successful hiring requires writing a job description and a candidate profile, then using appropriate sources for recruiting, and finally screening candidates skillfully.

Because you hire only occasionally, you have few opportunities to practice the techniques and acquire the skills. How many times have you said "I hired the wrong salesperson"? How often have you had to live with below-average results because you did?

In 1980 a new venture introduced an appealing long-distance telephone service with the potential to reduce customer direct dialing costs by 40 percent. Basically the user dialed into Watts-, MCI-, or SPC-leased lines, then dialed a customer charge code, and finally dialed the desired area code and local number. There were no connection costs or minimums. Salespeople sold the service by phone from various U.S. locations.

The company's management became concerned when its new salespeople opened only a few accounts and half the new hires quit within

1

ninety days. Management had recruited by running newspaper ads in targeted cities, then interviewing and hiring by phone any salespeople who responded. This hiring procedure allowed the company to expand its sales force quickly and inexpensively, but it did not produce positive sales results. The company had not outlined the type of person it wanted or employed an effective method of finding or screening applicants. It had not even bothered to meet applicants face to face. Later, by using the techniques described in this chapter (and this book), it obtained a productive sales organization that helped make this small company very prosperous. In the mid-1980s it sold out to a larger telecommunications company for a huge capital gain.

Hiring the wrong salesperson proves expensive because of the loss of potential sales and/or the eventual loss and replacement of the person hired. You can spend several thousand dollars of time and out-of-pocket expense finding, screening, hiring, and training a new salesperson. Losing such a person represents a nonrecoverable, nonproductive cost similar to a bad debt. Small businesses have limited financial and human resources and can ill afford expensive mistakes of this nature.

For a small, growing business to succeed, each salesperson must produce optimum results. A poorly selected salesperson allows competitors to make inroads, which leads to a loss of market share, and eventually he or she must be fired. Firing results in loss of continuity for the sales force and further reduces sales. Competitors target territories and companies with high sales force turnover. Customers must trust the salespeople they deal with, and continually replacing them destroys this confidence. A company with high salesperson turnover gets a bad reputation with customers, prospects, and potential salespeople and of course lowers the morale of its current sales organization. In a small company, sales force turnover can also have a direct impact on unemployment insurance rates.

Annual rates of turnover from resignations, discharges, and retirements generally vary from 15 to 20 percent of a sales force in consumer, industrial, and service industries. Turnover rates go up to 35 percent in instruments and office equipment, to 45 percent in construction, and as high as 100 percent in such door-to-door selling jobs as cable TV and aluminum siding. Industries with turnover below 15 percent include utilities, rubber/plastic, machinery, food products, and electronics. In general, the average length of service for salespeople is five years, and they are most likely to leave after four. Smaller companies achieve lower turnover percentages because there is a more personal relationship between the sales force and management and because their sales forces generally include fewer young people.

Of the people you've hired over the last three years, how many are still with you? How many are you happy with? How much greater do you think sales would be with a better group?

The basic techniques for reducing the risks of a bad hire and for reducing turnover are a realistic job description and candidate profile, contacting appropriate sources for attracting candidates, and skillfully screening and selecting from those who apply.

Job Description

Let's say that with your company's expansion into new territory you are faced with hiring a new salesperson. You cannot expect assistance from others within the organization. Tasks pertaining to sales or marketing are accomplished by you or not at all.

Because every selling job and company are different, you need a written summary of the person's anticipated duties. You can't go shopping until you know what you need. This job description also becomes a tool for sales training and later for evaluating the salesperson's performance. If your company sells milk, beer, soft drinks, bread, fuel oil, or a diaper or cleaning service through route delivery people to consumers, then the selling duties will differ from those involved if it sold Christmas ornaments, hosiery, window shades, lawn mowers, or office furniture through field salespeople to retail outlets. Similarly, if your company sells a refuse recycling service or ethical drugs through "missionary" salespeople, their duties will differ from those of sales representatives selling industrial robots, metal cutting fluids, gears, or nail-making machines to industrial users. Also, selling books, insurance, and advertising to corporations requires different duties and skills than are required for selling cosmetics, brushes, cable TV, a cleaner environment, aluminum siding, and household goods door to door.

Most selling positions can be divided into two major categories: passive order-takers and active order-writers. Passive order-takers sell a presold product, and their main job involves service. This category includes the "inside" customer service person, most retail salespeople, and delivery or route salespeople. Active order-writers must find and influence their customer. This category includes engineers selling a technical product to an industrial user, door-to-door sellers of reference books and cosmetics, sellers of intangibles such as IRA plans, and sellers of apparel to retail stores.

Most small-company managements do not bother with formulating well-thought-out, detailed job descriptions for their salespeople. At best, the job description is generic, inappropriate, or outdated.

Let's assume that the company for which you are sales manager sells expensive high-fashion ladies dresses to specialty stores in major cities. You take a pencil and paper and start writing a job description. The more detailed your job description is, the more likely your search will succeed. You expect your salesperson to be skilled in the following activities:

• *Selling.* The salesperson is expected to make twenty sales calls a week, fifteen to service and sell existing accounts and five cold or follow-up calls to prospect for new accounts. The salesperson must find new prospects without help from you. This involves qualifying accounts by phone and making appointments. Existing customers require servicing for reorders four times a year, and should review the entire line twice a year. The salesperson's objective requires unit sales to increase 10 percent annually. Orders are to be mailed in twice a week. During the busy season, reorders can be taken by phone and faxed to the mill. You want a mix of A, B, and C accounts, which are defined by potential volume. The salesperson sells a mix of products (skirts, slacks, tops, sweaters) at a variety of price points. Prices increase each season and a salesperson is expected to sell those price changes to customers. To accomplish these selling duties fifty-hour weeks and two nights a week away from home are required.

• *Servicing.* Where necessary, the salesperson assists the department manager or store owner with merchandising and displaying the dresses; reacts promptly to customer complaints; and educates the retail sales clerks on the selling points of your merchandise.

• *Community Involvement.* Because most specialty store owners belong to Kiwanis, the Elks, or the Masons, the salesperson is expected to be active in one of these groups.

• *Self-Organization.* You expect salespeople to plan each day and each call, dress neatly, and present a professional image.

• *Company Relations.* You expect salespeople to participate in sales meetings, comply with company policies, and work well with their colleagues.

• *Reporting.* Each Friday the salesperson submits an informative call report for the previous week, a route sheet for the next week, and an expense report. Twice a year, he or she submits a sales forecast, which includes a list of prospective new accounts along with a list of new items the salesperson plans to sell to existing accounts.

• *Administrative Chores.* You expect each salesperson to inform you of any significant competitive changes in the territory and to maintain a comprehensive customer record system, including profile cards. In a small business, your boss, the president, also handles credit and collection. Although the president hardly has time for this important function, present volume does not justify a separate credit manager. Therefore, you expect the salesperson to fill in credit application forms for new customers and to collect past due invoices.

• *Housekeeping.* You expect samples, sales literature, and sales aids to be maintained in mint condition. You expect the salesperson's car to be neat and clean.

Different territories may call for different job descriptions. A new territory you are trying to develop may require more prospecting than a matured territory, where account retention is the primary task.

Try to keep the job description to a page. Review and revise it each year to meet changing market conditions. Figure 1-1 presents a sample job description of the duties of a sales representative in a wholesale food distributing company.

To verify the job description, ask your current salespeople to list their duties/responsibilities, rank them as to importance, and note what percentage of their time is spent on each activity. The results may surprise you. If salespeople find this difficult, you should probably discuss it further or put it on the agenda for a sales meeting.

Candidate Profile

You must now translate the job description into a written candidate profile. The job description lists duties. The candidate profile describes the skills, experience, knowledge, and personal characteristics necessary for performing those duties.

As sales manager of a high-fashion ladies dress company, you want someone who:

1. *Knows the territory,* the customers (their problems and needs), and the buyers because he or she has previously been successful in selling a related line in that territory. Experience in selling a product is preferable to experience selling a service. Experience in cold calls, prospecting, and opening new accounts is essential along with experience in maintaining a large active account base. The person must have good communication skills.

Figure 1-1.   Sample sales representative job description (for a wholesale food distributing company).

List of Anticipated Duties

I. Selling

   A. Make 15 calls a day on proper mix of accounts.
      1. Retention and penetration route calls on present accounts.
      2. Cold calls or follow-up calls on prospects.
      3. Type of accounts to call on: bakeries, restaurants, grocery stores, hotels, in-plant feeders, food service.
      4. Sample and demonstrate daily.
      5. Attend appropriate trade shows.
   B. Sell all products, but concentrate on high margin groups.
      1. Continually learn new product knowledge.
      2. Continually acquire more selling skills.
      3. Keep abreast of competition.
   C. Manage a base of 150 diverse accounts.
      1. Call on each one to four times a month.
      2. Understand each account's problems, needs, people.
      3. When necessary, make emergency deliveries to customers.
      4. Handle service problems for customers.
   D. Meet or exceed sales goals.

II. Time Management

   A. Work a 12-hour day starting at 6:00 A.M.
   B. Work five days a week.
   C. Overnight travel.
   D. Maximize percent of time in front of customer.
   E. Use telephone where possible and necessary.
   F. Make optimum number of calls on the right customers and prospects.

III. Self-Organization

   A. Plan each day.
   B. Plan each call.
   C. Keep sales aids in mint condition.
   D. Dress neatly.
   E. Maintain a neat automobile
   F. Present professional image.

IV. Credit and Collection

    A. Fill out and submit credit form on new accounts.
    B. Collect past due balances.
    C. Collect money in advance on certain orders.

V. Paperwork

    A. Continually update customer prospect profile cards.
    B. Submit orders in a timely, accurate fashion.
    C. Submit daily planners/call reports in a timely, accurate fashion.
    D. Submit lost account report in a timely, accurate fashion.
    E. Submit quarterly sales plans.
        1. Target accounts.
        2. Growth accounts.

VI. Company Relations

    A. Participate in all sales meetings and make presentations at some.
    B. Comply with company policies on orders, credit, deliveries, terms.
    C. Work with and coordinate activities with other company employees in customer service, credit, warehouse, delivery.

In a recent survey of 160 sales managers conducted by TPF&C, 65 percent of the respondents required new salespeople to have both sales and industry experience.*

    2. *Owns a car,* can travel overnight, and lives near your major accounts. If Los Angeles represents most of your California business, hiring a salesperson who resides in San Francisco would obviously be a mistake.

    3. *Is mature and has career ambitions only in selling.* Because you are sales manager with no immediate intentions of leaving, and because there are no regional sales managers, no opportunities for advancement exist within your company for the sales force. A salesperson with ambitions to move into management would only be frustrated and quickly leave such a situation. Small-company management must be realistic about this limitation. Many excellent salespeople, however, are strictly interested in selling and

*From 1989/1990 Sales Compensation Survey, TPF&C, a Towers Perrin Company, Chicago, Ill.

in earning more money through increased sales. If these circumstances don't exist at your firm, you may want to look for someone who is promotable.

4. *Is a self-starter* who will enjoy the freedom, flexibility, self-expression, recognition, personal relationships, and feelings of belonging and usefulness offered by a small organization. Although you train, travel with, and supervise your people, there are not enough hours for you to monitor their everyday routines. You need someone who does not have to be pushed.

In a small, growing company, suggestions from the sales force can actually create satisfying and valuable changes in policy. The sales force often feels it participates in decision making. In a smaller company, each salesperson has met the president and dined with the sales manager. As sales manager, you must attract candidates whose needs for freedom and flexibility and a sense of belonging are greater than their needs for advancement into management.

5. *Has successfully performed under your type of compensation plan.* Your company pays commission, and your most successful salespeople have previously worked for companies that paid commission. The type of compensation system says a great deal about a salesperson's drive and confidence. As discussed in Chapter 3, the salespeople attracted to commission plans are very different from those who work on a salaried basis.

6. *Does not have a college degree.* A person with four years of college most likely would not find this job challenging. To sell industrial equipment often requires an engineering degree. To successfully sell ladies dresses requires intelligence and an ability to think on one's feet, but not a formal college education. Hiring overqualified people creates frustration resulting in high turnover.

In a recent survey of 400 medium-sized companies conducted by the Dartnell Corporation, 15 percent required their salespeople to have a high school education, 54 percent some college, 10 percent a college degree, and 3 percent a postgraduate degree.* By contrast, a recent survey of 160 Fortune 1000 companies conducted by TPF&C found that 75 percent of the companies required their salespeople to have four-year college degrees.†

7. *Does not necessarily know the product.* Except in highly technical industries, product knowledge is easy to obtain. Knowledge of the product or service represents a plus, but not a necessity.

---

*From *Sales Force Compensation, Dartnell's 25th Survey Edition.* Used with permission of the Dartnell Corporation, Chicago, Ill. All rights reserved.
†From Sales Compensation Survey, TPF&C.

Many companies overemphasize product knowledge because it is easier to assess, reduces the amount of training, and looks like a safe bet. Knowledge of the territory and customers together with a successful history selling related products or services, however, should rank much higher on the candidate profile. Whether the candidate has sold a premium product for a premium price is important because experience in minimizing price and emphasizing benefits helps sell this better dress line to better specialty stores.

8. *Displays empathy, enthusiasm, confidence, and drive.* A successful salesperson wins customers through empathy, enthusiasm, and confidence, and is motivated by a strong drive to succeed. These four qualities are probably the most significant personal characteristics to look for in a candidate. You can teach product knowledge and selling skills, but without the appropriate personal characteristics sales results will suffer.

Empathy, which requires a good listener, allows the salesperson to discover customer needs and build up trust. Once these are established, the salesperson can with enthusiasm and confidence present product or service benefits to satisfy these needs.

Successful salespeople possess tremendous drive. They derive satisfaction beyond the monetary rewards from closing a sale. Each selling experience represents a new challenge, and new challenges represent a necessary part of their daily diet. They are compelled to sell, which makes them behave like superstars and prima donnas. Some salespeople are terribly insecure, with a strong need to be liked and admired. Selling and the money derived from it satisfies this need. For whatever reason, financial or psychological or both, a salesperson must be hungry for success.

A legendary salesman became a star performer before the age of 30 for a giant men's shoe manufacturer. He invested his money well, married well, and accumulated a fortune that allowed him to live off his investments, but when his employer reduced the size of his territory, he quit and joined a smaller firm. In five years, he became their top salesman, and in ten years, the highest shoe volume producer in the country.

9. *Has an ego strong enough to withstand constant customer rejection,* and can be a team player when required. The successful salesperson enjoys solving customer problems, dresses neatly and makes a strong first impression, and is persistent, well organized, and honest.

Confirm the validity of your candidate profile by writing an actual profile of your most successful salespeople and then comparing the two.

Does a similarity exist? You can also check the validity of your candidate profile by comparing the future performance of the people you hire with their profile. The idea is to avoid making the same mistake over and over. If you wrote candidate profiles for your present salespeople and then placed them in two piles, the most successful and the least successful, what skills, experience, knowledge, and personal characteristics would each group have in common? Unfortunately very few sales managers do this. Figure 1-2 shows an actual sales candidate profile.

Determining whether a salesperson has the personal characteristics in your candidate profile can be difficult, because it is easy to be fooled by our desires and by clever candidates. The section on interviewing later on in this chapter discusses this in some detail. Look for successful work experience that requires the personal characteristics listed in the candidate profile. Does the candidate's past experience and performance indicate drive, enthusiasm, confidence, honesty, empathy, and that he or she is a team player, good listener, self-starter, people person, and good communicator?

The most unusual candidate profile I have encountered related to hiring a salesperson of precious gems for Central America. The position required a woman who could speak Spanish, English, and Arabic, could identify rare stones at a glance in poor light, was not afraid of carrying large amounts of currency, could handle a firearm and knew self-defense, and could travel one month out of two.

Equal Opportunity Laws

In writing your job description and candidate profile, and during the entire recruiting process, keep in mind that the 1964 Civil Rights Act and extensive legislation since then require that minorities, older people, women, and the handicapped receive a fair and equal opportunity for employment. Each requirement in your job description and candidate profile, and all the questions you ask at an interview, must be justifiable in terms of job performance.

You must be sensitive to the equal employment opportunity (EEO) implications of the questions you ask candidates, and of how you evaluate a candidate's job qualifications. Federal legislation prohibits withholding employment on the basis of race or color, sex, religious affiliation, national origin, age, handicapped status, or veteran status. The law restricts the questions you may ask and the topics you may discuss at an interview and the criteria you may use for selection.

Your objective is to identify people who can do the job. EEO legis-

Figure 1-2. Sample sales representative candidate profile (for a wholesale food distributing company).

I. Skills and Knowledge

  A. Knowledge of territory and customers
  B. Good listener
  C. Ability to use both hard and soft sell
  D. Ability to plan
  E. Ability to learn
  F. Good communicator
  G. Product knowledge

II. Experience

  A. Success in past sales positions
  B. Has sold a premium product/service at a premium price
  C. Has been paid 100% commission
  D. Has dealt with the public
  E. Has worked long hours
  F. Has handled a large diverse customer base
  G. Has done prospecting and made cold calls
  H. Longevity in previous positions

III. Personal Characteristics

  A. Ability to emphathize
  B. Endless need to increase income; high achiever
  C. Hungry, money-motivated; personal financial goals
  D. Determined
  E. Ability to live with rejection and show resilience
  F. Well-organized
  G. Honest, sincere
  H. Confidence and enthusiasm
  I. Aggressive, assertive
  J. Self-starter
  K. Neat, professional appearance
  L. Team player who can function as an individual
  M. Goal-oriented
  N. Optimistic
  O. Ambitious
  P. Creative, innovative
  Q. Persistent
  R. Dependable

lation does not restrict you from any bona fide job-related questions, but when in doubt consult an attorney.

Questions seeking the following information (as well as job descriptions, candidate profiles, and candidate evaluations based on this type of information) are illegal:

- Date of birth
- Maiden name
- Previous married name
- Marital status
- Name of spouse
- Spouse's occupation and length of time on the job
- Spouse's place of employment
- Number of children and their ages
- Arrest record
- Ancestry
- Age
- Sex
- Religion
- National origin (color)
- If child care has been arranged for
- Whether wages are garnished

In the light of equal employment opportunity legislation, it is interesting to note that recent surveys by *Sales & Marketing Magazine* and the Dartnell Corporation indicate that by 1989, women represented 28 percent of the average sales force. This ranged from under 10 percent in the chemical and fabricated metals industries to 40 percent in printing/publishing and 50 percent in communications.★

Sources for Attracting Candidates

Many small companies feel they lack the necessary financial resources to attract the best candidates. Often they merely do not know how or where to look for them.

★Reprinted by permission of *Sales & Marketing Management,* Copyright: Survey of Selling Costs, February 26, 1990; and from *Sales Force Compensation,* the Dartnell Corporation.

> Qualified applicants for sales positions can be found by—
>
> — Advertising in the classified sections of trade media and the local press.
> — Informing customers and employees that you are looking.
> — Contacting desirable applicants at competitors' companies.
> — Networking with vendors and friends and at trade shows.
> — Contacting professional organizations, educational institutions, and armed forces discharge centers.
> — Using employment agencies.

What source or combination of sources you use depends on your job description and candidate profile. Each job search is different, but if in the past one source has produced better results, start with that.

Advertising

Most companies advertise for candidates but complain of high costs and poor results. A small company can ill afford unproductive advertising expense. With financial resources limited, all expenditures must produce results.

A classified ad should produce qualified applicants for you to screen. If a great many unqualified candidates respond, your valuable time is wasted. If no qualified candidates respond, you also lose. Successful advertising for salespeople requires writing the correct kind of copy, then placing it in the appropriate media.

Copy

Your copy should include the company name, address, telephone number, and your name as the person to contact. Ask candidates to write or call you specifically if they feel qualified for the position. Your name humanizes the company and the ad.

Blind ads do not produce qualified applicants. Salespeople hesitate responding to them because they may have been placed by their current employer. Blind ads also cause suspicion: What sort of employer won't divulge its name in an ad? Replacing a current salesperson requires secrecy, but rather than placing an unsuccessful blind ad, I suggest using other sources.

Your ad must contain an honest description of the position. If too much information is given, qualified candidates might find something to discourage them from applying. If you include too little information, unqualified candidates are encouraged to apply. Remember that the ad's objective is not to hire and select the salesperson, but only to produce qualified applicants. You will do the selecting from those who reply.

An honest description of the position states the product or service to be sold, type of selling, territory available, type of customer, what experience is necessary, and amount of overnight travel, if any. I would not include a compensation range, since this generally varies greatly depending on the applicant's ability. I would not mention whether the territory contains established volume or requires pioneering. This information changes quickly, and can best be handled in a personal discussion.

The ad should contain words accurately describing the job's nonmonetary benefits such as "rewarding," "steady," "interesting," "challenging." Choose the words honestly. For example, a route salesperson's work is steady; a door-to-door salesperson's work is challenging.

An ad for the person described in our job description might read:

Challenging Rewarding Opportunity

Apparel Salesperson

Salesperson wanted to sell our line of high-fashion women's dresses to better specialty stores in Southern Florida. Prior related selling experience in the territory desirable.
Occasional overnight travel.

Call or write: Bill Dyer
ABC Company
1110 Sunset Boulevard, Boca Raton, Fla. 33432
(305) 555-0244

Personal interviews will be held in the near future.

Media

Some salespeople read the classified "lines offered" section of trade publications when job searching, but others read the "help wanted" section of their local paper. In certain industries, for example, advertising, apparel, and technical products, trade publications prove especially effective for reaching qualified candidates. Salespeople generally do not read financial publications, so advertising in the *Wall Street Journal* would be wasteful.

There will be one day a week when your trade publication specializes in your market segment or in employment ads. Therefore, you obtain better results by advertising on that day. In the local press for best results, advertise on Sundays, using newspapers with a circulation of more than 100,000. Generally, classified "lines offered" ads in trade publications cost less than "help wanted ads" in local newspapers. Only experience obtained from actual ads can show which media, trade or local, produce the best results for your company.

An effective technique for advertising in the Sunday paper involves asking the applicant to call you that Sunday. This requires your devoting that day to the project, but it produces results. If the ad is run outside your area code, it must specify a toll free number or that collect calls will be accepted.

In addition to the copy already suggested, your Sunday ad should state:

> Don't write, but pick up your phone now and call me, Bill Dyer, at this number. I am the sales manager of ABC, and will be at my telephone between 9 and 5 today. I will tell you about the job opportunity, and you can tell me about your qualifications. I will not ask your name unless you wish to tell me.

The personal aspect of this ad plus the easy opportunity it offers for immediate response produces qualified candidates. Also, it allows people who are currently employed to call without fear that their employer will learn of their interest. Most companies have greater success hiring currently employed salespeople than they do unemployed salespeople.

Certain advertising agencies—Nationwide Advertising Service Inc., Shaker Advertising, Bentley, Barnes, and Lynn (BBL)—specialize in employment ads. In exchange for the 15 percent commission collected from the media, they will advise you on copy and choices of publication.

Informing Customers and Employees

Informing customers and employees represents a very inexpensive way of producing applicants, but it cannot be used when privacy is important.

Often your customers know of an appropriate salesperson who wishes to change employment. As sales manager, you should call customers who could be helpful and explain the job's requirements. Choose customers with whom you have a personal relationship and in whom you have confidence. Otherwise someone might be offended by your request, or just recommend unemployed friends. Tell customers that you are asking their assistance because they will be dealing with your new salesperson.

This approach, asking for help, admits a certain amount of weakness to your customer, but most are flattered. Unless you wish to lose an account, never hire a customer's employee without first asking permission from the employee's supervisor.

One apparel firm has had great success hiring department store buyers who are familiar with its product and market. A metal polishing chemical distributor finds that its best field salespeople were previously manufacturing managers who had used its products. In both cases, the salespeople understood the customer's problems and needs. A firm that distributes bakery supplies to the food-service industry finds that previous customers perform poorly as salespeople. If you hire from customers' employees, be sure that the sales force candidates have the personal characteristics listed in your candidate profile, such as drive, enthusiasm, confidence, empathy, communication, and people skills.

Current employees of your own company often know qualified salespeople who might find the available position attractive. Use a bulletin to inform the sales force and other managers of the job's availability and requirements.

Your sales force probably knows other salespeople, currently employed elsewhere, who might be interested in the position. Salespeople trade stories, successes, problems, and opportunities over coffee and drinks. Similarly, if you know salespeople selling related lines for other companies, ask them for recommendations.

Occasionally, one of your company's employees in a nonselling capacity may be interested. A small refuse removal company lost a key salesperson and informed the staff of the job requirements. The controller recommended one of his accountants who knew the business, enjoyed people, and had trouble distinguishing debits from credits. The accountant transferred to sales, and all lived happily ever after.

Offering a bonus to the employee who finds a successful candidate acts as an incentive. Again be aware, however, that unqualified friends may also be referred.

On the other hand, some firms have had their greatest success hiring field salespeople from within their company. One refuse disposal firm only hires field salespeople from dispatch or operations. A Christmas decoration firm finds that its best field salespeople come from the showroom staff. A bakery supply firm promotes its field sales force from customer service. These people all understand the products/services and generally know the customers. Use whatever works for you, but again be sure the sales force candidates have the personal characteristics you put in your candidate profile. Don't recruit salespeople from operations, the showroom, or customer service unless they have drive, enthusiasm, good communication skills, confidence, can live with rejection, and enjoy people. One advantage of hiring from within is that you already know the candidate's personal characteristics. Salespeople from this background require more training in selling skills but less in product knowledge.

Seeking Salespeople From Competitors

Snatching a salesperson from the competition may look appealing, but this approach is often risky. Make sure you know why the competitor's salesperson wants to leave, or else you may inherit someone else's troubles. He or she may not be performing or may be having personal difficulties. Also, an individual who leaves a competitor may easily leave your company for yet another opportunity. Sometimes customers lose trust in salespeople who one month extol brand X and the next month brand Y. There are salespeople who have worked for almost everyone in an industry, leaving each job just before their employer wised up to their incompetence. In addition, you will have more difficulty changing bad selling habits, because the salesperson recruited from a competitor feels trained already.

On the other hand, a small company should not overlook a good candidate who works for a competitor. Often, mature salespeople leave a competitor because their territory faces reduction or because the competitor desires a younger, less expensive person who does not have large vested interests in a pension plan. Corporate mergers, market changes, new compensation plans, and recessions also make competitors' salespeople receptive to offers. When you're lucky, the right candidate can bring captive customers, no bad habits, good product knowledge, and little need for training.

Networking

Hiring ought to be looked at as a continuing process. You should always be looking for good salespeople. Don't wait until someone leaves. When an impressive vendor sales representative calls on you to sell printing or copy machines, get to know each other. Use trade shows and associations as a way of meeting appropriate candidates. The best interviews occur when a prospect is unaware of your interest and therefore not on guard. You obtain more candid information and opinions. You can learn a great deal by watching people work a trade show or sell you their products or services.

Always talk to qualified candidates who contact you, even when you have no position that needs filling immediately. Keep a file with names, phone numbers, addresses, and current employers for good candidates you have networked. Keep notes on their strengths, weaknesses, and backgrounds, and rank them as to desirability.

Then when you do need to hire, you start with a dozen prescreened qualified candidates. Several of them will probably be interested in the position. Networking and approaching hiring as a continuing process makes your job easier.

A packaged processed-meat company that sells corn beef and pastrami to grocery stores terminates one of its ten salespeople each year. Generally there is one weak salesperson who should be replaced. The sales force is thus constantly upgraded. The garden is weeded. The cream rises. The sales manager knows she must continually look for a new person each year. It is the leading small company in its field.

Contacting Professional Organizations, Schools, and the Armed Forces

These are inexpensive, productive sources of salespeople. Most industries have professional associations, occasionally just for salespeople, which publish lists of available positions for their membership. Many groups have a local chapter in each state or major metropolitan area. Such associations range from the Men's Apparel Clubs in each state to the Industrial Robot Division of the Society of Manufacturing Engineers. Be sure to list your job opening with the appropriate industry club or association.

Many small businesses do not take advantage of the free placement facilities offered by educational institutions. Junior colleges and technical high schools represent fertile ground for recruiting salespeople. Most colleges maintain a service for graduates who later in life wish to change jobs. List your job requirements with the appropriate educational institutions.

A traditional furniture manufacturer arranges to hire its interns every summer from the local junior college. Many of these interns later become permanent salespeople. The junior college has areas of study in interior design and business that fit well with the furniture company's salesperson profile.

Armed forces discharge centers offer placement services that prove effective for some selling jobs. It costs nothing to list your position with the local office. A company selling emission control devices to utilities experiences a high success rate in hiring young discharged military officers as salespeople. Selling a public utility requires understanding the problems of large, complex, slow-moving organizations, and ex-military officers can certainly appreciate these.

Employment Agencies

A capable employment agency earns its fee of 10 percent to 25 percent of a person's first-year compensation, but good agencies dealing with salespeople are scarce. Most agencies dealing with middle-level salespeople lack professionalism. Their main interest is in making a match, but not necessarily a good fit. A good agency can save you time in finding qualified candidates, and your time is money.

If you desire to use an agency, ask colleagues and other sales managers in related fields for references; then check them out. If you engage an agency, choose one you trust, and provide it with all the information available on job and candidate requirements. Ask to meet the person handling your account, establish lines of communication and the amount of your involvement. Be sure you have a written contract stating how the agency charges, whether on the basis of performance or front-end fee, fixed-dollar or percentage. Avoid surprises and fee bargaining once a candidate is hired. Be sure you establish a realistic time frame for performance, for instance, thirty, sixty, or ninety days. When candidates emerge, interview them immediately before they lose interest.

Choose your sources for attracting sales applicants according to how they fit the job and candidate requirements. Then maintain accurate records of the results obtained from each source. You will note a pattern developing. If you put emphasis on the most productive sources, in the future your task will become easier.

Screening and Selecting Those Who Apply

Choosing the best candidate from a qualified group requires not only intuition and insight but also structure and technique. The probability of success can be enhanced and the risk of a bad hire reduced by following certain procedures. Being the sales manager of a small growing company means you must absorb this extra work load on top of the demanding everyday tasks of running a sales force and producing sales. Most likely you receive no assistance from other staff members because they too are spread thin. Because of time limitations, there is a temptation to take shortcuts in the selection process; but shortcuts only increase the risk of failure, forcing you to accept a mediocre salesperson or eventually to seek a new one. Do it right, or do it again.

By using proper sources for candidates, you have obtained possibly thirty applicants. From some you have received résumés, but for others your notes from telephone conversations represent the only written record. The techniques and structure employed in successfully narrowing the field involve (1) preliminary screening of résumés and notes; (2) requesting personal history application forms; (3) preliminary personal interviews; (4) reference checking and background investigations; (5) testing; (6) a second interview for finalists; and (7) a physical exam.

Not every selling position requires all these steps, but as you can see, the process requires considerable time. The more time you make available to contact sources and screen applicants, the higher your probability of success.

To maximize the available time for recruiting, try to anticipate hiring needs. Don't wait for a salesperson to retire before you start looking. Set up a ninety-day program for the hiring process. If you suspect that one of your salespeople may leave, start looking now. Better yet, look at hiring as a continuing process to upgrade the sales force. Never cease networking to find better people. When you do, replace your weak performers. Should a salesperson leave or be terminated, you have a ready supply of qualified candidates.

Preliminary Screening of Résumés and Notes

You begin the screening process by reviewing the résumés received and the notes written from telephone conversations. Half the thirty applicants probably do not have sufficient experience for the position, or have a record of constant job shifting. You write a cordial letter to these people, expressing appreciation for their interest but informing them that their fine backgrounds do not meet the position's requirements. The hiring process represents an opportunity for the company to make friends. Job applicants sometimes become customers, suppliers, politicians, managers, or repeat applicants. I know of many situations where an applicant originally rejected for a selling position was hired years later for another. You should write rejection letters with this in mind, and keep a file for future reference of all résumés and notes.

Requesting Personal History Application Forms

You send the remaining fifteen applicants a letter asking them to fill out and submit the enclosed personal history form. Explain that after you receive the form, the applicant will be called for a personal interview.

The personal history form asks the applicant for the following information: name and address; educational background; employment history (including military) with dates and responsibilities; and outside interests. Keep it simple, and don't ask for unnecessary information. Time represents a valuable resource for you and the applicant. Even if you have received a résumé, each applicant should still submit this form. Often the information is different and not consistent.

If you do not already have this information for your current sales force, ask each salesperson to complete the personal history form. Then rank your salespeople by performance as strong, average, or weak, and analyze each group to determine what background characteristics seem most conducive to success and failure. This knowledge will be helpful in evaluating the applicants' backgrounds.

A small company that sold through telephone solicitation discovered that 70 percent of its most successful salespeople were divorced high school dropouts. Another business that manufactured transformers found that over 75 percent of its most successful salespeople were college dropouts whose hobbies involved citizens band radios. A company that sold sailboats learned that sailors represented their worst sales performers and skiers the best. Many companies discover that their best performers have had previous experience selling a related product or service in their current territory. By using this technique, you may uncover obvious or obscure clues that will assist you in screening applicants. The information is available at no cost.

Preliminary Personal Interviews

Of the fifteen applicants who received your personal history form, let's assume that eight have replied. The other seven have lost interest. Now you begin the art and black magic of interviewing. If applicants live nearby, you can make arrangements for the interview in your office. If the available territory is out of town, interviews should take place at a hotel in that area. Some small companies use telephone interviews to save time and money, and make selections based on these conversations. However appealing this shortcut may appear, you really require a face-to-face interchange to obtain the appropriate hiring information and to develop intuitions.

Interviews prove more productive if you know exactly what type candidate you are seeking and if you prepare a written list of questions based on the candidate's personal history. Again, you may seek people similar to your current best performers. Most of us spend too much time interviewing applicants who are not qualified.

The most reliable guide to a salesperson's future performance is his or her past record; therefore, obtaining a reliable picture of the past record represents the most important aspect of screening. In your interview, ask the candidate to comment on specific past achievements with each employer. Compensation history becomes an extremely important indicator of past performance.

Unfortunately, people seldom change their bad working habits. The mediocre sales performer continues to perform at mediocre levels. The job hopper continues to hop. The person with financial problems usually finds new ones. The salesperson who works four days a week seldom switches to five, in fact often regresses to three.

Interview Format and Sequence

To make applicants comfortable and more willing to talk, immediately establish rapport by discussing some common interests or making small talk. Don't dive into the interview. Take a few minutes to establish a bond and dissipate nervousness.

Next, state the purpose of the interview and how long it will take. You wish to gather information on the candidate, tell the candidate about the position, and answer any questions he or she might have. You are not making a hiring decision today, and have a number of candidates yet to interview. This relaxes applicants and outlines what they can expect.

Discussing the job description is an effective means of starting an interview. Answering questions about the position provides an effective means of closing the interview. Ask the candidate why he or she feels capable of performing the job. Find out why the candidate has changed jobs in the past, and why he or she wishes to change jobs now. As the interview progresses, discuss past compensation and future opportunities. If health or personal difficulties appear to be a job-related problem, discuss them at the preliminary interview. Tailor the questions to the candidate. Don't use canned questions unless you want canned answers.

You may ask any job-related question that does not express willful prejudice toward the applicant's religion, race, sex, age, disability, veteran status, color, or national origin. Often open-ended questions produce answers that would be illegal to ask for directly. When in doubt, consult an attorney because Equal Employment Opportunity law suits against small businesses are common and expensive to defend.

The more the applicant talks, the more you will learn. Know what information you seek, and what questions you wish to ask; then listen openly and concentrate on the meaning of the responses. You can discover a great deal about applicants' skills, motivation, and experience by asking how they organize their day, what they think of their current employer, what they liked most and least about past positions, and through self-analysis questions that elicit their own opinions of personal strengths and weaknesses, areas to change or develop further.

Ask open-ended probing questions that cannot be answered with a yes or no. "What were the major responsibilities in your last two positions?" "Give me an example of a difficult problem you solved or a decision you made." "What motivates you?" "Tell me about your selling skills." "At work, what kinds of things do you enjoy the most?" "What is it that you are looking for in a company?" "Why did you choose selling as a career?" How candidates choose to answer these questions and the amount of time they devote to an answer reveals a great deal about their personal characteristics and what is important to them.

Don't ask leading questions that signal the response you hope to hear, such as "Do you like to work with people?" Questions that ask "why," "how," "what," or "tell me" elicit more complete answers.

If you create a nonthreatening atmosphere in which candidates feel free to talk, they will volunteer all the information you desire. You can best put the candidate at ease by being punctual, not accepting phone calls, not rushing through the interview, not putting a desk between the two of you, and sitting in chairs of equal status. Display empathy and understanding, but don't talk about yourself. A good interview requires you to listen 80 percent of the time and not to interrupt the candidate. Also, don't criticize the candidate, or you will find future responses guarded. When you want more information on a subject, agree with the applicant. When the conversation veers from the subject at hand, subtly steer it back in the desired direction. Once you have established rapport, keep the candidate talking about himself or herself, and don't let the conversation lapse into the World Series.

If you nod your head or say "uh huh," the candidate senses you are listening and will talk more. By occasionally stopping to summarize a prospect's point or answer, you give feedback to confirm understanding and interest. Don't feel compelled to fill voids caused by silence. Often applicants bridge a silence with significant information. Instead, use silence to put pressure on the prospect. You want to know how he or she would react to this in a selling situation.

Occasionally a candidate will give fuzzy replies or no replies to such questions as "Why did you leave your last job?" or "What was your compensation?" To elicit a more forthright response, drop the question for a while and go on to something else. Then return later to the subject and probe further by phrasing the question differently, for example, by asking "What sort of a person was your boss?" If related questions continue to produce indistinct or weak replies, you have found a problem area, which after the interview will require independent investigation through reference checking.

When possible, record in writing your impressions and key information immediately after the interview. After six interviews, as after six sales calls, information and impressions merge, unless you have made notes. If you wish to take notes during an interview, ask the salesperson's permission, and make your notes at regular intervals, not after revealing statements. Candidates attach importance to what you record so don't tip your hand.

As you record information, it is a good idea to mark each item with a plus, minus, or zero, depending on its bearing on the candidate's desirability. Try to look for information that helps you reject or accept the applicant. After the interview, organize this information in two columns with pluses on one side and minuses on the other.

I know of one instance where a sales manager hired the wrong candidate of two finalists because he relied on his memory for the requisite information. When the candidate, now employee, reported for his first day of work, the sales manager realized his mistake, but decided not to admit it. The story has a happy ending, however, because that salesman proved highly successful. When the sales manager retired, he told the story at his farewell dinner, while his successor, the wrongly hired salesman, listened in astonishment.

What to Look for Behind the Answers

You have prepared questions for the interview based on the candidate's personal history application, possibly a résumé, previous phone conversations, and of course the company job description and candidate profile. With luck, the interview will produce answers to these questions, plus useful unsolicited information. Don't waste time asking questions about where the candidate went to high school, which have already been answered on the résumé or personal history application. What the person does not say, or the manner in which information is conveyed on a résumé or personal history form, is what you want to discuss. Review résumés and applications for completeness, accuracy, misspellings, gaps in employment, and insufficient or inconsistent responses.

Be cautious of candidates who frequently move from one company to another or who have gaps in their employment record, such as a salesperson who left a job in June and did not find new employment until November. Be careful of candidates whose records show no improvement, such as a salesperson whose shipments and compensation have remained unchanged for many years, or a salesperson who traded a good line with a top company for an inferior line with a second-rate organization.

Domestic and money problems interfere with a salesperson's job performance. A general open-ended question concerning family, vacations, and expenses sometimes elicits information in these areas.

Salespeople who criticize past employers and bosses signal a problem that requires further investigation. The fault often does lie with the previous employer, but you need more information. Ask whether their previous boss would rehire them, or what that boss would say about them.

The rigors of some sales positions require a great deal of energy, which not all people possess. In such a situation, look for active people who channel their energy into work and don't just talk about working hard. A person who works long hours and Saturdays generally meets this requirement. Salespeople at a bakery supply distributor make their calls on independent bakeries from 6:00 A.M. to 9:00 A.M., then call on restaurants, grocery chains, and hotels from 9:00 A.M. to 3:00 P.M., and end their long day by calling on ice cream and yogurt shops from 3:00 P.M. to 6:00 P.M.

During the interview, watch for verbal slips or for stories and anecdotes that reveal personal weaknesses. A candidate once told me about a "funny" incident that involved missing an important selling date because he had accidentally walked under a sprinkler and gotten his suit wet. Another candidate told me that every Friday he "got gassed," then corrected himself to say that every Friday he "bought gas."

Watch for body language when your candidates answer certain sensitive questions. Do they look you in the eye, wet their lips, wring their hands, sit erect, play with their pen, grimace? Most people can't hide anxiety, and anxiety points to problem areas.

Just because you happen to be the interviewer, don't assume that you are cleverer than the applicant. Some salespeople have taken more interviews than you have given, and some have even read books on interviewing techniques. Often this person dresses well and speaks well but cannot close a sale. He or she drifts from job to job, is likable, charming, wonderful at interviews, and sometimes proficient at twisting facts. A clever recruiter spots this person because of constant job changes, lack of increased compensation, and by proper reference checking.

To end the interview, ask the candidate to summarize why he or she feels qualified for the position and if he or she has any more questions for you. Tell the candidate what your next step is and when it will occur. "I will arrange for you to meet my boss in two weeks." "Your skills and background are great, but we need someone who has traveled the territory." Don't make false excuses for not hiring someone.

Major Interviewing Errors

Although candidate profiles are essential, don't stereotype the ideal applicant. We have a tendency to hire people we like, who don't threaten us, and who fit the company mold. I recently attended a sales meeting where no one was taller than the sales manager, who was 5'1".

Many of us make judgments early in an interview and then look for information to support that decision. Public relations professionals claim that lasting personal impressions, often based on appearance, are made in the first ten seconds of an interview. "I sized him up as a phony the minute he walked in." "I liked her style and confidence the moment I saw her." Use the interview to obtain a complete, well-rounded profile of the candidate. Save your decision until the end.

Often a single favorable or unfavorable item will warp our judgment. "He is friendly with the purchasing agent at our largest account." "She drives an old car." Look at the whole picture before making a decision.

Often a glib, egocentric, evasive, talky, or argumentative candidate forces us to lose control of the interview. Be direct. Tell the applicant the questions you want answered. Don't hesitate to end the interview if this disruptive behavior continues.

Reference Checking and Background Investigation

You have now finished the eight preliminary personal interviews and, based on the information obtained, have eliminated four candidates. During the interviews, you asked for personal references who could be called and for permission to contact past employers, customers, and competitors. If the applicant currently holds a job, you usually cannot contact the employer. If the applicant asks you not to contact past supervisors, customers, and competitors, ask why. This could be a red flag. What is the applicant hiding?

Because checking references is time-consuming, burdensome, and awkward, most small business sales managers neglect it. Next to the personal interviews, however, reference checking represents the most important screening technique. If you don't have the time or inclination to contact references, then try flipping a coin or throwing darts to choose the best applicant.

A sales manager's aversion to reference checking stems partially from mistrust of references and partially from misunderstanding of the technique. Sales managers typically complain that "Candidates only give us the names of people who give good references." I agree, and so you must call references the candidate has not provided. Many sales managers also feel that reference checking challenges their infallible judgment based on personal interviews. As you will see, reference checking helps make preliminary interview information more meaningful and provides questions for the final interview.

Disregard written references provided by the candidate, because obviously these represent a form of advertising. Telephone interviews with past employers, customers, and competitors, however, will provide useful information.

In calling past employers, speak first with the applicant's supervisor and then with his immediate supervisor's boss. Reaching these people can prove difficult; sometimes they have changed employers, or company policy prohibits giving telephone references. Also, since you cannot call the applicant's current employer, all information remains somewhat dated. Still the information gained from past employers can prove invaluable in evaluating candidates.

Introduce yourself and explain the reason for the call. Explain something about your company and the position available. Then try and establish rapport in order to elicit more candid responses. You undoubtedly have common friends or interests. Next verify dates of employment and salary level, and ask why exactly your applicant left this former employer. What were his or her work habits, strengths and weaknesses, responsibilities and performance record? Find out the referee's title and past relationship to the applicant; I once discovered the referee was the applicant's ex-brother-in-law.

Last and most important, ask, "Would you rehire the candidate?" Company policy often prohibits rehiring. In this situation ask, "If company policy allowed rehiring, would you rehire this individual?" This is the moment of truth, when previously withheld information comes tumbling forth. I have encountered reactions such as "Never," "Only if his father-in-law made me," and "I would, but my boss would not."

As with the candidate interview, listen carefully to the previous employer's responses and tone of voice. Phrases such as "unfortunate circumstances," "personality clashes," or "chose to resign" usually indicate problems.

If the previous employer is a competitor, you may receive a false recommendation. The competitor may wish to burden you with one of its previous problems.

Customers on whom the applicant has previously called often provide useful information, because they have dealt with the applicant in a selling situation. When calling them, ask about the candidate's ability to present ideas, his or her work habits, follow-through, enthusiasm, and confidence. Customers feel less inhibited in candidly answering these questions than previous supervisors do.

If the candidate sold a product or service noncompetitive to yours, and you know competitors in that industry, their input could be useful. They can provide information on the applicant's employer and possibly on the applicant as well.

Background investigations on the finalists are a useful precaution. Equifax Inc. of Atlanta, Trans Union Credit Information Co. of Chicago, and TRW of Orange, California, all offer a service that investigates appropriate court and financial records and if necessary, verifies places of residence and past employers. These credit reports cost $15 each, and large credit agencies offer online computer access to their databases. Through such an investigation, one sales manager discovered that the finalist had just lost his driver's license. The job required extensive use of a car. Knowing how applicants handle bills, loans, and other financial obligations helps predict their responsibility on the job. A salesperson who is preoccupied with lawsuits or overdue loan payments will be distracted from selling customers. One company was won over to background checks after a new hire was apprehended stealing from a customer.

Under the Federal Fair Credit Reporting Act of 1971, you must advise candidates that credit reports will be used. Should the report provide information leading to rejection, you must supply the candidate with the source's name and address.

Testing

Intelligence, personality, and interest tests for salespeople can be administered and scored either by yourself or by outside services. Such tests provide insight into the subject's learning and reasoning ability, emotional stability, confidence, and occupational interests. The problem lies in interpreting the results. Which test results can accurately predict positive or negative job results? As with the personal history applications, you might have your current sales force take the test, then correlate their individual test results with their individual sales performance. You can then use your best performers' test results as a standard by which to evaluate candidates.

A sales manager obtains from testing what he or she puts into it. If you are willing to devote time and energy to this area, you can obtain useful information. These tests are available from distributors for a number of companies, including Strong Vocational Interest, Minnesota Vocational Interest, Martin Bruce Test of Sales Aptitude, Thematic Apperception Test, California Personality Test, Guildford-Zimmerman Temperament Survey, John G. Geir Personal Profile System, Otis Quick-Scoring Mental Ability Tests, Wesmon Personnel Classification Test, Adaptability Test, Concept Mastery Test, Wonderlic Personnel Test, Caliper Human Strategies, Inc., Personality Dynamics, Inc., and Kolby Conative Index.

Testing is a tool to help you hire the best candidate, not a crutch to make the decision for you. Don't substitute test results for your judgment. Narrow the field to the three best candidates, test each, and compare results. Use tests to eliminate certain candidates, not to hire the best.

Tests cost between $100 and $200 per applicant. Turn-around times varies from a day (using a Fax or overnight delivery) to a week (using regular mail).

Second Interview for Finalists

You have now completed reference checks, background investigations, and testing on the four remaining candidates. Based on information obtained from these sources, you have narrowed the field, and now must choose between two excellent candidates. You make appointments with them for a second and, most likely, final interview.

Based on reference checking and a reexamination of résumés, personal history forms, and notes from the previous interview, you prepare a written list of questions to ask. Differing from the first interview, these questions are specific, not general. If one former boss has reported employment dates and a reason for leaving that differ from what the candidate gave you, what explains the inconsistency? Or, although the candidate has a marvelous past record selling established products for large companies, how will he or she adapt to selling a relatively unknown product for a small company?

Use the same interviewing techniques suggested for the preliminary meeting, but occasionally inject some stress-producing factor to see how the candidate reacts. Imply that some of the former employers were not overly enthusiastic about the applicant's performance record or reject an applicant's idea. Does the candidate become hostile, argue with you, or start divulging previously undisclosed information, or politely call your bluff and try to change your mind?

If possible, introduce the finalists to your boss, the company president. The applicant will be impressed, and the president might help in the final choice. No salesperson should be hired without at least one additional opinion.

Some sales managers have the finalists interviewed by several of their top salespeople. A chemical waste disposal firm insists that each finalist spend a day in the field with a key salesperson. The finalist receives a firsthand look at the job, and the key salesperson can evaluate the candidate at the moment of truth.

Make sure that you have honestly answered all the finalist's questions about the company and the position. Allow the applicant several opportunities to ask. When inviting finalists to a second interview, send them product or service literature and general company information. End the interview by telling the applicant that within a certain time frame, you will call.

In making your final choice, classify each item listed on the job description and candidate profile as a "must" or a "want" with a numeric value as to importance attached. For each duty, skill, level of knowledge, or area of experience and for each of several personal characteristics, decide which are the "musts," which are the "wants," and how each ranks in importance in selecting a salesperson. Any finalist possesses all the "musts," so in making your choice review which finalists have the most important "wants." And never be rushed into a dubious decision by the need to put a warm body on the street.

One last word of caution: Before hiring your final choice, invest several hundred dollars in a thorough physical exam. This represents a nice opening fringe benefit for the candidate, and one more filtering process for the company. If the exam produces no surprises, the screening is complete. Should the exam raise job-related health questions, you may wish to hire the other finalist. Many companies require drug, liver, and AIDS testing.

Hire Only the Best

You should be aware that most sales managers prefer salespeople who share their background, make a nice appearance, and do not threaten them. Most sales managers hire people they enjoy; but this natural selection does not necessarily result in the best sales force. First-rate people hire first-rate people. Second-rate people hire third-rate people. I once attended a company sales meeting where everyone wore a striped tie and was bald.

You should also be aware that most sales managers, being sales types themselves, oversell the job. Overselling the candidate results in unmet expectations, disappointment, resentment, and high turnover. If the territory requires a great deal of missionary selling, or sales are declining, admit it.

During the entire hiring process you should maintain accurate and adequate records so that later you can compare candidates' actual sales performance with their interview responses, personal histories, references, and test results. What characteristics did the strong performers have in common? This knowledge makes future hiring easier and produces better results.

Occasionally, after you have completed the steps described in this chapter, only a best candidate will emerge, not a good candidate. Don't hire the best of a weak group. This will not solve your problem. A weak salesperson can prove more expensive than no salesperson. It is less expensive to continue looking than to hire, fire, and look again.

Hiring competent salespeople is a process with a beginning—the job description/candidate profile; an end—the medical exam; and steps along the way such as advertising the position, personal interviews, and checking references. If you view recruiting as a process, and consider all appropriate steps even if you decide against using all of them, the probability of success increases. Viewed as a process, you realize that hiring requires thirty to ninety days to recruit the right person. Hiring requires planning and anticipating needs.

Recent studies show that 55 percent of the people holding sales positions have little or no ability to sell, while 25 percent have sales ability but are attempting to sell the "wrong" product or service. The remaining 20 percent are doing the job most appropriate for them and their companies. These are the 20 percent of the sales force that account for 80 percent of the sales. The hiring techniques described in this chapter are designed to help you beat these odds.

2

Training Salespeople

The most important resource in a small growing business is people. As sales manager your most important task is hiring competent salespeople; your second most important task is training them. Hire the right people, train them well, and the rest of your job is much easier. Willy Loman, the tragic hero of Arthur Miller's play *Death of a Salesman*, worked for a small family-owned business. In preparation for his selling position, he received only a calling card and a sample case. The rest was up to him. Willy represented the end of a romantic era for salespeople. Today you need more than friends, a good shoe shine, and a pleasant smile to obtain orders.

As the sales manager for a small growing business, you probably feel continual pressure to allocate the bulk of your time and energy to closing sales, opening new accounts, and the day-to-day details of operating a sales force. There are only so many working hours in a week, and the company does not employ anyone else to help in sales management. Therefore you allocate time to the areas where results are immediate and predictable. No business can exist without orders and customers.

Your job is to make heroes, not to be one. Six competent salespeople can sell many times more goods or services than one sales manager. But to get work done through other people means you must train them. When sales managers do not devote the proper time, energy, and skills to hiring and training the sales force, then they must continually perform extra sales duties to back up a weak organization. Such sales managers transform themselves into line salespeople. Sometimes a small-business sales manager actually enjoys competing with the sales reps, because he or she can usually outperform them. Such behavior does not reflect good management, but rather uncontrolled ego. Small-company sales managers must

sell, but at the management level, and not in direct competition with the
sales force.

Sales training, like any form of education, is a continual process that
should never end. Not only do newly hired salespeople require training;
so do those who have been with the company for some time. Even the
best salesperson needs current input on product knowledge and the competition. A well-cast and thoroughly rehearsed play has a higher probability of success, as does a company with a properly hired and well-trained
sales organization.

New hires start with an initial four- to eight-week training program
that continues with field coaching and sales meetings. What percentage of
your time is devoted to training salespeople? Make a list of your anticipated duties as sales manager. Keep a log of how much time you spend
on each. At least 20 percent of your time should be spent training. Depending on geography and the size of your sales force, you should spend
from five to twenty-four days a year in the field with each salesperson.

A sales organization is no better than its management. Management
begins with hiring and continues with training, compensation, motivation, communication, and appraisal. A good training program produces
confident, enthusiastic salespeople who make the sales manager's job easier, not harder. A well-trained sales force not only generates more orders
but results in less turnover. Invest time in training, and you will have to
replace fewer salespeople.

Salespeople can learn from experience, but it is more efficient to hit
the deck running. They will make fewer costly initial mistakes with customers, such as quoting wrong prices or recommending the wrong service
or product, if they are properly trained. Sending new hires out before they
are ready creates frustration, confusion, and disappointment and gives them
excuses for poor performance. A good training program motivates salespeople to perform.

Don't delegate sales training to your best salesperson even though this
option may appear attractive. The best salesperson may not be the best
trainer. Even the best salespeople develop bad habits, believe some misinformation, and, most important, possess selling styles peculiar to their
personalities. If you delegate training to other salespeople, their habits,
misinformation, and styles will be passed along. As sales manager, you
alone possess the skills, knowledge, and authority to train others properly.
Having a new salesperson travel with an experienced person or with several experienced people makes sense, but this should be a small portion of
the total training program.

A sweater company discovered that its sales of Orlon sweaters were declining each year while sales of natural fibers increased. This did not coincide with overall market trends. In questioning the sales force, management discovered that the salesperson who trained new recruits liked natural fibers rather than synthetics and passed this bias along.

In 1989 the Dartnell Corporation interviewed 400 companies employing a total of 55,000 salespeople concerning their training programs. The average length of the initial program was reported as four months, but ranged from one month for pharmaceuticals to seven months for fabricated metal. These companies spent an additional fifty-six hours a year training experienced salespeople. Of this training, 74 percent involved individual instruction, 87 percent involved on-the-job training, 63 percent external seminars, and 66 percent in-house classes. Of the content of this training, 90 percent involved product/service knowledge, 88 percent selling techniques, 72 percent company matters, and 55 percent relationship building.*

The 1990/91 Sales & Marketing Personnel Report (ECS/A Wyatt Data Services Company) involving 424 companies showed that 37 percent of the respondents had initial sales force training programs lasting under three months, 21 percent had programs of between three and five months, 20 percent programs of between six and eight months, and 22 percent programs of over eight months. Banking and service firms had the shortest initial training periods, utilities and retailers the longest. The same report shows that 45 percent of the sales force training involved some individual instruction, 63 percent some in-house classroom instruction, 13 percent home assignments, 86 percent on-the-job training, and 48 percent seminars.†

Customizing the Program

To be effective, any sales training program must accommodate the specific type of salesperson and product/service involved. A training program for route delivery people calling on bakeries will differ from a program for people calling door to door offering educational books; it will differ also from a program for industrial computer salespeople, which in turn will differ from a program for men's neckwear salespeople calling on department stores.

*From *Sales Force Compensation, Dartnell's 25th Survey Edition.* Used with permission of the Dartnell Corporation, Chicago, Ill. All rights reserved.
†From the 1990/1991 Sales and Marketing Personnel Report (Ft. Lee, N.J.: ECS/A Wyatt Data Service Company).

Moreover, a sales training program can't be mass-produced. It must accommodate the salesperson's background, skills, and experience level. In dealing with seasoned salespeople, you need to recognize their worth, ask their opinions, and spend less time on basics. For newcomers, you should slow the pace and expand the subject matter. A salesperson hired from a competitor, from inside your company, or from a customer requires less product/service knowledge, but at the same time, in the case of the latter two, more selling skill knowledge. A salesperson hired from Xerox or Procter and Gamble to sell advertising might require more product/service knowledge, but probably little training in selling skills.

Base your training program on the needs of those to be trained, not on your particular interests. You are the expert and your job is to transfer your knowledge to your salespeople. Consider what you wanted to learn when you first came to the company.

A good training program requires goals and objectives that reflect the job description. Review the job description, which lists anticipated duties, and decide what training is necessary to meet these requirements. Also review the candidate profile for training goals and objectives. Based on the candidate profile, a software firm set three additional training goals: Teach salespeople to be order-writers and not order-takers, to be price-givers and not price-takers, and to sell a premium product at a premium price.

Salespeople often resist training for the same reasons that adolescents resist sex education: They really think they know it all, and they are afraid to admit what they don't know. You can overcome this resistance by creating a nonthreatening participatory atmosphere in which information is shared rather than taught. Don't present the sales training program as a penalty or as remediation for weak or potentially weak performers. Present it as an aid to strong performers. Present the sales training program as a sharing of proprietary information about the company and the industry. A proper training program motivates salespeople by making them feel useful, important, wanted, and privileged. It gives you and your company a more professional appearance. It can reduce the salesperson's cost per call through efficient time and territory management. He or she should understand that learning these skills and obtaining this knowledge will result in increased sales and compensation. Inform your sales force of other peoples' increased sales and effectiveness through training.

Wherever practical during the training process, outline in advance how you will spend the time, what information you will discuss, and what the objectives are. After each step, summarize your outline, information, and objectives. Present material in logical order. For example, when discussing selling skills, don't talk about closing the sale before you talk about qualifying leads.

Make sure that the salespeople ask questions, and you too should ask questions periodically, use role play and even multiple choice self-graded tests to establish that they understand the material. Encourage their participation and discussion. Tell the trainees in advance what feedback and participation you expect.

The structure of this program allows it to be inexpensively and efficiently administered by one person, the sales manager. Basically, salespeople require training in product/service knowledge, competitive advantages, customer knowledge, customer service and nonselling activities, pricing, time and territory management, company background and organization, company policy, and selling techniques. Salespeople receive this training by visiting the home office, by the sales manager visiting the field, by group sales meetings, and, to a lesser extent, through bulletins, telephone calls, tapes, and manuals.

Product Knowledge

A salesperson requires enough product knowledge to feel confident in presenting the benefits and features of the goods or services. Confidence is an important characteristic of successful salespeople. Salespeople feel confident when their product knowledge exceeds that of the customer's. A salesperson should feel capable of answering in depth any reasonable customer question relating to the products or services offered. Customers respect and trust salespeople who have complete product knowledge. A salesperson should also know where to obtain additional information when required.

Refer to the job description for assistance in determining how much product knowledge is required. If your sales force offers a technically based product such as industrial robots to plant engineers, the salespeople must possess very complete product knowledge. For example, they must know the electrical characteristics of all components and the alloys and thickness of all metals involved.

But if your sales force offers a technically based product such as hand-held calculators to department store buyers, then the salespeople need only limited product knowledge. They must know how to operate the calculator, its uses, and its performance capabilities. However, component and construction knowledge are unnecessary because the department store buyer is not an engineer and his or her concerns pertain to product features, benefits, reliability, and saleability. Advertising allowances, return privileges, and point of purchase displays are more important to the buyer than which type of transistor performs the calculations.

If your sales force offers a cleaning service to hospital purchasing agents, the salespeople require a knowledge of the people to be employed and the chemicals to be used. They don't need to know what gauge metal is used in the buckets.

If your sales force offers life insurance to individuals, the salespeople need to understand tax benefits, term versus whole life features, cash values, balloon payments, life expectancy tables, inflation rates, interest rates, and double payments under certain conditions. They do not need to know the risk ratings of rare diseases, or which banks accept insurance policies as loan collateral, or the name of the insurance company's founder.

One leasing firm that specialized in financing used computers taught its salespeople a great deal about the equipment, but nothing about figuring monthly payments. Customers and prospects were impressed by their knowledge until the discussion turned to numbers.

Essentially, then, you must teach the sales force whatever product/ service knowledge the customer requires in order to make the buying decision. Initially, basic product/service knowledge can best be learned by asking the new recruit (or established salesperson who needs assistance) to spend time at your office. Send pertinent catalogs and manuals to the salesperson for review before your meeting. Make a list of the information you wish to discuss. If possible, have pictures, models, prototypes, videos, audiotapes, charts, graphs, or samples of your service/product, and spend whatever time may be necessary explaining its pertinent details.

Next, where appropriate, accompany the salesperson on a tour of your factory, warehouse, or processing facilities to see the product manufactured or service prepared. Don't delegate the tour, because then you lose control of the situation, and your salesperson may receive information not appropriate to the selling process.

If possible, take the salesperson with you to see the product or service in use. If you sell a hospital cleaning service, visit the hospital and watch the service being performed. If you sell garbage disposal, have the trainee ride the garbage truck for a day and visit the landfill. If you sell sweaters, visit some stores that offer your merchandise. If you sell industrial robots, visit some factories that employ them. To save time and money, visit customers near your office.

Too much product knowledge, however, can confuse customers and deceive salespeople. Most small firms overemphasize product knowledge because most sales managers are experts in the subject and information is readily available. Most small firms are product- rather than customer- or need-oriented. In any case, salespeople need equal amounts of training in many other subjects.

Competitive Advantage

Salespeople require knowledge both of their own products or services and of their competitors'. To sell effectively, a salesperson must know the competitive advantages or disadvantages of each style, model, or service in the marketplace. Do your company's automatic welding robots cost more than your competitors'; do they work faster, last longer, move up and down as well as sideways? Do your company's wool/nylon sweaters require hand-washing when competitors' sweaters can be laundered in a machine? Does your service clean hospitals two shifts a day as opposed to your competitor's one shift only? Does your refuse removal company pick up twice a week while the competition picks up only once? Does your firm's life insurance policy offer dividends or dividend reinvestment while others do not?

After you and the salesperson have discussed product information, reviewed company sales literature, looked at models, visited the appropriate facilities and a customer or two, you should compare the features, benefits, and image of each of your firm's styles, models, or services with what major competitors offer. This can best be accomplished by means of information sheets.

Use one page for each major product, product group, model, major service, or service group. List your company and all competitors across the top. Down the left-hand side put appropriate topic headings relating to competitive issues such as price, reliability, durability, yarn content, delivery, colors, dividend reinvestment, welds per minute, components, double indemnity, gauge, drying time, availability, or cost per hour. Fill in each space with the appropriate information and with how it compares with your product or service features. Is it more, less, better, worse?

Explain and discuss this information with the salesperson and leave him or her copies of the sheets for future reference. As material on competitors requires continual updating, you should save and update competitor's catalogs and product/service brochures, then make this material available to any person receiving training. Friendly customers and suppliers as well as your seasoned salespeople can provide a great deal of competitive literature and information. Collect newspaper and trade magazine articles on the competition. Obtain a credit report on each competitor.

You should also discuss with each salesperson the strengths and weaknesses of your company's size versus that of the competition. For example, being medium-size within your industry, your company is more reliable than smaller competitors, but more flexible and personal than larger ones. Your company policy on returns and credits may be more lenient than that of larger firms. Possibly your president personally answers any complaints. You use in-house customer service representatives to support field salespeople, whereas some competitors use answering machines. With less bureaucratic paperwork, possibly your company's orders can be shipped within twenty-four hours versus seventy-two for your competitors, and decisions on product/service variations to meet customer needs can be made in hours rather than months. In a small or medium-size company, each customer receives more attention and is more important.

A partial checklist of competitive issues to discuss with salespeople would include the following:

Prices	Type of distribution
Length of contracts	Major customers
Terms	Availability
Return privileges	Delivery time
Advertising allowances	Support staff
Prepaid freight	Years in business
Variety of product/services offered	Financial stability
Quality and reliability of product/ service	Policy concerning ethics or collections
Number of salespeople	Image and reputation
Sales techniques	Specialization
	Strengths and weaknesses

It is not sufficient merely to say, "Our quality exceeds the competition's." Salespeople must know the key words, the benefits and features that represent quality to a customer, for example, "Our sweater contains 80 percent cotton," "Our cherry pie filling contains 40 percent fresh cherries," "Our Christmas ornaments are handmade," "Our nail-making machines weigh over 1,000 pounds," "Our landfill is lined with clay and plastic." Obviously salespeople need to know how their product stacks up against the competition's.

Many companies hold sales meetings to discuss competitor comparisons for each product/service offered. At such meetings salespeople share information and learn from each other. Figure 2-1 shows a competitor comparison format used by a small garbage company.

Be honest in appraising your competition. All companies' products and services have strengths and weaknesses. Accurate knowledge allows the salesperson to call on customers with the greatest need for the particular strengths your product offers. Accurate competitive knowledge allows the salesperson to feel more confident, to present features and benefits more effectively and forcefully, to make price less of an issue, and to sell the risk of a bad job. Knowledge increases the probability of success, ignorance the probability of failure.

Customer Knowledge

You and the salesperson should next review and discuss the customer and prospect list. Ask the salesperson who the most important person in your organization is. If the answer is anything other than "the customer," he or she needs an instant course on company philosophy

For each customer in the salesperson's territory, review sales by product or service in units and dollars. Is the trend up or down, and why? How can sales to each customer be expanded—by increasing usage of current services/products or by attempting to sell the customer new ones?

For each customer and major prospect, discuss who does the buying, what the best time for reaching that person is, his or her personality, likes and dislikes, and "hot button," company buying policies and procedures, the highest- and lowest-ranking person involved in the purchasing decision, credit issues, and corporate culture. What is the buyer's or purchasing agent's attitude toward our company? Did we ever disappoint them? If so, what are the details?

When you call on the head engineer at a major Ohio auto plant, he turns a sand glass over, and you have five minutes to make a presentation. You will make the head engineer a friend by calling his employees associates. When you call on the head architect at a major Ohio utility, be prepared to talk about the Cleveland Browns and Cincinnati Reds for thirty minutes before your presentation. Knowing these little personal idiosyncrasies as well as the birthdays and the names of spouses of your contacts makes selling that much easier. When possible, we buy from our friends. In the end, it is people who choose between vendors, not computers or software.

Does your customer or prospect have special problems, such as running a seasonal business, or specific needs, such as for overnight delivery?

Figure 2-1.   Competitor comparison format used by a refuse removal company.

Competitive Issues	Competitor A	Competitor B	Competitor C	Competitor D
Price				
Length of contract				
Frequency of service				
Condition of containers				
Type equipment				
Number of trucks and containers				
Number of salespeople and drivers				
CSR, dispatch, telemarketing staff				
Years in business				
Variety of services				
Landfill access and ownership				
Disposal costs				
Markets serviced				
Policy concerning: Ethics Safety Credit and collection				
Financial stability				
Reliability				
Image, reputation				
Specialization				
Number of customers				
Key accounts				
Strengths and weaknesses				
Thinks and acts				

What competitive product/services are bought? How are they priced? Is there a contract? Is the customer's or prospect's business growing? What drives it? Do they pay their bills on time?

Supply the new salesperson with the addresses and telephone numbers of all customers and major prospects along with the names and titles of all people involved in the buying process. What is the best time to reach them? Who are the gatekeepers? Who makes the buying decisions? Don't allow a salesperson to waste time calling on the purchasing agent if it's the maintenance manager or head engineer who makes the buying decision.

A new salesperson can learn all this on the street through trial and error, but it is more efficient and less expensive to learn it before contacting the customer or prospect. Imagine how impressed you would be if a new salesperson knew your personal preferences and your company's problems and needs. Customers are impressed by salespeople who do their homework.

For each customer/prospect, you should have a profile card or a file containing this information. Some companies store this information on their computers. Salespeople need to know how to obtain this data. If you don't have a formal system for storing customer/prospect information, start one. It is the heartbeat of your business. Do you or your competition know more about each customer?

If your company sells cable TV or educational books door to door, or magazine subscriptions by phone solicitation, new customers generally are more important than repeat sales. For such services/products, knowledge of existing customers or prospects becomes less available and less important.

Customer Service and Nonselling Activities

Besides knowledge of the product, of competitors, and of customers, salespeople also require skills in nonselling activities, including customer service. A salesperson for a sweater manufacturer must help the retailer display merchandise and help count it for reordering. A life insurance salesperson assists in handling claims and in processing paperwork for cash value loans. An industrial robot salesperson assists in installing and maintaining the equipment. A garbage disposal salesperson handles customer complaints on missed service, misplaced containers, and damaged property.

Consult the job description and make a list of the nonselling activities and customer service functions that your salespeople should handle, and of the information/skills they need to perform these functions. If possible, review these functions during a customer visit when the salesperson sees the product/service in use, and then again in your office.

Most small, growing companies complain that their salespeople often write orders and service contracts incorrectly, requiring clerical help at the office to rewrite them, or causing the factory to ship the wrong goods or provide the wrong service, or causing the computer to incorrectly calculate inventory figures or available service hours. This happens because most small companies don't take the time to instruct their salespeople on proper order-writing. So while you have your salesperson's attention, hand him or her an order form and describe the proper procedure for writing and submitting orders. Let them write some trial orders or spend half a day working in order processing and shipping. One company eliminated a part-time order clerk, while another reduced delivery time by 25 percent, simply by educating salespeople in the fine art of proper order-writing.

Using the job description, prepare a list of other nonselling activities required of the sales force, and then instruct new employees on their use. If you require route sheets, call reports, prospect lists, credit applications, expense reports, customer profile cards, account files, and sales forecasts, this is the moment to inform your people. Give them a copy of the form, show them how to fill it out, and when and where to send it. If you use a computer for any of these functions, show them how to input and access the data. One small company complained that only half the sales force sent in call reports. I discovered that the other half didn't know how to fill them out, and were embarrassed to ask. Occasionally devote a sales meeting to customer service and nonselling activity.

The use and care of sales aids, audiovisuals, the company car, presentation material, testimonials, references, and premiums need to be discussed. If sales aids are to be kept in mint condition, if the car is to be washed once a week, if videotapes, story boards, and demos are to be updated monthly, talk about it as part of your training program.

Salespeople's compensation is based primarily on sales, not customer service, proper use of order forms, or prompt submission of call reports. You should use this initial sales-training session to explain why these nonselling activities are nevertheless important to the salesperson. After all, good service creates business, referrals, and a positive reputation. All this benefits the salesperson. Call reports enable you to help salespeople to use their time properly and thus to increase their sales.

If you require salespeople to collect overdue accounts, be sure and train them on how to do this. Collections put the salesperson in an awkward position. A number of one-day seminars teach salespeople the key words, phrases, steps, and questions to use in collecting money and how to keep customers at the same time. Let salespeople spend a half day in the credit office or with your controller learning about credit applications and overdue collections.

Pricing

Salespeople also need training in pricing. Salespeople complain that they don't understand pricing policies, quantity discounts, bundling, two-tier prices, pricing windows, or how to sell price increases. Yet pricing errors and confusion make customers suspicious, influence profit margins, and cause expensive mistakes. Some time spent working in order processing, customer service, and with the controller helps salespeople understand these issues. Laptop computers can also assist salespeople with pricing.

A Christmas decoration firm offers "early bird" discounts for all holiday orders placed before March 31. Discounts vary with the dollar amount of the total order. In addition, there are substantial discounts based on the quantity ordered in each category: lights, ornaments, or artificial trees. A refuse removal service prices every customer separately based on type of waste, weight, volume, frequency of service, and distance to the landfill. Both firms have created a matrix to which salespeople can refer for the variables and quickly find the price.

Some industries, such as waste disposal, paper products, and chemicals, continually raise prices. Salespeople need training in how to sell price increases. To take the edge off, some firms announce price increases thirty to ninety days ahead of the effective date. This is done by letter or through the salesperson.

Price increases, although unpleasant, should be looked at as an opportunity to resell the customer. As sales manager, you must sell the price increase to your salespeople before they can sell it to the customer.

Salespeople should be prepared for objections to price increases and possibly deflect them by offering alternative products or services. You can maintain the price by trading down in quality of features or by providing less service. Offering alternatives shows that the salesperson understands the customer's problems. It also gives you the opportunity to resell the benefits of your better product or service.

You can offer the customer a blended cotton and dacron sweater to replace the 100 percent cotton style that has increased in price. You can offer the customer a personal computer without graphics capabilities to offset a price increase. You can offer the customer a larger garbage container but less frequent pick-up service to offset a price increase. Generally, customers see the benefit of their current product, model, or service and decide to accept the price increase.

If what you sell to customers has only a small impact on their total costs, salespeople should point this out. They must also explain the reason for the price increase. They need to allude to other vendor prices that have risen, including the customer's prices, as well as to rising elements in the cost structure of their own companies.

Often to sell a price increase the salesperson need only listen and let the customer blow off steam. By talking too much, the salesperson can get backed into a corner. Often it takes two trips to sell a price increase—one to discover what the customer wants, the second to offer alternatives and resell benefits.

Selling a price increase means understanding competitive advantage, making price less of an issue, and alluding to the risk of a bad job, the cost of change. Sales meetings and role playing are excellent ways to train salespeople in selling price increases.

Time and Territory Management

Time represents another important resource for salespeople; therefore, correctly organizing their time represents an equally important skill. Although management decides on a territory's boundaries, it is the salesperson who decides each day how best to utilize a finite amount of time within the territory. Chapter 4 discusses these matters in greater detail and Chapter 10 discusses how computers can assist salespeople with time management.

Depending on the job description, the salesperson allocates time between calls on prospects (new accounts) and calls on established customers (retention), between qualifying leads and calling for appointments, between visiting large accounts and visiting small ones, between several product lines, and between one geographic part of the territory versus another. In addition, salespeople have to organize their travel to minimize the time between calls and to maximize the time spent with customers. Ask your established salespeople what percentage of their time they spend eyeball to eyeball with customers. The answers may frighten you; the time averages 25 percent to 40 percent. Imagine by how much sales would increase if a salesperson could make just one more call a day, open one more new account a week, or spend 10 percent more of the day in front of customers?

As sales manager, you know what time allocation and call frequency produces the best results for your particular service/product. You know that prime selling time (two to four hours a day) is far too precious to waste. Share this knowledge with your people. If trade shows are important, tell them which ones they should attend.

Keep a map of each territory showing locations of major accounts and prospects. Discuss with the salesperson which clusters of accounts can be called on in one day and which highway systems are good for moving between accounts.

If appropriate, suggest parking the car and walking between accounts. Map the territory into quadrants or grids or slices and suggest working one quadrant or slice or grid each day. Suggest using the clover leaf system to call on accounts closest to home in the early morning and late afternoon. Or start at the far end and work back. Suggest using the mornings for retention calls on current accounts and the afternoons for cold calls, prospecting, new accounts, past due collections, service problems and complaints. Act in the morning, react in the afternoon. Suggest leaving one afternoon a week open for accounts the salesperson missed and for emergency calls. Teach your salespeople how to plan their day, and consider making time management a subject for a sales meeting as well.

An office furniture distributor that did a magnificent job training its sales force in product knowledge and competition nevertheless experienced a high turnover among sales reps. New salespeople with previous strong performance records in other industries expressed frustration with weak sales. Finally, the sales manager spoke to her three best and three weakest established salespeople about how they allocated their time. The best performers spent more time with small accounts than large, more time with established business than in prospecting, more time on the phone than in the car. The worst performers allocated their time in just the opposite manner. The sales manager adjusted this information for differences in the six territories, and a strong pattern evolved. Then as part of the sales training program, she suggested this successful time allocation. Turnover of new salespeople dropped in half, and orders from new salespeople doubled.

Company Background and Organization

A customer purchases both your product or service and your company at one and the same time. Therefore, a salesperson selling home smoke-alarm systems door to door in Chicago will find it easier to close a sale after telling the prospect that the company has been making industrial smoke

alarms for fifty years, that it installed the first home system in California
ten years ago, that it makes the detector for the portable Sears unit, that
it has been owned and managed by the same family since inception, and
that it has never had a year when sales increased less than by 10 percent.

So share pertinent company information with each salesperson. You
can do this in a two- to five-page writeup. This writeup might include
such information as years in business; growth; ownership; management
background and experience; major technical, sales, and manufacturing
achievements; major milestones and events; acquisitions; new product/ser-
vice introductions; and key financial data and market share.

Salespeople do not function in a corporate vacuum. For instance, they
require information on customer deliveries and credit, and they must know
who in the organization has these responsibilities. If they want information on the group insurance plan or commission checks, they need to know
to whom to write. Salespeople perform better when they feel part of their
company, and this involves knowledge and understanding of the organization's structure.

In a smaller firm you have an opportunity to make salespeople feel
they are truly part of the company. Share the entire organization chart
with each new recruit. Explain who does what from the president on down.
Point out what person they should contact for certain information, and
who should not be bothered. If practical, introduce your salespeople to the
appropriate administrative people and company officers. Meeting the president shows that the company cares about its employees. A salesperson
remembers this in the field after a disappointing day.

Company Policy

To sell some products or services effectively, a salesperson must understand company and competitor policies on allowable returns, advertising
allowances, freight costs, payment terms, collections, available displays,
cancellation penalties, contract enforcement, and minimum orders. Again,
consult the job description to determine what policy information a salesperson requires, present the policies in writing and review them with the
new employee.

Your policies on returns, minimums, and cancellation penalties may
represent the competitive advantage that allows a salesperson to close the
sale. Similarly, salespeople can't be faulted for misstating payment terms
if those terms have never been explained to them. A dog food company
established one truckload as its minimum order, but neglected to notify

the sales force in writing, and then wondered why most orders were written for smaller quantities.

Salespeople not only need information on company policy as it relates to customers, but on company policy, procedures, and philosophy as they relate to employees and ethics. What is the company policy on gifts, entertainment, drinking, expense receipts, car mileage, seat belts, safety, car phones, hard hats at construction sites, dress codes, antitrust legislation, fire extinguishers in cars, civic participation, local politics, vacations, fringe benefits, and sick days? Review the policy manual with each new salesperson, and occasionally devote a sales meeting to key policy or procedure areas. If your company does not have a policy manual, at least write an outline of key policies and procedures that effect salespeople.

Selling Techniques

Every industry, product, or service involves the individual use of certain broad selling techniques. A sales force that understands these individual uses and broader techniques produces superior results. Often, large businesses with large market shares neglect these techniques in favor of clout. For very little cost, the smaller-business sales manager can gain an advantage by teaching and utilizing these skills. The techniques involve selling benefits, using empathy, being organized, qualifying prospects, obtaining appointments, employing a proper presentation format, using written presentations, working with group decision makers, negotiating, and postcall self-analysis.

Selling Benefits

Customers purchase benefits; as sales manager, you must teach salespeople what competitive benefits most appeal to your customers and prospects. The automotive manufacturing engineer and procurement agent purchase welding and painting robots because they reduce costs and increase reliability. Families buy educational books from door-to-door salespeople so that their children can do better at school. Auto owners buy undercoatings to increase the life and resale value of their cars. Family heads purchase life insurance for protection and tax relief.

Effective salespeople know why their company's robots are more reliable and cost-efficient than their competitor's; or why their encyclopedia rather than a competitor's gives youngsters an edge in world history; or why their form of life insurance rather than another creates more after-tax cash. Effective sales managers teach these benefits to their sales forces. Benefits shape the customer's image of your company and can include on-time, on-budget guarantees, deep pockets, excellence in engineering and follow-up, a wide variety of products or services, one-stop shopping, greater reliability, less downtime, safety, and EPA compliance.

The sales presentation must be need- or benefit-oriented, customer-oriented rather than product- or service-oriented. However, a salesperson requires complete product/service knowledge to adequately show how the product/service benefits fill the need. Convert product/service features into customer benefits and teach them to the sales force.

A temporary clerical help service sells productive employees who get the work done on time. Employers want courteous, reliable, neat temporary office people who arrive on time, fit in, and are dependable. The temporary service salespeople must understand word processing, but what they sell is reliability, productivity, trust, and minimal risk of a bad job. Testimonials, guarantees, and customer evaluation sheets help sell these benefits. Selling benefits makes the price less of an issue.

Using Empathy

Salespeople close sales when the benefits of their product or service meet a need or solve a problem for the prospect. To define the problem or locate the exact need, salespeople must be empathetic.

A yarn manufacturer has lost its head dyer, who had formulated all of its colors. Your company sells an automated dye machine that uses a minicomputer to formulate, weigh, and dispense dyes. If your salesperson can discover this yarn manufacturer's problem, your product has the means to solve it, which might result in a sale.

A retailer must carry high inventories of imported calculators because deliveries from the current overseas supplier are erratic. Your calculators are manufactured domestically and delivered a week after order receipt. If your salesperson, through empathetic listening, uncovers this problem, a sale is likely.

Empathetic selling involves listening, concentrating, and responding. Teach your salespeople to ask key questions that lead the prospect or customer to discuss problem areas. The questions might involve returns, deliveries, retail markup, labor shortages, inventory levels, downtime, reliability, manufacturing margins, or plant size. With minimum encouragement, most people will tell you a great deal more than you need to know. Remind your salespeople that customers respond to personal warmth and a real interest in their situation. After the buyer perceives that the salesperson has an honest concern, a positive sales relationship develops.

Once the customer or prospect starts talking, your salespeople must know what problem areas to listen for. Complaints about high turnover of minimum-wage help in a hospital probably translate into a need for an outside cleaning service. A retailer's complaints concerning unexplained inventory loss might indicate a need for security devices. Complaints about high turnover of bakers in a restaurant may suggest it's time to turn to frozen mixes. Complaints about overflowing garbage containers and no lids probably means the need for a new disposal firm. Concerns with turn-over and absenteeism in the typing pool mean a need for temps on short notice.

You should also teach salespeople that all buying behavior is a com-plex mixture of reason and emotion that can result in both corporate and personal gain. Purchasing agents, plant managers, food-service managers, design engineers, architects, retail store buyers, and merchandise managers all want their company to succeed. They participate by buying goods and services that lower costs, improve sales, and, most important, increase corporate profits. These people also want to move up the corporate ladder toward management. They fulfill this need by drawing attention to them-selves through making successful changes. These individuals also want to make their jobs easier by obtaining as much service as possible from ven-dors, and avoiding problems and mistakes by dealing with reliable re-sources. They are influenced by the risk of a bad job and the cost of change. Your job is to make the buyer a hero. Many buyers and purchasing agents develop strong egos, and most have a need to feel important and re-spected. Any salesperson who fails to "massage" the buyer's ego loses a certain amount of effectiveness. When the purchasing decision is made by the owner/manager of a business and advancement is not an issue, other personal factors such as convenience, comfort, security, envy, fear, and pride become more important. People make buying decisions, not orga-nizations or computers. We buy from people we like. Salespeople need to understand both the company and the people.

Being Organized

Remind your salespeople that they must appear, act, and be organized. A neat personal appearance and appropriate attire convey a sense of organi-zation. A salesperson's appearance represents a kind of personal packaging that reflects on the entire company. Many companies suggest that sales-people dress a little better than their customers, which may mean a sports shirt or blouse with slacks for bakery suppliers and a suit for medical suppliers.

If you sell a consumer product that can be worn, make sure your salespeople wear it. If your company manufactures ties, your salesmen should not wear sport shirts. If your company manufactures dresses, your saleswomen should not wear slacks.

Before each call, salespeople should organize their material into smooth-flowing presentations. Before speaking during the call, they should organize their thoughts. Salespeople visit the customer or prospect for a specific purpose. Before sitting down with the customer, the salesperson should know what questions to ask and what statements to make. What is the objective of the call? Is it to gather information, explain a service, add another model to the program, meet the buyer's boss, open a new account, or sign an agreement? What problems or objections might the salesperson encounter? The competition has presented a lower cost system. Our last shipment was late and incomplete. What additional opportunities might be available? Teach salespeople to think about the "what ifs." Anticipating problems and opportunities takes the emotion out of surprises and allows people to respond more professionally. Anticipating problems allows them to come up with contingency plans and alternatives for accomplishing their objectives. The homework should have been done before the visit.

Profile cards with up-to-date information on each customer and prospect (Date of the last visit. Date of the last shipment. Any overdue payables? The buyer's spouse's birthday. The buyer's boss's name. The major competitor for that account. Special pricing.) are very useful tools that should be reviewed before each customer visit. These cards allow a salesperson to quickly obtain customer/prospect information when taking over an existing territory, and they help salespeople to organize their day. If the visit pertains to a reorder, the salesperson often needs a stock count. If the visit pertains to expanding a current service, the salesperson should have the benefits down pat.

A small office supply concern employed a saleswoman who made sixteen calls a day but sold only half as much as another who made just eight calls. The first woman would walk into the purchasing agent's office and say, "What do you need today?" The second woman opened with questions about paperwork flow specifically relating to the customer, then mentioned that based on previous orders, certain stocks must be low. She then suggested specific fill-ins and wrote up the sale.

Before each sales call, a salesperson's demos, videos, story books, graphs, brochures, photos, samples, and sales aids also require organizing.

To a customer, the samples and sales aids represent the product or service being sold. A worn sample, a wrinkled chart, even a dirty calling card create a negative impression. You should train new salespeople to keep these aids in mint condition.

A new salesman for a small company selling clear plastic window shades was not performing up to his potential. The sales manager discovered many fingerprints and smudges on the salesman's samples. This immediately reminded potential customers of problems, not benefits. With clean samples, the new man's sales rose.

You also need to train new salespeople on how and when to use sales aids to their best advantage. The timing of course varies according to product and situation. For example, in selling industrial robots, always wait until after the plant tour to point out cycles-per-minute in the product brochures. In selling life insurance, the salesperson may lose the potential customer by presenting a cash value and premium schedule before first establishing the customer's need. The door-to-door salesperson must offer the free gift when first greeting the prospect, not after the prospect has rejected the sales pitch. The software salesperson never uses a demo on the first call. The temporary office help salesperson only presents testimonials and guarantees when asking for the order. One sales manager suggests writing down a customer's key problems, needs, and benefits and then re-presenting them just before closing.

Qualifying Prospects

You and your new salesperson have previously discussed the strengths, weaknesses, and personalities of current customers and certain prime prospects. For revenues to increase, the new salesperson must know how to efficiently find additional prospects with greater than-average needs for the product/service. You must teach the proven unique techniques that have produced qualified leads for your more successful salespeople or develop and test new techniques yourself. Prospecting creates growth, but the time required and risks involved are not worth the reward unless leads are qualified. You must find efficient ways to reach the target customer.

Some businesses, such as those selling smoke alarms, emergency lighting, or hot tubs, rely heavily on new customers because repeat orders are few. Here the ability to produce qualified leads inexpensively, to efficiently reach target customers, means survival.

The sales manager for a small distributor of ice-making machines initially instructed salespeople to call on all restaurants, taverns, and food processors. Only one out of every hundred calls led to a sale. Sales force turnover was high, and those salespeople that stayed were marginal. One day the sales manager realized that following an ice delivery truck and then calling on the establishments that purchased ice could produce more select prospects with greater potential needs. Each salesperson was informed of this technique, which results in one out of every ten calls eventually producing a sale. Turnover decreased and salesperson caliber rose.

The sales manager for a small distributor of solar heat-reflecting window shades had similar problems. Salespeople made cold calls on building managers and interior decorators. One saleswoman began calling directly on offices with large windows and southern exposures. She eventually closed one out of every four calls. The sales manager informed the other three salespeople, and their business prospered.

A software company with a unique program for tracking leads, prospect databases, call reports, route sheets, and advertising results could not justify the expense of full-time salespeople. Their closing ratio was 20 to 1. By targeting sales-driven companies with large sales forces and a constant need for new accounts, the hit ratio improved to 10 to 1, and full-time salespeople paid for themselves.

You should inform salespeople of appropriate lists for prospecting. If you sell a cleaning service to hospitals, you should make use of a publication that lists all private and public hospitals by state and city, giving telephone numbers and addresses. If you sell men's belts, you should make use of a publication listing major men's wear retailers by state and city. Trade publications, trade associations, and certain specialized business publishers sell such lists. The local Yellow Pages also have listings that can prove an invaluable help for selling certain products/services.

Supplying salespeople with a list of inactive accounts and previous customers sometimes produces good results. A giftware company discovered that 33 percent of its accounts turned over each year. It replaced these accounts by opening new ones, but it never recontacted the inactive customers. One year the company sent a letter to all its inactive customers asking why they had left and offering a 10 percent discount on the next order. Salespeople had to follow up on each inactive customer. That year the sales volume increased dramatically.

Similarly, salespeople should not neglect qualified prospects who currently buy from a competitor. Business is a dynamic process, and buyers, needs, salespeople, quality, service, and prices change continually. You never know when a prospect will become unhappy with your competitor. Caution your people not to attack the competitor's product/service, because then they insult the customer's judgment. Instruct them merely to sell your benefits and to listen to the prospect's needs, problems, and comments on the competition.

Remind your salespeople that referrals from satisfied customers represent an excellent introduction to qualified prospects. Suggest that the sales force ask for referrals; there is no charge. A small garbage disposal firm gives discounts to customers when a referral leads to a sale.

Remind your sales force that noncompetitive salespeople can supply excellent leads. The institutional food purveyor might know which hospitals need a cleaning service. The hosiery salesperson calling on retail outlets might know a buyer who is dissatisfied with her current sweater source. Encourage your sales force to exchange market information with noncompetitive salespeople.

Some small growing businesses produce qualified leads for their sales force through media advertising, trade shows, and direct mail. One small company that sold hot tubs produced leads by advertising on cable television, giving a number to call, and in TV guides with a return coupon. Another small company produced leads for a unique industrial cutting fluid by exhibiting in regional machine tool trade shows. If your company produces leads for salespeople, explain the process, train them in efficient follow-up, and ask them to evaluate the quality of prospects.

Most salespeople disregard leads produced by advertising. They complain that the leads are a waste of their time because too many are not qualified buyers. Yet you have incurred considerable expense producing those leads, and if used correctly they represent future sales revenues.

To efficiently use these leads, develop programs that qualify them by phone and then send them certain information by mail. Before forwarding any advertising or trade show leads to salespeople, have someone in the office call the prospects with some specific questions as to need, problems, size of operation, present resources, and names of decision makers. This immediately eliminates literature collectors, third parties, duplications, poor credits, and nontarget prospects.

For the remaining qualified leads, send them a letter signed by you or the president. This letter quickly outlines some benefits, but, even more important, gives the name of the salesperson who will be calling them. A copy of the letter goes to the appropriate salesperson, who then has two weeks to see the prospect and report back to you.

Obtaining an Appointment

Salespeople with delivery routes don't require appointments, and salespeople calling on repeat customers for reorders have little difficulty arranging them. However, salespeople who depend on a constant stream of new customers or call on customers only infrequently must be taught proven techniques for selling the appointment. These techniques vary for each company, product, service, and industry. Even salespeople who don't make appointments can benefit from sending advance-notice postcards to customers announcing the date of their next visit.

If your company falls into the new customer or infrequent customer category, remind your salespeople that successfully selling an appointment by phone does not mean selling the product by phone. Trying to sell the product/service by phone generally fails. The objective of the phone call is to obtain an appointment; a by-product is to further qualify the prospect. In the phone call, the salesperson should stress the value of the proposed visit and the sizzle of the product/service. The call should stimulate the prospect's curiosity, add a certain element of mystery, and of course mention any referral. Teach salespeople the key phrases and words that produce the desired result—an appointment.

For example, in calling establishments that purchase ice, the ice machine salesperson would mention that this machine could save the prospect money, time, and space. The prospect might ask what the machine costs. The salesperson should reply that the price depends on the prospect's needs, which they can discuss at their appointment.

Similarly, in calling establishments whose large windows have southern exposures, the solar heat-reflecting shade salesperson would mention that these shades could reduce the prospect's room temperature ten degrees in summer, reduce glare, and prevent fabric fading without reducing necessary sunlight. The prospect might ask how the shades affix to the windows. The salesperson should reply that that would depend on the particular shade and window, subjects they can discuss at their appointment.

The telephone appointment request can also result in a "No" or "Call me later." The ice purchaser might say no because his nephew drives the ice truck. The shade prospect might say no because the company is moving out of state in ninety days. But the telephone call requesting an appointment has allowed these salespeople to quickly determine that these two prospects are not qualified. Should the prospect reply "Call me later," this information is recorded on the customer profile card and referred to in the future for the callback. Encourage your people to maintain profile cards on each prospect with all appropriate information.

Some salespeople prefer not to make appointments because it gives customers an excuse to say no. However, it's generally better to find this out over the phone than to risk a wasted personal call. Some salespeople prefer not to make appointments with small businesses (restaurants, cleaners, specialty retailers) because the owner/manager is always present. However, asking for an appointment is a courtesy that gives your call more importance. The rule of thumb is to do whatever produces the best re-sults, and this may vary from customer to customer.

A giftware company discovered that its salespeople who had made appointments wrote twice as many orders per retailer call as those who had not made them. Thereafter, it insisted that salespeople use appointments made over the phone or during a personal visit, and results improved dramatically.

On the other hand, a garbage disposal firm discovered that salespeople with appointments wrote no more service contracts than those without appointments. The sales manager thus let each salesperson decide on his own approach.

Presentation Format

Every product or service has a unique selling presentation format that produces the best results. Salespeople will of course vary it to fit their individual style and the customer's needs. Some salespeople will not use it at all. As sales manager, however, you must teach all your people this proven basic format, including the key phrases and power words. An engineering firm found that the following words evoked positive customer responses; *unique, proven, market leader, reliable, stable, experienced*. Other words drew negative responses: *probable, usually, approximately,* and *maybe*.

The sales manager of a small men's tie company realized that few retailers purchase an entire line of ties from one manufacturer, preferring instead to buy the best styles from a number of resources. Therefore, the four salespeople currently employed by this tie company were trained to analyze a retailer's selection, find weak areas, and show only strong styles that filled a need in one of these weak areas. The sales manager then hired a fifth salesperson from a shoe company, whose previous shoe customers had wanted to see and purchase an entire shoe line from one source. The sales manager neglected to inform him about analyzing needs, and about presenting selected styles, not the entire line. The new salesperson performed poorly until the sales manager made a field visit, realized his mistake, and corrected the problem.

Teach your new salespeople how to be task-oriented, how to understand customer needs, and the ways in which your product specifically satisfies those needs. Suggest certain questions to ask concerning customer problems and opportunities that will elicit information on needs. Warn salespeople not to present the product/service before they have identified customer needs. Then show salespeople how to completely and clearly explain the major benefits associated with your product/service. Show them how to make benefit statements that clearly demonstrate the value of the product/service in meeting customer needs. Explain which product features concern the buyer, and which do not. Explain how to relate customer needs learned earlier to benefits and product features.

Share the type of objections the salesperson is likely to encounter, and techniques for overcoming them. Objections show buyer interest and are an invitation to resell the benefits. One sales manager gives new salespeople a book of objections and how to overcome them. The more experienced salespeople *wrote* the book at a monthly sales meeting. The key to handling objections is proper preparation.

Objections may reflect a prospect's need for more information, confusion over your benefits versus those of competitors, or pressure from a superior to buy from a competitor or a friend in the business. The prospect may be testing your confidence and enthusiasm or testing to see if you are listening. There may be budget constraints or important information you have not asked for. Possibly you have not established trust, or your company disappointed this customer in the past. Teach salespeople to probe for the reason behind the objection and to think about it before answering it.

One sales manager does not accept price as a legitimate objection. She rightly claims that price is relative and has its own benefits. Price is part of the product/service image. Customers feel that items that cost more are worth more. As a salesperson you must explain why. Quality and value, not price, must be sold. If you can solve the customers' problems, meet their needs, establish yourself as a friendly expert, price is secondary.

For example, if your small company sells ice-making machines to concerns currently buying their ice, you might suggest the following approach or presentation format to your sales force. After introductions and small talk to establish rapport and get the buyer's attention, the salesperson should ask the customer what he uses the ice for, how many pounds are purchased each week, and how often it is delivered. The customer might respond that deliveries are irregular in the summer but three times a week in winter. Purchases average a ton a week, and the ice is used for processing certain meat products.

You would advise the salesperson to acknowledge the difficulties and inconvenience of irregular ice deliveries. Then suggest that the salesperson show a picture of a machine capable of producing 350 lbs. of ice daily, two of which would satisfy the buyer's needs. Next you would recommend that the salesperson discuss the space needed for the machines, their electrical requirements, the type of ice made, and their reliability. The salesperson should point out that the machines would solve the delivery problem because ice would always be on hand, and then (showing a chart with the information), that after energy costs were deducted, money would, in fact, be saved. If the customer asks for exact figures on savings, you teach the salesperson how to calculate them.

The buyer might complain that their last ice-making machine broke down often and was expensive to repair. You should give the salesperson information on frequency of machine failures and the cost of a maintenance contract. Suggest that the salesperson remind the buyer that breakdowns will be less of a problem with two machines. The buyer might contend that machines break down in summer when repair people and ice delivery outfits lag days behind. You suggest countering by explaining that your repair staff will deliver ice made at your facility at no cost until the machine has been repaired. The salesperson could refer to other customers who have been happy with the service.

This buyer might ask the cost of these two machines with installation, and then possibly complain about the funds needed for such a purchase. You suggest that the salesperson mention a lease plan and figure out suitable monthly payments.

The ice-machine sales manager had salespeople practice this presentation format using role play. At sales meetings, while one salesperson played a customer, another used the presentation format to make a sale. Sometimes these role plays were videotaped and rerun. The other salespeople present were always asked to comment on the presentations' strengths and weaknesses.

Remind your salespeople never to lose their temper or argue with a customer. Demonstrating patience and courtesy accounts for many orders. Saying "you have a good point" shows that you recognize the prospect's position. If disagreement occurs, keep it polite and friendly. An infamous chain-store buyer gave all salespeople who argued with him two orders: "Get out" and "stay out." Whether an order is written up or not, salespeople should always leave a good impression if they want to return some day. To win an argument but lose the order makes no more sense than to win a battle but lose the war.

Remind your salespeople to obtain buyer agreement at each stage of the presentation by asking questions, for example, "This machine would save you money, wouldn't it?" Once agreement is established, the salesperson applies positive reinforcement, for example, "That savings would amount to over $10,000 a year." Remind your salespeople that a presentation in which the buyer does not raise objections or ask questions indicates that they have lost contact, and this must be reestablished. Salespeople should know that letting the buyer talk without interruption helps establish good rapport. A good salesperson is a good listener. Most buyers complain that salespeople talk too much.

Tell your salespeople not to answer questions if they are unsure of their facts. They should admit this to the buyer and promise an answer later by phone.

Next, suggest the key phrases, questions, and unique techniques that close sales for your product/service. Remind your people that if the previous selling process has been handled correctly, closing, asking for the order, develops naturally. Many salespeople resist closing because they fear rejection and feel asking for the order is "pushy." You must emphasize the importance of closing techniques. For ice machines, the salesperson might ask, "Where would you like the machine installed?" (assumptive close). The door-to-door hot tub salesperson might ask, "Would you like redwood or oak?" (choice). The tie salesperson might point out, "An order today can be shipped at once, but because of limited inventories an order taken next week might take longer" (delivery date). The hospital cleaning service salespeople might just say, "What action would you like to take? We are ready if you are" (action). The office temp salesperson might say, "You will discover that our word processors are highly trained and always on time and pride themselves on a good job" (assurance). The waste disposal salesperson might say, "With your signature affirming the program we just discussed, I will schedule your service to begin next week" (ask for the order). Other closes include using a testimonial; summarizing the needs, problems, and solution; giving instructions on use; asking for a purchase order number; and guaranteeing a price.

Once the salesperson has closed and made the sale, remind him not to buy it back by gratuitously continuing to sell. Overselling creates doubt in the customer's mind. Your salesperson should thank the customer for the order, set a date for the next appointment, confirm the timetable for follow-up action, and leave.

When salespeople have not made a sale, they should not overstay their welcome. Customer personnel want their time respected. However, remind salespeople not to leave without selling the next appointment or obtaining a commitment to a timetable for action.

Finally, remind your salespeople that selling is a process, which starts with prospecting, moves forward with a sale, and ends with service. Using the suggested presentation techniques improves the probability of success, but no more than do the salesperson's enthusiasm and confidence. If a salesperson is not enthusiastic about the product/service, why should the buyer be? If a salesperson fails to look the buyer in the eye, does that indicate a lack of confidence? And if so, how can the buyer have confidence in the person selling? Salespeople must establish relationships that create long-term customers, not just short-term sales. Salespeople don't just sell a product or service; they must sell themselves.

Written Proposals

Salespeople generally dislike written proposals because they are time-consuming and cumbersome. However, in many industries they are part of the selling process. If your customers want written proposals, teach your salespeople how to prepare them.

Proposals must be personal and professional and reflect the customer's needs. Remind salespeople that word processors allow them to write time-saving standard paragraphs, which can then be rearranged so as to customize each proposal. On a word processor all proposals look like originals that have been written exclusively for the prospect. But make sure your salespeople proofread all outgoing correspondence that they sign.

A proposal should restate the prospect's needs and how the benefits of your offer will satisfy those needs. It should allude to relevant competitive advantages.

Be sure salespeople explain specifically what they are offering, its cost, and the time frame. If necessary, include a signature line for the prospect to approve any action.

Include a follow-up date in the proposal stating when your salesperson will call the prospect. When practical, hand deliver it and explain the proposal.

Working With Group Decision Makers

Because many buying decisions are made by groups, salespeople need training in dealing with a group as the buying entity. Some groups contain up to six people, each with different roles. Salespeople must identify each person's role so that they can meet their needs. Generally, although only one person in the group can say yes to a vendor, the rest can say no, which is equally important.

A small pollution-control engineering firm targeted a dozen utilities needing wet scrubbers to meet the 1990 acid rain SO2 emission legislation. In each case the decision was made by a group composed of an engineer, an architect, a lawyer, a financial officer, an operations person, a safety engineer, a purchasing agent, and a member of top management.

Although it varied somewhat by company, each utility buying committee contained at least one person with the following role: the "initiator," who recognized that the utilities problem (meeting the acid rain emission standards) could best be solved by using an outside service (an engineering consultant to design the specs for a wet scrubber); the "gate-keeper," who determined which vendors went on the approved list, and who was the most knowledgeable about vendor/supplier offerings and usually controlled the information available to other group members; the "influencer," who had the most power in determining what was to be bought and from whom; and the "purchaser," who was actually in charge of buying the service/product. In this situation, everything salespeople had been taught about selling benefits, using empathy, being organized, satisfying needs, and solving problems had to be customized for each member of the group.

Negotiating

To answer objections and close sales, salespeople require training in negotiating. Negotiation is the give-and-take process by which a customer who needs the product/service tries to obtain the best terms for the price; in which you agree upon the final conditions of the purchase; and by which differences as to price, deliveries, terms, and conditions are resolved in order to gain customer commitment. A successful negotiation is one in which the customer, supplier, and salesperson all win.

Teach salespeople how to use the five basic types of negotiating alternatives: making a trade-off, adding an enhancement, splitting the difference, making a concession, or walking away. The first two alternatives satisfy both parties, the last three only one.

When a large department store asked its giftware company for 5 percent off list prices, the company agreed only on the condition that orders be confirmed six months before delivery dates (a trade-off). When a large restaurant asked its refuse removal contractor for more frequent pickups at the same price, the garbage company offered an enhancement instead—the same frequency of service but a larger container. When a hospital offered to buy all its bakery supplies from one distributor in exchange for 10 percent off list prices, the distributor offered to split the difference and give the hospital 5 percent off in exchange for buying 100 percent of its bakery supplies. When a large insurance firm said it would try the office temp service, but wanted the right to test and possibly refuse any temps, the service agreed to this concession. When a chain store agreed to carry some of a neckwear company's styles in several of its branches if the freight were prepaid, store labels and retail price tickets placed on each tie, stock counted each week, and deliveries made within twenty-four hours of order receipt, the tie company walked away from the offer.

Teach salespeople how to deal with customer negotiating ploys and strategies. Most small companies buy from and sell to larger companies, which train their personnel in negotiating. Your salespeople are at a disadvantage unless they understand the art and skills that go into this game.

When a high-pressure customer intimidates a salesperson by making demands, and then says, "Take it or leave it," your salespeople must know how to sidestep the demand and review what is being "taken" or "left." By doing this they can focus on the value offered and the potential loss to the customer if the deal dies.

When a customer pleads with a salesperson that although the company wants the product/service offered, there is no more money available, teach your representatives to express concern and understanding and then to prorate their proposal downwards to meet whatever money is available. The temporary help service would reduce the proposed number of people and then explore other department budgets.

When a customer responds to your salesperson's proposal by saying nothing (strategic silence), the salesperson usually starts attacking the proposal mentally in favor of concessions. Teach salespeople that in such situations "he who speaks first loses," that it is preferable to say nothing, to wait, to remain positively focused, and not to show self-doubt or discomfort. Teach them instead to take the attitude that an agreement has been reached and to continue closing: "I am glad you see the value of our service; we could start work tomorrow."

When a customer appeals to higher authority by saying, "My boss will only deal with vendors who can private-label merchandise," ask to meet with the boss to help sell your proposal. When a customer responds with phrases like, "You gotta do better than that," or "There is fat in your price," teach salespeople to refocus on value and the fact that price is relative and only one factor in the buying decision.

When a customer plays your proposal against a competitor's to obtain concessions, your salespeople must know what the competition is in fact offering. Rather than attacking competitors, teach them to sell your competitive advantages.

When your salesperson is calling on two or more people at a customer's and one takes the role of the tough guy attacking your proposal, teach salespeople not to fall victim to the tactic or to let it distract them. Rather teach them to acknowledge the concern but immediately to refocus on how these attacks address each point.

When a customer makes a phony demand that he will give up in exchange for a meaningful concession on your company's part (the bargaining chip), teach your salespeople to immediately present alternatives that supersede it. If the customer asks for an unreasonable guarantee, the salesperson counters by offering to ship sample quantities for testing.

In strategic negotiations, customers will fragment your proposal to gain concessions in each area. A major industrial company might try for concessions from the refuse removal company in price, size and type of container, terms of payment, frequency of service, and length of contract. Teach salespeople to present the total package and to discuss concessions only in relation to the total package.

When customers offer to "split the difference" or say "let's bargain," teach salespeople that this only benefits the customer. Basically, you are lowering the price or compromising terms. Teach salespeople to counter by focusing on the value of the entire package, but if necessary to introduce preferred alternative trade-offs.

Teach salespeople to give concessions reluctantly, to make the prospect feel that he or she has received the best deal, to understand that concessions are irreversible, to know always what the bottom offer is, and to negotiate only with the decision maker. Negotiation is a subject to be discussed with a new hire but also makes an excellent presentation for a sales meeting. Your larger customers are probably trained negotiators, so your salespeople must know how to deal with these tactics.

Postcall Self-Analysis

You have already taught salespeople precall planning, but once the call ends, you must teach them postcall self-analysis. Did the salesperson achieve his or her objectives? What went well, what went poorly? What follow-up action is required? Did he or she forget to ask about labor problems, to use sales aids, or to present a key benefit or testimonial? Did the sales rep get the order, obtain the information, meet the boss, find out about a problem, or get surprised by a demand? When leaving an account, salespeople should fill in the appropriate information on the customer/prospect profile card and call report. What happened, what was learned, and what is to be the objective and strategy on the next call? We learn and improve by self-analysis. Discipline your salespeople to conduct a postcall critique, and your own job becomes simpler.

Field Training

Much of the training discussed so far relates primarily to newer salespeople and is handled by the sales manager in the course of numerous two- to five-day visits by the salesperson to the main office. Unless the training continues via field visits, however, its value is limited. Within thirty days after the home office training sessions, the sales manager should spend a day or two with each new salesperson calling on accounts in the salesperson's territory. Then, at least twice a year, the smaller-company sales manager should visit customers and prospects with each salesperson in his or her territory. Because your sales force probably contains between five and twenty people, this does not represent an unmanageable task. The fewer the salespeople and the closer their territory is to your office, the more days you can spend with each. The sales manager for a local garbage disposal company employing three salespeople spends a half day a week with each.

How much time do you spend calling on customers/prospects with your salespeople? What prevents you from spending more? Are these excuses or reasons?

Field visits have a variety of functions. They are an opportunity for continued training and salesperson evaluation at the moment of truth, help to humanize the company, establish personal relationships with customers and rapport with salespeople, give the salespeople a feeling of belonging and a feeling that you care, and allow you to engage in personal selling at the appropriate level. Field training and supervision give salespeople confidence in you as a sales manager and make them feel important, which creates personal motivation. Field visits also give you a firsthand chance to learn more about problems and opportunities with customers, with products or services, with salespeople, and with competitors. When a customer complains about deliveries to you in person, it has more impact than when a salesperson complains over the phone. Often a salesperson teaches you an effective technique, or a customer gives you information that can be successfully employed elsewhere. Field visits to customers and prospects create buyer's confidence in your company. Field visits, including training and supervision, present smaller concerns with an inexpensive way of outperforming larger competitors by maintaining superior sales organizations and good customer relations. Many larger-company sales managers don't have the time or inclination to travel with salespeople and call on accounts.

Before the Sales Call

You should call the salesperson at least a week ahead to arrange a mutually convenient day or two for your visit. Depending on circumstances, you may wish to spend one day visiting large prospects or customers that you choose, and another calling on smaller accounts that the salesperson chooses.

Choose a variety of accounts. Decide which of you will set up appointments with specific buyers, and then schedule appointments to fill the same full day you expect your salespeople to work. If your company sells door to door or uses prearranged routes, appointments may not be necessary.

If the sales force resides locally, you may occasionally have an unannounced ride-with. This way you see a typical day and how the salesperson plans each day. Salespeople dislike this approach, but it is effective.

Be sure you arrange field trips with both new and experienced salespeople, and with both weak and strong performers. Field visits represent a unique personal opportunity to build rapport with your people. Strong performers need the relationship, if not the training. They need to know that you care. Salespeople with whom you don't travel may feel insulted or begin developing bad habits. Also, if you ride only with weak people, you condition the sales force to resist field coaching. It becomes a punishment rather than a reward. Sometimes strong performers want to show you off to their customers; sometimes they want to show off to you. You may learn successful techniques from strong performers, which can be passed on to other salespeople. Since strong performers write a larger percentage of your business, the time you spend with them may show more dramatic and immediate sales results than the time you spend with a weak performer.

A small furniture company employed a star salesman whom the sales manager chose not to visit because he posed no problems. Although the salesman's shipments grew each year, he never called on the two major department stores in his territory. When questioned by the sales manager, he claimed that other customers kept him busy. His boss correctly suspected that it was a fear of rejection, because department stores were more difficult to sell. The sales manager arranged a visit to the territory and had the salesman make appointments with the two "majors." Once in the buyer's office, the salesman did a magnificent job and left with an order. Having overcome his fear of rejection and gained confidence, he went on to open many other department stores.

A small sweater manufacturer employed a woman over sixty-five to represent the company in New Jersey. She resented the sales manager, thirty years her junior, and resisted any visits to her territory. On his initial trip, they called on retail customers in Atlantic City and then checked into a casino hotel on the Boardwalk. When the reservation clerk asked if they were married, everyone had a good laugh. Suddenly they had shared a funny experience, become friends, and, thereafter, sold together for many years.

With new salespeople, the sales manager should make the presentation with the first few customers, then allow the salesperson the opportunity to do it. The new salesperson will learn from watching you in action and from your analysis of his or her performance.

With seasoned salespeople, let them make the presentation unless otherwise agreed upon, but define your role. You may occasionally help or be a silent partner. An experienced salesperson may ask you for specialized assistance selling a particular product/service or type of account. In this case you would make the call as an expert but allow the salesperson to show what he or she has learned on a similar account.

Because your presence could make your salespeople uncomfortable, before the call express confidence in their ability. This sets them at ease. One sales manager found that her salespeople often locked keys in their cars when they traveled together.

Sometimes major customers or prospects prefer to be sold by management. Similarly, when you are calling on management rather than on the buyer, purchasing agent, or design engineer, a presentation by sales management or a dual presentation by you and your salesperson may be preferred. Dual presentations allow you to share the responsibility so that no customer need or benefit is missed. Discuss with your salesperson before the call who will make the presentation and what your role will be. Discuss how you will be introduced—as an associate, as the sales manager, or in some other capacity. Customers are complimented by the sales manager's presence, but then all conversation is directed toward you rather than to the salesperson.

Regardless of who makes the presentation, it is necessary before each call to discuss the objectives, the plan of attack, and background information. The objective might be to see if the customer needs another ice machine, to see whether the current robot installation performs as promised, to count stock for a fill-in order on ties, to determine the insurance needs of a doctor who responded to a direct-mail piece, or to sell educational books on a cold call. The plan of attack includes specific questions that determine customer needs, a list of benefits you offer that satisfy known needs, answers to objections that might be raised, what ifs and contingencies. Background information appears on the salesperson's customer or prospect profile card and might include the buyer's name, personality traits, past purchases, credit issues, current resources, and known needs. This precall analysis and review of information allows for proper planning. Hopefully the salesperson does it when you are not present.

During the Sales Call

When the salesperson makes the presentation, try not to interfere; and if you must interject something, be gentle. You accompany the salesperson on this call primarily for training purposes, not necessarily to write an order. Salespeople learn from failures as well as from successes. If you interfere, the buyer becomes confused and the salesperson embarrassed, which strains the relationships. You may gain an order but lose a customer and a salesperson. You may travel with a particular salesperson for four days annually, but on the other 236 he or she travels alone. When the sales manager sells for the sales force, the sales force stops selling.

Salespeople prefer that you take over on a field trip. It takes them off the hook. Your instinct in front of a customer is to sell, but the purpose of this trip is training.

When you must interrupt, use a question to make the point indirectly. For example, if the salesperson suggests the wrong model, ask if the customer might also be interested in the correct model. If the salesperson concentrates on price when another benefit should be emphasized, ask if the customer might wish to have the other benefit explained.

If the customer directs questions to you, turn them over to the salesperson. Sit farther away from the buyer than your salesperson does. Take yourself out of the conversation. Lean back rather than forward in your chair. During a joint sales call never speak to a customer/prospect as "executive to executive" or do anything else to make the salesperson feel less than equal in the customer's presence. Don't volunteer concessions to a prospect/customer simply because you have the authority. Avoid "piling on" when the salesperson is trying to close.

After the Sales Call

Critique each call immediately afterward and before making the next one. You can accomplish this on your way to the next customer or over coffee. A good salesperson will eventually employ self-analysis after each sales call, but to help develop this faculty, ask the salesperson how he or she felt about the call. What went well? What went poorly? Were the call objectives met? They will do most of the work for you. Agree on the follow-up action and the objectives for the next call on this customer.

After this self-analysis, share your thoughts on the strengths and weaknesses of the presentation. If you first tell the salesperson what was done right, it will be easier to accept criticism on what was done wrong. Reinforce skills used effectively. Review the extent to which call objectives were met. Give the salesperson credit for any positive accomplishments, including writing the order. Your comments should be logically organized, easy to understand, and action-oriented so that corrective steps can be taken on the next call. You will obtain best results through analyzing major issues rather than by outright criticism or by trying to cover too many areas. The fewer the messages, the better they will be understood. Use questions to make points. "Do you think you emphasized their lease plan enough?" To emphasize points, do some role playing before the next call. Salespeople are self-conscious and often not at their best when accompanied by their sales manager. You must factor this into your evaluation.

The curbside analysis for a solar heat-reflecting window shade sales call might proceed as follows. The sales manager begins:

S.M.: Well, Joan, how do you feel the last call went?

Joan: We found out the problem areas—high air-conditioning costs in summer, high heat loss in winter, ultraviolet damage to furniture, too much sunlight in the morning, not enough in the afternoon; and I presented the benefits of our solar shades to solve those problems. But I didn't feel their objection to price was handled well.

S.M.: You did an excellent job of determining their needs, and getting the purchasing agent to talk; but the presentation would have been stronger if you had mentioned that the shades reduce summer air-conditioning costs 25 percent and winter heating bills 15 percent. This information also could have been covered when the buyer questioned the price.

Joan (smiling): That's right, I forgot, but I'll use that material on our next sales call.

A door-to-door Bible salesman was making household calls with his manager. The company offers attractive editions of the Old and New Testaments along with other religious items. The salesman wanted to close a sale for the Old Testament by showing pictures from the edition. Without thinking, he picked up the New Testament, unintentionally offended the customer, and lost the sale. The two men walked in silence to the next prospect because a verbal critique was not necessary.

At the end of each day, write notes for yourself on how the calls went so that on your next field visit with the salesperson you have a basis for comparison. Sometimes checklists prove helpful in evaluating salespeople's strengths and weaknesses and in determining areas that require further development. Based on a field visit, you may schedule some role play on closing. A checklist might include time and territory management; appearance; organization; product, customer, and competitor knowledge; selling skills; paperwork; enthusiasm and confidence. Base your checklist on the training agenda, training record, and performance evaluation format. When you return to the home office and write to the salesperson, you can both acknowledge certain strengths and remind him or her of specific weaknesses. Make sure you have agreed on action, objectives, and a time frame for correcting these weaknesses.

Management Selling

Certain major customers and management-level decision makers prefer to be sold by vendor management rather than by a field salesperson. In a smaller company, this process, known as management selling, becomes part of most sales manager field visits and therefore part of sales training. Major customers or management represent an appropriate level for the sales manager to sell on. With these accounts you help the salespeople; you do not compete with them. They require your help, and appreciate it. On most field trips, at least one major account requires a visit by the sales manager.

Before the call, you again discuss objectives with the salesperson, along with a plan of attack, background information, and possible objections. You do a complete precall analysis. But on these calls, you, the sales manager, make the presentation. If obtaining an order represents the objective, you use all your skills to obtain it. This call belongs to the sales manager, but the salesperson participates when appropriate. The salesperson might provide information on customer usage and local conditions, and the salesperson will most likely be responsible for follow-up. Salespeople handle some calls on major accounts themselves, but once or twice a year your presence is required.

After the call, decide on the timetable for follow-up action, and who will be responsible for it. Also, ask your salesperson how it went. His or her suggestions will help in future customer visits and provide further insight into the sales process and self-analysis. At one such critique, the salesperson told the sales manager that he had forgotten to mention the same product feature that she had forgotten the previous day. The sales manager asked why she had not corrected him with the customer. She replied that he had not embarrassed her with the customer yesterday, and she was returning the courtesy today.

Sales Meetings, Manuals, Bulletins, Tapes, and Telephone Calls

You spend two to five days or more initially training a new salesperson at your office, and then two to four days or more a year in continued field training. Often this leaves long periods between visits. Between field visits, training takes place by means of sales meetings, manuals, bulletins, audiotapes, videos, and telephone calls. This makes sales training a continual process with a logical progression of events. Unfortunately, sales training in many companies ends after the first sixty days of employment.

In a smaller company, you generally hire one or two new salespeople per year, which does not facilitate initial group training. Therefore, you must train each person individually unless, by coincidence, several are hired at once.

However, at periodic sales meetings you engage in training a group, or the members engage in training each other, which represents a more efficient use of time and requires different techniques from individual training. (There is an entire section devoted to sales meetings in Chapter 6). At a sales meeting you must limit the training subject matter to such broad topics as new product knowledge, opening new accounts, and follow-up service. Time is limited, and subject matter must be applicable to the entire group. Group training loses its effectiveness unless all participants share a similar level of proficiency. Training the most experienced salesperson with the least experienced, and the strong performer with the weak, often dilutes results. For certain training, you may remedy this problem by forming subgroups at the sales meeting.

The sales manual presents in writing much of the training material you have already presented orally, and thus becomes a salesperson's reference book. Bulletins keep salespeople informed on such items as new policies, competitive advantages, product developments, and market changes. Through periodic telephone conversations and/or audiotapes, the sales manager discusses matters relating to each salesperson's individual territory, such as specific orders, customers, or prospects. Much of the material discussed in Chapter 6 involves a continuation of the training process.

Training Agenda

Some sales managers find it helpful to prepare an agenda when initially training a new salesperson. For the trainee, the agenda outlines the material to be covered and the activities to be engaged in. The trainee feels more comfortable knowing what to expect. For the sales manager, the agenda serves as a schedule allocating appropriate time to various subjects and deciding who will present them. The agenda makes your company look more professional and gets the trainee off on the right foot.

Be sure the trainee understands the specific objectives of each session. For example, customer and prospect knowledge helps us identify needs, problems, and opportunities. We visit retailers to see how the product is displayed, sold, and used. We ride through the territory to identify efficient travel routes. We spend time in the controller's office to learn about credit and collections. Figures 2-2 and 2-3 are examples of training agendas.

Training Record

Because sales training is an ongoing process, you require a means of recording each salesperson's progress. Often a one-page form outlining the training program proves helpful. Such a form might list the training subject matter (a checklist) down the side and the types of training sessions across the top. The sales manager would fill in dates and remarks where appropriate. Should disciplinary action or terminating a salesperson become necessary, the training record, showing the time you have spent with the trainee, might save thousands of dollars in legal fees. Records of driver or safety training become important for insurance. Figures 2-4, 2-5, and 2-6 show the training records used in three different kinds of companies.

In order to train your salespeople or salesperson properly, you the sales manager must have a thorough understanding of all the material involved, because unless you possess this knowledge your training program will fail. Even if you are a sales manager with no sales force—not uncommon in a small business—you must still have this knowledge.

Measure the results of your training program just as you did with hiring, and change the program accordingly. Smaller businesses have the competitive advantage of being flexible and can change quickly. Use role play and multiple choice self-graded tests to measure salespeople's training

(*Text continued on page 75.*)

Figure 2-2. Sample sales training agenda for an apparel company.

Salesperson's Name _____Date _____

Monday, April 27
 9:00–12:00 Review our product line.
 1:00– 5:00 Review competitors' product lines.

Tuesday, April 28
 9:00–12:00 Visit Bloomingdale's and Macy's to see how our merchandise and competitors' merchandise is displayed.
 1:00– 5:00 Visit our factory to see goods being made.

Wednesday, April 29
 9:00–12:00 Discuss customers and prospects.
 1:00– 3:00 Review customer stock taking, merchandising, order writing, prospect lists, call reports, route sheets, forecasts, and appraisals.
 3:00– 5:00 Discuss how to allocate time between customers and the most efficient way to travel the territory. Review a road map of the territory and show where customers and prospects are located.

Thursday, April 30
 9:00–10:30 Discuss our company's organization chart and personnel.
 10:30–12:00 Discuss our company's history and achievements.
 12:00– 1:30 Lunch with the president.
 1:30– 3:30 Discuss our company's and competitors' policies on terms, advertising allowances, promotions, box sales, returns, freight, display racks, and minimum order size.
 3:30– 5:00 Review the sales manual and bulletins.

Friday, April 31
 9:00–12:00 Present the line to the salesperson as if he or she were a customer.
 1:00– 4:00 Have the salesperson present the line to you, as if you were a customer. Critique the presentation. Review selling techniques.
 4:00– 5:00 Discuss sales aids, qualifying prospects, and making appointments.

Figure 2-3. Sample sales training agenda for a refuse removal company.

Week One

Salesperson's Name _____ Date _____

Date/Activity   *With Whom*   *Objective*

Monday, September 11
        Ride with driver on
            garbage truck.

Tuesday, September 12
8:00–12:00 Half day in dispatch.
1:00–5:00 Half day with customer service rep.

Wednesday, September 13
8:00–12:00 Ride through territory.
1:00–3:00 Review customer profile cards.
3:00–5:00 Discuss allocation of time in territory.

Thursday, September 14
8:00–12:00 Visit prospects with sales manager.
1:00–3:00 Read equipment brochures.
3:00–5:00 Review information on competitors.

Friday, September 15
8:00–10:00 Visit sanitary landfill.
10:00–12:00 Review pricing parameter.
1:00–3:00 Review selling techniques.
3:00–5:00 Discuss nonselling activities.

Figure 2-4. Sample training record for a trucking company.

Salesperson's Name _____ Date Hired _____

	Home Office	Field Visits	Sales Meetings
Product Knowledge			
Competitive Advantage			
Customer Knowledge			
Customer Service			
Pricing			
Nonselling Activities			
Time and Territory Management			
Company Background and Organization			
Company Policy			
Selling Benefits			
Empathy			
Organization			
Qualifying Prospects			
Obtaining Appointments			
Presentation Format			
Driver Safety			

---

progress along the way. If salespeople fail to present benefits, if salespeople are losing more accounts than they are opening, find out why and make adjustments in your training. If 20 percent of your sales force accounts for 50 percent of your sales, reexamine your training program. If

(*Text continued on p. 81.*)

Figure 2-5. Sample training record for a refuse removal company.

Salesperson's Name _____

	Date Completed	*Comments*
I. ORIENTATION		
Job Description		
Personnel File		
Company History		
Sales Goals		
Compensation		
Division Personnel		
Drivers/Trucks		
Landfills		
Dispatch		
Maintenance		
Safety		
Controller		
Customer Files		
Company Policy		
Antitrust		
Expense Account		
Community Involvement		
Territory		

Supplies	Date Completed	Comments
-Map		
-Presentation Binder		
-Calling Cards		
-Literature		
-Car Phone/Radio		
-Price Sheet		
-Proposal Letters		
-Call Reports		
-Grid Cards		
-Service Agreements		
-Car Files		

(Continued)

Figure 2-5. *(Continued.)*

	Initial Training Date	Skills Rating (1–10)	Date Review	Comments (Further Training)
II. ADMINISTRATION				
Sales Forms				
Record Keeping				
Collection				
Service Agreement				
Computer				
Sales Leads				
III. SELLING				
Price Sheet and Parameters				
Sales Skills				
Major Customers				
Major Prospects				
Compaction				
Competitors				
Roll-off				
Commercial Services				
Medical Waste				
Recycling				
Features and Benefits				
Time and Territory Management				

Figure 2-6. Sample training record for a giftware company.

Salesperson's Name _____

Subject	Date Completed	Comments

PRODUCTS

CHRISTMAS
    Christmas Lights
    Gifts
    Trees
    Garlands
    Ornaments

GIFTWARE
    Mexican
    Pottery
    Ceramics
    Frames
    Dolls
    Glass
    Brass
    Floral
    Holly

HOLIDAYS
    Valentine's Day
    Halloween
    Christmas

COMPETITION
    Christmas
    Giftware
    Holidays

COMPETITIVE ISSUES
    Price
    Quality
    Delivery
    Service
    Reliability
    Strengths
    Weaknesses

CUSTOMERS
    Decision Maker
    History

(Continued)

Figure 2-6. (*Continued.*)

Subject	Date Completed	Comments

Personal
Needs
Problems

PAPERWORK
Order Writing
Call Reports
New Account Credit

TIME AND TERRITORY MANAGEMENT
Number and Type of
    Calls per Week
Clustering Accounts
Route Analyses

COMPANY POLICIES
Pricing
Entertainment
Autos
Ethics

SELLING TECHNIQUES
Prospecting
Problem Solving
Needs, Problems
Benefits
Referrals
Objections
Closing
Listening
Objectives
Self-analysis

COMPLAINTS, SERVICE PROBLEMS

COMPANY BACKGROUND

COMPANY ORGANIZATION

IT = Initial Training
FT = Field Training
SM = Sales Meeting

30 percent of your new salespeople leave within two years, reexamine both your training program and your hiring program.

Hire the right salespeople, train them well, and the remainder of sales management becomes much easier. As you can see from these first two chapters, hiring and training involve considerable time and energy. However, if they are performed correctly, you obtain a tremendous advantage over your larger competitors. Aside from your time, doing these tasks correctly does not require much more money than doing them incorrectly.

3

Compensation

Many smaller businesses inherit their salesperson compensation plans from previous management or industry tradition, or they merely copy plans used by their larger competitors. Because correct compensation represents an important ingredient in attracting, retaining, and motivating good salespeople, you, as sales manager, should review the compensation plan annually. Business is a dynamic process, and the plan must meet changing human and commercial requirements. Each company, and even each salesperson, has different and changing needs. Other ingredients for retaining and motivating salespeople include achievement, recognition, freedom, status, personal relationships, belonging, company policy, and fear of failure.

Smaller businesses, because of their flexibility, can compensate salespeople as well as or better than larger concerns. Proper recruiting and training, discussed in Chapters 1 and 2, also influences compensation. If you hire the correct people and train and manage them well, they perform better and can be well compensated. A good compensation plan proves useless for a weak or badly trained sales force.

Creating a compensation plan involves setting objectives, determining compensation mix, creating an expense policy, and determining fringe benefits. The particular combination of salary, commission, and bonus you select for your company's compensation plan should reflect the objectives you most want to stress.

Setting Objectives

The objectives of a sales compensation plan include balancing the needs of the company and salespeople, quickly and effectively rewarding positive action, simplicity, fairness, rewarding superior performance, and establishing a minimum level of stability.

Balancing Company and Salespeople's Needs

Basically, the company needs to attract, retain, and motivate salespeople who produce desired levels of sales at a cost that generates profits and allows necessary percentage returns on sales and invested capital. A company can be generous with its compensation plan, but if the business isn't profitable, the mix is obviously wrong. For example, one small company manufactured silver-coated reflective plastic film for application to windows, using an adhesive. In the winter, the film reduced heat loss through windows. In the summer, the film blocked some of the sun's rays, reducing indoor temperatures and air-conditioning expense. With energy costs skyrocketing, this was a good product for the 1970s.

Management tried to sell the product through window applicators, air-conditioning representatives, and retail shade departments, but none had the interest or knowledge to be effective. Finally the company hired its own full-time field sales representatives and devised an "ingenious" compensation plan that included base salary plus a commission on sales plus bonuses for achieving quotas. Every year sales doubled, until the company went out of business! The compensation plan had equalled 20 percent of sales, which did not leave enough cash flow to support increased inventories and accounts receivable.

Good salespeople need a compensation plan that relieves them of basic financial worries, gives them pride in what they earn, reflects their qualifications and experience, and equals or betters that of the competition. Compensating salespeople on the basis of the cost of replacing them—or just the cost of keeping them from leaving—does not satisfy these needs. You will obtain better results with fewer but more qualified and more highly paid salespeople than you will with a larger sales force that includes less qualified, lower-paid people.

Rewarding Positive Action

To fulfill this objective, return to the job description and establish the specific goals of your compensation program. What positive action do you want the compensation system to quickly and effectively reward? Select specific objectives that are important to company success, measurable, realistic, and achievable through salespeople's efforts.

If, for instance, your business sells Bibles door to door, the compensation plan should quickly reward sales and only sales. The job description calls for no customer service after the sale and no missionary work preceding the sale.

If, on the other hand, your company sells underwear to retailers, the compensation plan should quickly and effectively reward not only the initial sale but also fill-in orders, display work with clerks, credit and collection activities, handling complaints and delivery information, sales forecasting, record keeping, and call reports. The job description requires salespeople to engage in all these activities.

If your company sells industrial gears for oil-drilling equipment, the compensation plan should reward not only the initial sale but also replacement orders, the missionary work with customer design engineers that led to getting your gears specified, and the follow-up work with customer production engineers teaching the correct application. Again, the job description requires salespeople to engage in all these activities.

A new territory requires a compensation plan that places more emphasis on opening new accounts and less on servicing existing ones. In recessionary times, the compensation plan should place more emphasis on collections than it would in prosperous times. These examples show why compensation plans require annual reviews and a flexible approach.

Simplicity

A universal objective for all sales compensation plans ought to be simplicity. Salespeople do not understand or remember complicated plans, and companies have difficulty administering them.

A small company that sold abrasive grinding wheels fired its sales manager after two successive years of declining orders. The new sales manager discovered that the compensation plan included a different commission rate for each of twenty major products, a different bonus system for each month, and a salary that was adjusted each quarter to reflect the last quarter's shipments. The program totally confused the sales force and required one full-time administrative person. Each month the salespeople and the administrator would waste a day arguing over the accuracy of paychecks. The new sales manager established a different commission rate for each of five product groups, one bonus system for summer, one for winter, and a level monthly salary. Orders immediately began increasing, and half the administrator's time became available for other tasks.

Fairness

A good sales compensation plan must have fairness and equitableness built into it. For example, orders that customers phone or mail directly to the office should be credited to the salesperson's account just as if they had been written in the field. Also, nothing dulls a salesperson's enthusiasm more than "house accounts." Taking lucrative accounts out of a territory for handling by management or family members hurts morale.

Similarly, paying lower commissions on certain sales that involve the same effort as those on which you pay higher commissions generates resentment. Also, not splitting commissions on orders that have involved a joint effort is not equitable. One sales meeting held by a food purveyor ended abruptly in a hot-tempered fistfight between two salesmen over commission splitting.

Salespeople displaying equal ability and effort, but with different type territories, require compensation plans that take this into account. It is not equitable, for example, to pay a person in a new territory with no accounts on a straight commission basis just because you pay straight commission to the people in established territories with many accounts. It would not be fair to compensate the New York salesperson who rides the bus between accounts on the same basis as the Colorado salesperson who drives hundreds of miles between customers.

Rewarding Superior Performance

A good sales compensation plan always rewards superior performance. Using the job description, you have decided which positive action the compensation plan is to quickly and effectively reward. Now you must build into the compensation plan means for the superior performer to receive superior pay. Don't place an upper limit on salespeople's compensation, because this dulls motivation. Earning potential for salespeople should remain open-ended.

If you employ six salespeople in well-developed territories with similar potential and one salesperson's orders grow much faster than the others, then your compensation plan should pay that person more money. If, from the job description, you decide that the compensation plan should reward the opening of new accounts, and if one salesperson opens twenty new accounts in six months versus ten for the other salespeople (assuming equal territory potential), your compensation plan should pay more money to the salesperson with twenty new accounts.

Providing Stability

A good compensation plan provides a certain level of stability so that salespeople have some downside protection for their incomes. The income of a salesperson who loses a large account should decline, but not to a level that threatens his or her ability to meet mortgage payments. Such a salesperson requires time to obtain another major account. The income of salespeople selling to cyclical industries such as the auto, aircraft, steel, and farm equipment industries should be less in bad times than in good, but not so much less as to threaten their ability to put food on the table. Such salespeople must survive the bad times in order to write orders when business improves. Rewards must reflect results, but a certain minimum level must be assured.

Outlining the Objectives

Take a few minutes to outline the objectives of your particular sales compensation plan. If your small business sells custom-printed forms for data processing, your objectives might read:

- Reward salespeople for opening new accounts and expanding existing ones through developing forms that solve customer problems. Reward salespeople for diligently seeking reorders.
- Encourage salespeople to assist in obtaining credit information, collecting overdue balances, occasionally delivering small orders, and handling complaints.
- Provide a guaranteed minimum monthly paycheck for new salespeople, new territories, and weak sales periods.
- Require administration by current payroll clerk, monthly payments, and simple reporting to each salesperson.
- Require commission splitting on regional accounts where two salespeople share the work.
- Provide 5 percent more compensation than the competition, but do not exceed 10 percent of company sales.
- Do not limit top earnings.

Compensation Mix

The particular combination of salary, commission, and bonus you select for your compensation plan should reflect the overall objectives you have set. Remember, your compensation plan should reinforce positive behavior and encourage productive activity, which achieves these objectives and satisfies salespeople's needs. Your choice also depends on the type product or service you sell and the type salesperson you wish to attract. Your compensation plan tells salespeople which activities and results the company regards as most important. Management in fact communicates its priorities to the sales force through the compensation mix.

The 1990 Dartnell "Sales Force Compensation" report on 400 medium-size American companies shows that for senior salespeople only 5 percent of the companies surveyed employed straight salary, while 12 percent used straight commission, 7 percent a combination of commission and bonus, 34 percent a combination of salary and commission, 18 percent a combination of salary and bonus, and 24 percent a combination of salary bonus and commission. The companies employed 55,000 salespeople, and 70 percent of the companies had annual sales under $25 million. Median compensation for trainees was $22,820, for entry-level salespeople $28,291, for semi-experienced salespeople $35,734, and for experienced salespeople $46,209.* *Sales and Marketing Management* magazine reports the average annual 1989 compensation for a sales trainee at $25,079, for a middle-level salesperson at $37,073, for a top-level salesperson at $58,981, and for a sales supervisor at $62,282. By industry group, sales trainee average annual compensation ranged from $22,506 for services, to $23,297 for consumer goods, to $28,455 for industrial goods. For middle-level salespeople, compensation ranged from $35,082 for services, to $37,882 for consumer goods, to $39,614 for industrial goods. For top-level salespeople, compensation ranged from $54,573 for industrial goods, to $56,764 for services, to $63,355 for consumer goods. These compensation figures include salary, commission, bonus, and other incentives, but do not include expenses or fringe benefits.†

A 1990 survey of forty large consumer goods companies conducted by TPF&C showed that 67 percent of all intermediate direct salespeople were compensated by salary plus bonus, 10 percent were compensated by salary plus commission plus bonus, 10 percent by base salary only, 7 percent by salary plus commission, and 3 percent each by salary plus bonus or commission against a draw. The same survey of sixty large industrial products companies reported that 46 percent of all intermediate direct sales people were compensated by salary plus bonus, 19 percent by salary plus bonus plus commission, 23 percent by salary plus commission, 10 percent by base salary only, and 2 percent by commission against a draw. For forty large industrial process component companies the survey reported 54 percent of all intermediate direct salespeople were compensated by salary plus bonus, 20 percent by salary plus commission, 14 percent by base salary only, 10 percent by salary plus bonus plus commission, and 2 percent by commission against a draw. For twenty large all-service companies the survey reported that 36 percent of all intermediate direct sales people were compensated by salary plus bonus, another 36 percent by salary plus bonus plus commission, 23 percent by salary plus commission, and 5 percent by base salary only.* Thus compensation varies considerably by industry.

The 1990/91 Sales & Marketing Personnel Report (by the ECS/A Wyatt Data Service Company), which surveyed 630 organizations, showed that 78 percent of all sales representatives were compensated by salary plus incentive, 17 percent by salary only, and 5 percent by commission only. The same report on 479 organizations showed that the annual total compensation (salary plus incentive) for the highest-paid sales representatives in durable-goods manufacturing averaged $54,000, in nondurable-goods manufacturing, $51,000, in energy, $52,000, in trade, $48,000, in services, $49,000, in utilities, $47,000, in banking and finance, $41,000, in insurance, $50,000, in nonprofits, $36,000, and in all industry categories combined, $51,000.†

Salary Plans: Advantages and Disadvantages

Salary provides salespeople with a fixed amount of pay per period regardless of their recent activities or results. Nonetheless, when results exceed or fall short of expectations, you can adjust the salary accordingly. However, the reward for good performance or penalty for weak results is not immediate or direct.

Straight salary provides the salesperson with a steady income and does not stress the immediate importance of writing orders. Salary emphasizes the importance of certain nonselling activities and encourages the salesperson to engage in these activities. Often a salesperson must perform services after the sale that will not necessarily result in a reorder. For example, the salesperson for a small concern renting expensive tropical plants to offices may be required under the rental agreement to check and treat the plants monthly.

Because payments are the same each period, salary is easy to administer, and direct selling expenses remain fixed regardless of volume. Before

*From 1989/1990 Sales Compensation Survey, TPF&C, a Towers Perrin Company, Chicago, Ill.
†From the 1990/91 Sales & Marketing Personnel Report (Fort Lee, N.J.: ECS/A Wyatt Data Services Company).

each month begins, you know the exact amount required for your salespeople's compensation.

Salary compensation for salespeople, however, contains certain theoretical advantages that in practice do not exist. In practice, salary does not allow greater control over the sales force or greater flexibility in realigning territories. Nor does it develop a greater sense of company loyalty. Regardless of the compensation plan, no salesperson readily accepts a weaker territory or reassignment of a major customer. Control, flexibility, and loyalty are thus not reasons to use a straight salary plan, but excuses because straight salary is so simple.

The correct level of compensation, whether salary, commission, bonus, or some combination of two or more elements, helps maintain proper control over the sales force and builds loyalty. A salesperson receiving $70,000 annually in straight commission is more likely to respond to your directions than a salaried person receiving $25,000, and will certainly display more company loyalty. In smaller companies, proper control and loyalty also result from nonmonetary factors such as personal relationships, recognition for achievement, a feeling of belonging, fear of dismissal, and the use of communication tools like call reports and route sheets.

The major disadvantages of salary plans are their lack of financial incentives, their tendency to reward poor performers at the expense of strong performers, and their lack of a proper percentage relationship to sales volume. Salary does not offer that special incentive required for extra effort. It encourages adequate but not superior performance. Generally, salaries overpay the unaggressive salesperson and underpay the hustler, thus favoring the less productive.

Salaried compensation as a percentage of revenues can vary drastically depending on sales. When sales rise, the percentage falls; but when sales decrease, the percentage increases painfully, and this may prove critical to a small business's profits and/or survival.

Type of Person and Selling Related to Salary Plan

Salaried compensation plans generally attract salespeople who are team players, ambitious to climb the executive ladder, steady rather than top performers, more professional than commercial, and prefer presold products. Once hired, salaried salespeople often develop rigid but comfortable routines and often expect considerable sales assistance from management. The type of sales compensation plan you choose acts as a natural filter or selection device in attracting candidates. In this way your job description, candidate profile, and compensation plan objectives become interrelated.

Salaried compensation plans lend themselves to selling products or services that are presold or cyclical; that require considerable prospecting, missionary work, or long negotiating periods; that call for service not related to reorders; and that involve team selling. Salary is also appropriate for trainees, new undeveloped territories, and situations with no adequate measure of performance.

For example, sales of durable goods, such as machine tools or equipment for utilities, fluctuate dramatically with business cycles; require considerable time working with customer engineers, purchasing agents, and plant managers to make a sale; often require the salesperson to be accompanied by a sales engineer; and involve the salesperson's assistance with installation. Machine tools or equipment for public utilities, like many big-ticket technical products that involve few orders but many dollars, lend themselves to salaried sales compensation. Items presold through national advertising such as pharmaceuticals, soap, toothpaste, liquor, and petroleum lend themselves to salaried sales compensation. In these situations the salesperson functions as order-taker, not active seller.

Some new salespeople require salaries during their training period because they could not survive financially on the basis of their performance. Salespeople assigned to new territories with no established business require a salary until they can build up volume. People selling to government agencies or other businesses that require bids operate in conditions with no adequate measure of performance. Was the salesperson or the bid responsible for the sale? Here again, salary proves appropriate.

Commission Plans: Advantages and Disadvantages

A commission provides an immediate reward for successful performance. If sales increase, your people make more money; if sales decrease, they make less. Commission emphasizes the importance of writing orders and encourages the salesperson to engage in activities that culminate in order-writing. Increased sales often require the salesperson to perform many tasks besides writing orders, including prospecting for new accounts, setting up display fixtures, counting stock, calibrating equipment, and solving a data entry problem.

Generally, commission plans are easy to understand and to compute. You multiply a fixed percentage times dollars of sales, or a fixed dollar amount times units of sales. Each day your salespeople know their earnings. Each month the payroll department clerk performs simple multiplication to arrive at each person's compensation.

Where commissions have to be split, because the sale involved more than one person's efforts, or when different rates are used for different products, administration proves more difficult. To prevent arguments, details of commission splits must be decided before a sale, not afterwards.

With commission plans, sales compensation costs remain a fixed percentage of your revenues whether they rise or fall, thereby protecting profit margins and helping cash flow. When sales decline, the company is not saddled with a large fixed expenditure. For smaller companies and start ups with limited capital, this feature is very important. New ventures especially benefit from commission because initial sales costs are lower, reflecting the low sales volume.

Commission provides the sales force with an incentive to work hard and earn a great deal of money. Only time, energy, and territory restraints limit the salesperson's compensation. Because no career ladder exists in the smaller-business sales force, the opportunity to earn large sums on commission takes on added importance. In some small and medium-size concerns, top salespeople earn more than the sales manager or president. Commission also proves more appropriate for smaller businesses because their sales forces are often smaller but the territories are larger and have unlimited potential. Don't place an upper limit on compensation, because it dulls motivation. Earning potential for salespeople should remain open-ended.

The major disadvantages of commission plans are that they lack emphasis on non-selling activities and encourage highlighting, or calling on a small number of large accounts at the expense of a large number of smaller ones. They can also result in high sales force turnover during weak sales periods, in excessive income from large nonrecurring sales, and in salespeople overselling unneeded features in addition to overloading customers with inventory. Commission compensation stresses the benefits (immediate orders) of shorter-term customer relations rather than the longer-term benefits of a growing relationship. However, proper sales training and supervision can overcome many of these disadvantages.

It is difficult convincing commissioned salespeople to collect past due accounts unless their commissions are penalized for bad debts. It requires more salesmanship on the part of management to obtain weekly call reports from commissioned people than it does from salaried; the salespeople must believe that call reports help their performance. Commission attracts salespeople with a need for freedom and independence, people who feel they are in business for themselves.

Because large accounts generate more sales and commission dollars, a nonsalaried salesperson often concentrates his or her efforts on the majors and neglects small accounts. Through proper training and supervision, management must convince the sales force that smaller accounts also have virtues. For example, smaller accounts often take less time to sell, remain loyal, and require less service.

Large fluctuations in sales cause large fluctuations in dollars of commission income, leading to high sales force turnover. Few salespeople quit when their commissions rise, but many leave when their income falls.

When unusually large windfall orders create unusually large commissions, problems may occur. Sometimes the salesperson rises to the next tax bracket, or just becomes complacent, and the following year's results are sure to be a letdown. The additional compensation may also upset fellow employees, who feel entitled to more money. A commission salesman for a small industrial gear company increased his income tenfold on one order from a conveyor concern. He used the six-figure commission check to buy out the family that owned the small gear company.

Some commission salespeople sell customers unneeded features and overload inventory. Proper sales training can prevent this. Commission people must understand that there will be less commission next year if they mistreat customers this year—because their sales will be lower. Over the long term the salesperson must satisfy customer needs.

If a compensation plan allows commission people to earn a good living, then management can obtain their cooperation in correcting some of these disadvantages. A salesperson earning a good living does not wish to loose his or her job. A commission sales force that trusts and respects management will modify its behavior.

As prices rise for a product or service, so do commission dollars. A salesperson gets paid more dollars for selling the same units this year than last if the unit price increases. However, a decrease in unit volume because of the price increase can offset this gain. Commission rates require annual review to measure the effects of inflation and unit sales.

Commissions can cause frustration when small territories or realigned territories limit or decrease sales volume. In such a situation you may have to consider guarantees.

Type of Person and Selling Related to Commission Plans

Commission compensation plans generally attract aggressive career salespeople with no ambition for promotion into management. These salespeople are lone wolves, top producers but erratic, and more interested in the sale than selling technique. Sometimes these characteristics strain customer relations or result in a salesperson who prefers to highlight a large territory rather than saturate a smaller one.

Because of all these characteristics, commission plans do not lend themselves to selling products or services that are cyclical, that require a great deal of nonorder-related service, or that involve missionary work or team selling. Commission plans do lend themselves to nontechnical, unsophisticated products and services for which reorders create a steady flow of business and unit prices are not high. The commission represents an incentive to return for reorders.

For example, sales of some soft goods such as men's white underwear to retail stores are a nonfashion, nontechnical, unsophisticated low-ticket item involving frequent orders, little missionary work, and no team selling. Men's underwear, like most apparel, lends itself to commission selling. Door-to-door salespeople and part-time salespeople almost always receive commission.

Rates of Commission

The rate of commission must allow a salesperson to earn a competitive and living wage from average results, but a superior wage from superior results. Also, the rate of commission must allow your company to maintain necessary profit margins and return on capital. Commission rates vary from 3 percent on the sale of commodity food products and lumber to 20 percent on software, medical supplies, and scientific research equipment.

Some concerns dramatically vary commission rates on different products or services as an incentive for salespeople to push slow sellers or high-margin items. Some concerns pay commission on a product lines gross margin rather than its sales dollars. In practice this does not achieve its goal. A salesperson's job involves finding customer needs or problems and then selling a product or service with benefits that meets those needs and solves those problems. Management's job includes pricing products and services to create a desired return, developing products and services that meet needs in the marketplace, and eliminating products or services that no longer meet customer needs or company profit goals. Commission plans that encourage salespeople to sell something that is not best for the customer or that is not wanted by the customer generally do not work. When you vary commission rates according to gross margin or product, salespeople complain about the lower commission rate rather than selling the items with a higher rate, customers complain that salespeople push inappropriate items, and administrative and salespeople complain about the difficulty of understanding such a system and computing monthly paychecks.

However, large quantities of goods sold off-price or large service contracts sold at below list price sometimes justify a lower commission rate. The company and the salesperson share the cost of such a discount. Many concerns pay only one rate even on large off-price orders. They feel a salesperson should not be penalized for large off-price orders because if some orders are less profitable management does not have to accept them.

Some concerns pay a lower commission on the first dollar of sales, progressive rates; other pay lower commissions on the last dollar of sales, regressive rates; others use constant rates. Progressive and regressive rates tend to confuse and discourage salespeople and complicate administration. A salesperson puts the same effort into the first sale of the month or year as into the last and deserve equal compensation for both. If you pay more for the first sale than the last, salespeople may lose enthusiasm toward the end of a sales period. If you pay more for the last sale than the first, salespeople may concentrate their orders in one period at the expense of another.

Many businesses pay a higher commission rate on annual sales in excess of last year's actual figures, or in excess of this year's forecast or quota. Even with commission compensation plans, some salespeople reach complacency plateaus. Their current sales level is constant and dollars of compensation meet their needs. In this situation commission becomes more like a salary, with little financial incentive to grow. To overcome this situation, one software company lowered its commission rate from 10 percent to 9 percent on last year's volume, but raised it from 10 percent to 13 percent on any annual increase. Your compensation plan sends a strong message to salespeople.

Bonuses

A bonus provides an extra, deferred reward for some form of outstanding performance. Generally, bonuses are paid once a year, once a quarter, or once a selling period over and above salary or commission. You decide on a specific activity that most benefits the company and then set realistic goals or quotas with each salesperson relating to performance of this activity. If goals are approached or exceeded, the salesperson receives a predetermined sum of money. Generally, salespeople who reach 125 percent of their goal or quota receive a larger bonus than those who have reached only 100 percent.

Base the salesperson's goals on expected performance and territory potential. Setting unreachable goals frustrates salespeople, dulls their motivation, and defeats the purpose of a bonus.

Because bonuses are not paid frequently or immediately after the successful performance of a task, they lose some of their motivational value. The loss of motivation can be partially offset by informing salespeople monthly about their performance progress toward their annual goal and resulting bonus. Also, a portion of the annual bonus can be paid quarterly if the previous quarter's performance exceeds a proration of the annual goal.

Bonus plans can be difficult to administer, but they do allow a great deal of flexibility. You can reward different activities at different performance levels with varying sums for different salespeople. Depending on your company's needs, you can pay a bonus to the Wisconsin salesperson for new accounts, to the Ohio salesperson for increasing average order size, and to the Florida salesperson for increasing dollar sales. Depending on company needs, bonus arrangements may be changed annually. Make sure each salesperson understands the ground rules.

A processed meat company allows salespeople to earn a third of their income from bonuses based on a territory's profitability. This incentive is important because salespeople have some flexibility in setting prices. A temporary personnel service pays salespeople a bonus equal to 50 percent of their salary for making their revenue quota. Revenues not only depend on new business but on servicing current accounts after the sale. A supplier of big-ticket equipment to utilities pays sales engineers a bonus equal to 25 percent of their salary for making a specified number of qualified bids or proposals.

The flexibility of a smaller business allows it to custom design the bonus for each territory. The lack of management opportunity makes the bonus especially important for smaller business salespeople. The bonus rewards an outstanding performance in lieu of a promotion. Also, bonus compensation being contingent upon proven performance creates less resentment among nonselling employees over certain salespeople's higher income levels.

Combination Plans

Some combination of salary, commission, and bonus represents the most widely used form of sales compensation. Dartnell Corporation's 1990 Sales Force Compensation Report shows that 81 percent of the 400 American companies surveyed (employing 55,000 salespeople) employed a combination of salary and incentive.

Because the objectives of a compensation system usually involve quickly and effectively rewarding a combination of positive actions, rather than one simple action, combination plans prove most appropriate. Combination plans can be tailored to encourage the specific behavior most beneficial to your sales effort and to eliminate the disadvantages of straight commission or straight salary. Because smaller concerns are more flexible and can even use different compensation plans for different salespeople, combination arrangements prove particularly suitable for them. What motivates one salesperson may not motivate another. Combination plans provide security plus incentive for salespeople at a cost that most smaller businesses can afford.

Combination plans lack the simplicity of straight commission or straight salary plans, however, and this makes them more difficult for the company to administer and for the salespeople to understand. A common mistake of combination plans involves offering a specific compensation for too many activities rather than emphasizing the most important ones, for example, paying a bonus for new accounts, a commission on sales increases, plus a base salary for retention. Because of their complexity, combination plans require more frequent revision than either straight salary or straight commission.

An office furniture company in St. Louis employed five local full-time salespeople, all on a straight commission basis. Two of the salespeople, who had ten years with the concern, earned a good income but only sold large customers in their territory. The other three salespeople had less than two years with the company and replaced a previous parade of representatives who had quit. The president, who was also the sales manager, kept himself busy selling "house" accounts, but worried because total company sales had stopped growing.

After attending a sales management seminar in Hawaii, the president decided to make some changes in his sales compensation program. He set sales goals or quotas 20 percent higher than previous actual figures for the two older salespeople and established a bonus that would start when they achieved 90 percent of quota and would become very substantial if they achieved 110 percent of quota. He also paid these men a small bonus for every new account they opened.

For the three newer salespeople, he guaranteed a base salary in addition to commission but lowered the previous commission rate. He added a bonus based on achieving certain percentages of their sales quotas or goals. He also agreed to split commissions on what were previously house accounts. As a result of this new plan, revenues grew and turnover declined.

An emergency lighting company in California employed salaried full-time salespeople in Los Angeles, San Francisco, and Sacramento. They made a good living, but sales had stagnated and selling expenses as a percentage of revenues had increased, producing lower profit margins. The company enlisted the help of a consultant who recommended more incentive compensation. The sales manager put each salesperson on a draw equal to his or her previous salary. A monthly commission was paid against the draw. The rate and dollars of commission at current sales levels would have left each salesperson 20 percent overdrawn at year's end. The sales manager agreed not to limit higher compensation, but he also informed his people that draws would be reduced each year to equal the previous year's actual commission earned. One salesperson quit and had to be replaced, but two years later company revenues started increasing and selling expenses as a percentage of revenues decreased.

A person who leased guard dogs required his salesmen to deliver and pick up the animals as well. This service activity was as important as opening new accounts. He paid his people a fee for each animal delivered and returned, plus a commission on each sales dollar, plus a bonus on new accounts. His business thrived, but at the expense of several bookkeepers.

Individually Written Compensation Plans

Because smaller businesses are flexible, you can tailor-make your compensation plans according to individual needs. Each salesperson has different and changing needs, and each territory presents different problems and potential. What motivates and is appropriate for one salesperson may not motivate or be appropriate for another.

In creating a compensation plan, you may wish to consider each salesperson separately. For instance, the New York salesperson may sell primarily to major department stores that require considerable stock-taking service, or to corporate headquarters that require considerable missionary selling. The Ohio salesperson may be pioneering a new territory, and the New England salesperson may sell to many established small accounts. Therefore, you may decide to pay the New York salesperson primarily on the basis of salary with a small commission, the Ohio salesperson primarily on salary with a small bonus, and the New England salesperson on straight commission against a small draw. You may reimburse all travel expenses up to $1,000 a month for the Ohio person, pay the New York

Figure 3-1. Sample compensation arrangement for the New York salesperson.

Name:	Bill Locke	Time period: Calendar 19___
Salary:	$4,000 a month payable every other week.	
Commission:	2% of sales when shipped less uncollectible accounts receivable, returns, and advertising allowances. Payable on the 20th of each month for the preceding month.	
Expenses:	$250 a month for travel and entertainment, payable on the 15th; expense reports required each week.	
Fringe Benefits:	Social Security, unemployment, group life, disability, and health insurance.	

salesperson a flat $250-a-month travel allowance, and have the New England salesperson pay his or her own expenses.

Whatever the individual plan, each salesperson should receive a complete written presentation of the compensation arrangement. Figures 3-1, 3-2, and 3-3 represent the written forms appropriate for the three different salespeople.

Expenses

According to Dartnell's 1990 Survey of Sales Force Compensation report, 79 percent of all companies surveyed paid all or some of their salespeople's expenses in addition to salary, commission, and bonus compensation. For these companies' salespeople, travel and entertainment expenses averaged 24 percent of their direct compensation. Industrial goods companies were above the average and service companies below. For these firms, sales force compensation plus expenses averaged 12 percent of their annual sales volume, but ranged from 3 percent for the chemical, rubber, plastics, and construction industry to 20 percent for business services, communications, and sales to retailers. Expense categories include travel by automobile, air, and rail; lodging; telephone; car phone; entertainment; product samples; local promotions; office or clerical help; and home FAX machines and photocopies. Thirty-seven percent of the respondents give an auto mileage allowance, 22 percent lease company cars for salespeople, 16 percent own

Figure 3-2. Sample compensation arrangement for the Ohio salesperson.

Name:	George Geroan Time period: Calendar 19___
Salary:	$3,000 a month payable every other week.
Bonus:	$2,000 if shipments exceed 90% of quota, $3,000 if shipments exceed 100% of quota, $4,000 if shipments exceed 125% of quota. Maximum total bonus $4,000 payable on January 30, 199___.
Expenses:	Up to $1,000 a month cumulative for travel and entertainment payable two weeks after expense reports are received. The difference between 12 months actual expenses and $12,000 to be split 50/50 if actual is under $12,000.
Fringe Benefits:	Social Security, unemployment, group life, disability, and health insurance.

Figure 3-3. Sample compensation arrangement for the New England salesperson.

Name:	Kevin Kelly Time period: Calendar 19___
Commission:	10% of sales when shipped less uncollectible accounts receivable, returns, and advertising allowances. Payable on the 20th of each month for the preceding month.
Draw:	$2,000 a month payable every other week against commission earned.
Expenses	All travel and entertainment and expenses are paid for by the salesperson.
Fringe Benefits:	Social Security, unemployment, group life, disability, and health insurance.

company cars, 18 percent pay for salespeople's car phones, and 10 percent provide home photocopiers and FAX machines. Most companies pay between $6,000 and $14,000 of annual expenses per salesperson, with the average at $9,363; and so this becomes a major selling cost which must be kept under control. Over the previous five years salespeople's expenses had risen faster than their commissions, salaries, and bonus compensation.*

Sales and Marketing Management magazine's 1990 "Survey of Selling Costs" reports that in 1989 annual auto, travel, and entertainment expenses averaged $6,721 for sales trainees, $9,514 for middle-level salespeople, and $11,855 for top-level salespeople. Travel and entertainment expenses averaged $8,988 for consumer goods salespeople, $11,172 for industrial goods salespeople, and $7,938 for salespeople selling services. The same survey reports that the average cost of meals, lodging, and auto rental for a salesperson rose from $50 per day in 1972 to $137 a day in 1983 to $176 a day in 1989. New York, San Francisco, Chicago, and Washington ranked as the most expensive cities, Dayton, Canton, Omaha, and Wichita as the least costly.†

The 1990/91 Sales & Marketing Personnel Report (ECS/A Wyatt Data Service Company), which surveyed 240 organizations, showed that total salesperson travel and entertainment expenses averaged 1.9 percent of annual company sales for services, 2.1 percent for retail/wholesale trade, 1.3 percent for nondurable manufacturing, and .9 percent for durable goods manufacturing. The same report, but including 580 responses, shows that 16 percent of the companies provide salespeople with company-owned cars, and 44 percent with company-leased cars. For employee owned-cars, 69 percent of the companies use a single rate mileage reimbursement, 11 percent a flat reimbursement, and 20 percent a combination of the two.

The same report, with 440 responses, shows that the average salesperson cost of travel with overnight accommodations runs approximately $124 a day and without overnight accommodations approximately $40 a day.‡

The TPF&C 1989/1990 Sales Compensation Survey of 160 Fortune 1000 firms reports that 65 percent of intermediate direct salespeople in the consumer products, industrial products, and industrial process components industries are provided automobiles at no expense. However, in the service industry only 14 percent of the companies provide cars at no ex-

*From *Sales Force Compensation,* the Dartnell Corporation.
†From *Sales & Marketing Management,* Survey of Selling Costs.
‡From *Sales & Marketing Personnel Report,* ECS.

pense to the salesperson. For all companies surveyed, the report shows that 90 percent reimburse salespeople for out-of-pocket expenses.*

A smaller business does not possess the financial resources of a larger concern and so must selectively put its available resources to the best use. A small electronics company that manufactured components for cable television and microwave transmission hired three new field sales representatives, one to cover the government market in Washington, one to cover the West Coast from Los Angeles, and one to cover Europe from London. Each person received a modest salary, plus a commission based on sales; but each also received an open-ended expense account because these new territories required a great deal of travel and entertainment. These three salespeople accounted for $200,000 in expenses in two years in addition to their salaries and commissions. Although they wrote $1 million worth of orders, they almost put their employer out of business.

A company that employs part-time salespeople to sell cable television door to door must reimburse a different variety of expenses at a different level than a concern that sells office supplies by phone or one that uses representatives to sell wallets to chain stores, or one that employs full-time people to sell cleaning services to hospitals, or a concern with one salesperson covering the entire country selling nail-making machines to steel mills. This section discusses the objectives of an expense plan, the various types of plans available to obtain those objectives, and proven means for lowering salespeople's expenses.

Objectives of Expense Plans

Regardless of your product or service, any expense plan should be fair, controllable, fast, simple, easy to understand and administer, and flexible. Salespeople should have an economic incentive for controlling their expenses, for using expense money productively and efficiently. If no economic incentive exists, if expenses are open-ended, salespeople use them as an additional form of compensation. Similarly, management cannot ask its sales people to pay for expenses when this would lower their total compensation to an unacceptable level.

Salespeople should be paid and expenses reimbursed promptly. Many smaller companies finance themselves by remaining months behind in paying portions of their sales force's compensation or expenses. Such behavior

*From Sales Compensation Survey. TPF&C.

increases turnover of salespeople, and certainly hurts morale and productivity.

Salespeople must thoroughly understand what is included in the expense plan so they can act appropriately. An industrial gear salesman who lived in Los Angeles covered the entire state of California by auto. His employer reimbursed auto expenses. On one trip he flew to San Francisco and submitted his expense report for the plane ticket only to find out his employer did not reimburse air travel.

Make your expense plan as simple as possible to facilitate administration and understanding. A small securities brokerage firm paid all of its institutional salespersons' air fare, plus 80 percent of the first night's lodgings, 70 percent of the second night's lodgings, and 60 percent thereafter. In addition, it reimbursed 50 percent of breakfast expense, 80 percent of lunch, and 70 percent of dinner. The expense reports and vouchers looked like physics formulas.

A good expense plan requires a certain amount of flexibility for exceptions. Your Denver salesperson receives a call from a hot prospect asking him to be in his Salt Lake City office at ten o'clock the next morning. The salesperson flies both ways to save time, since he also has appointments in Denver the day following the Salt Lake City visit. Your company policy reimburses auto expenses but not airfare. You might consider making an exception in this case.

Types of Expense Plans

Salespeople can be asked to pay all their own expenses out of their basic compensation, the firm and the sales force can split expenses, or the company can reimburse the salespeople for all their expenses. Many variations exist within each of these possibilities. Expense policies, like salespeople compensation plans, require annual review and constant updating to reflect changing conditions.

Salespeople can be asked to pay all their own expenses if the level of compensation takes this into account. Commissioned salespeople in the apparel business, for example, receive a rate of commission high enough to pay all their own expenses. The rate of commission varies according to the level of anticipated expenses. The New York salesperson who travels between customers by subway might receive a lower commission rate than the Iowa/Nebraska salesperson who drives fifty miles between accounts.

If possible, making the salesperson responsible for his or her own expenses proves best for the smaller business. Under such a plan, the salesperson, who has the most to gain or lose and is the best judge, has total responsibility for expenses. Money will not be wasted on unnecessary trips or entertainment. If salespeople feel that money spent on travel or entertainment will result in orders, they will spend it. Certainly this arrangement is the easiest to administer and understand.

A similar but more complicated arrangement involves the salesperson submitting reports and receipts for certain designated expenses, which the company reimburses until the total reached a specified percentage of sales volume. Anything over that percentage becomes the salesperson's responsibility. At year's end the salesperson receives a portion of the amount saved should expenses total less than the agreed percentage. Here again the salesperson has an economic incentive to spend wisely. The percentage rate varies according to the territory, volume, and expense requirements. The sales volume figure against which you apply the percentage rate to arrive at a dollar expense limit may be last year's actual, this year's forecast, or this year's actual cumulative to date.

Some concerns agree to pay a predetermined percentage of allowable expense items. For example, they may agree to pay 65 percent of all the salesperson's entertainment, travel, and telephone expenses. Salespeople submit invoices, receipts, and reports verifying their expenses, and the company then reimburses only 65 percent. Company and salesperson share the expense.

Some concerns merely give salespeople a flat monthly expense allowance to use as they see fit. Others allow a flat amount for certain expenses, for example, $60 a night for lodging and $40 a day for food. Both arrangements must vary dollar amounts to accommodate different expenses in different territories. A hotel room in Omaha will not cost as much as a hotel room in San Francisco. The flat monthly allowance allows you to accurately forecast this expense item. Both these plans are easy to understand and administer.

Some capital goods companies allow salespeople unlimited expense accounts on certain items, but such an arrangement can put a smaller concern under tremendous financial pressure. A good expense plan gives the salesperson an incentive to spend wisely and limit expenses.

Some expense plans involve combinations of the above choices. Airfare might be 100 percent reimbursable, but lodging and meals are paid for with a flat allowance.

Expense plans that require vouchers, receipts, invoices, and reports involve a great deal of administrative time on the part of salespeople and the sales manager. The salesperson must submit accurate information, and you must verify its correctness. This is necessary not only for internal controls but for reporting to the Internal Revenue Service as well. However, expense reports provide important information both on costs and on where the salesperson travels and who the salesperson calls on.

Unless salespeople pay their own expenses or you pay a flat monthly allowance, these costs are difficult to forecast. It is difficult to estimate in November what travel expenses might be incurred during the following year. For a smaller concern this can prove especially problematic.

Reducing Expenses

The following specific suggestions should help your salespeople reduce their expenses. When possible, they should use the telephone rather than a personal visit to qualify prospects, arrange appointments, handle service items, answer specific questions, or write small orders. They should plan the day ahead so as to see more customers and travel fewer miles. They should travel only economy class by air and, where possible, stay at budget-class lodgings. If the same city is frequently visited by air, consult your travel agent as to discount tickets. Some discount tickets can't be canceled and others involve penalties. Lastly, they should make fewer but longer trips. Also, management should try to negotiate special corporate hotel, auto rental, airline, and telephone rates for the sales force.

As salespeople and buyers have become more professional, entertainment has become less important as a selling and promotional tool. Personal relationships established over lunch and dinner continue to be extremely significant, but golf in the afternoon, gifts, paid vacations, theater or sporting event tickets, and expensive night clubs have given way to price, quality, and service. Many concerns frown on any entertainment or gifts for their buyers or purchasing agents beyond a business lunch. As sales manager you can reduce expenses by discouraging salespeople from engaging in excessive entertainment. There are ethical issues involved here and in some industries legal concerns.

Company-owned or leased cars and company credit cards are difficult for the smaller concern to control and administer. Reimbursing travel and entertainment expenses is one thing; having primary financial responsibility is another. When the company provides a car and a credit card, it initially pays for the salesperson's personal and business use of both. The salesperson then reimburses the company for personal use. When disputes result, the company must prove the salesperson wrong. When the salesperson owns the car and credit card, personal use is expected; but the company does not pay for it. When disputes result over mileage, travel, auto, and entertainment expenses submitted for reimbursement, the burden of proof lies with the salesperson. Although Dartnell and Wyatt report that 52 percent to 60 percent of the 400 firms in their survey provide salespeople with company-leased or company-owned cars, as sales manager of a smaller firm you can reduce expenses by not providing company-owned or leased vehicles and by not issuing company credit cards.

A few smaller concerns do allow personal use of certain sales expenses such as a company-owned automobile or credit card as a fringe benefit because these items often can escape income taxation. If you choose to do this, however, be sure to consult the company accountant.

Fringe Benefits

The total direct cost of your sales force includes salaries, commissions, bonuses, expenses, and fringe benefits. In 1989, average compensation for experienced salespeople whether paid through commission, salary, bonus, or some combination was $38,000, with annual reimbursed expenses averaging $10,000. Smaller companies are generally at the upper end of the commission, salary, and bonus scale, but at the lower end of the reimbursed expense scale.

Now you must add to these figures the cost of primary fringe benefits such as social security, unemployment compensation, medical, life, accident, and disability insurance, and vacations, and possibly the cost of secondary fringe benefits such as profit sharing, pension plans, personal use of company car and credit cards, club and association memberships, reimbursed educational expenses, dental/vision insurance, and reimbursed moving expenses. Fringe benefits vary from 15 percent to 40 percent of salary, commission, and bonus, and thus represent a significant expense item.

In 1989, according to Dartnell Corporation, the cost of a sales call including compensation, expenses, and fringe benefits averaged $115, up 57 percent from 1979. The average cost of a sales call varied from $25 in the tobacco, office equipment, trash removal, and beverage industries to $250 for nonferrous metals, transportation equipment, instruments, rubber and plastics.*

The 1990/91 Sales & Marketing Personnel Report, which surveyed 217 companies, shows that the total cost of a sales force (compensation, expenses, and fringes) averaged 4.3 percent of annual company sales for durable goods manufacturing, 3.5 percent for nondurable good manufacturing, 7.2 percent for retail/wholesale trade, and 7.5 percent for services.†

*From *Sales Force Compensation,* the Dartnell Corporation.
†From *Sales & Marketing Personnel Report,* ECS.

The TPF&C 1989/1990 Sales Compensation Survey reports that 96 percent of the 160 Fortune 1000 participating companies paid for their salespeople's group life and medical insurance, 92 percent paid for dental insurance, and 74 percent had profit-sharing or thrift plans. The same survey shows that 90 percent of the participants also pay for long-term disability, short-term disability, and pension plans.*

Primary Fringe Benefits

Regardless of the compensation mix, most smaller businesses pay their share of a salesperson's social security and unemployment taxes if the salesperson works more than half-time. Protection against major illness, accidents, disability, or death through group insurance can be purchased less expensively by the employer than by the individual. Some companies offer coverage for dependents, some just for the salesperson. These primary group insurance benefits are necessary to attract competent salespeople in today's business environment, and they promote good morale and peace of mind. Because premium payments are tax deductible for the company but not taxable to the insured, these benefits are more valuable to both parties.

If your smaller business does not possess the resources to pay the entire cost of premiums for primary group insurance benefits, ask the sales force to share the cost. If the company pays half and the salesperson pays half, he or she still benefits and gets the necessary protection at group rates. Major medical insurance with a $1,000 or $2,000 deductible and health maintenance organizations represent other means of lowering medical insurance costs.

Vacations represent an inexpensive fringe benefit for salespeople. Generally, customers write larger orders to cover themselves before or after the period when your salesperson takes a vacation. During the latter part of December and the early part of July many buyers and purchasing agents vacation themselves or close their order books. Encourage your salespeople to take their vacations when business is seasonally slow. Salespeople require a rest from the rigors of their work and generally return from such a rest with renewed vigor. If you schedule vacations correctly, no business will be lost.

Secondary Fringe Benefits

Because most smaller companies remain privately owned, profit sharing is not practical. For competitive or personal reasons, most smaller-business

*From Sales Compensation Survey, TPF&C.

owners don't care to divulge their profits. For tax purposes the owner often takes out any profits in the form of a bonus, reimbursed expenses, or a higher salary. Most small-business salespeople want a reward for selling performance instead of company profits because they have little control over profitability. Profit sharing in good years causes unmet expectations and disappointment in bad years. For these reasons, profit-sharing plans in smaller businesses cause more disappointments than motivation.

Because pension plans involve complicated and rigid legal requirements and excessive reporting and administrative work, most smaller businesses do not employ them. A pension plan for the sales force would also have to be available to all other employees on the same basis. You may desire a pension plan for executives and salespeople only, but generally it must be offered to hourly help too. In addition, pension plans require establishing reserves, hiring actuarial consultants, and filing reports on your financial condition with various governmental agencies.

For smaller businesses, selectively paying certain salespeople more and encouraging them to use IRA (Individual Retirement Act) or SEP (Self-Employed Pension) plans for retirement proves more practical. You can assist key salespeople in establishing IRA or SEP plans by introducing them to financial institutions that offer these services.

Also, you can purchase life insurance for a salesperson that converts to an annuity at retirement. These whole life policies carry a cash value that belongs to the salesperson and becomes an incentive for continuing employment. However, the company premium payment on such policies becomes taxable income for the insured. Universal and Incentive Life Insurance use term policies and then invest the excess funds to produce the same benefits.

Because pension-plan benefits grow with years of employment, they represent an incentive for good salespeople to continue with their present employer. When a person terminates, he or she loses a significant portion of the pension-plan benefits. Because smaller concerns generally cannot offer pension plans, the incentive to stay must come from other sources, such as current income, achievement, status, personal relationships, and generally pleasant working conditions.

In a smaller company, because opportunities for advancement do not exist, nontechnical educational costs does not produce positive results. To reimburse salespeople for attending classes in sales management only causes frustration, and might even lead to the loss of key personnel. However, if you offer a technical service or product, for example, chemical compounds used in metal plating or software used for financial analysis, technical courses would improve a salesperson's effectiveness. In such a situation reimbursed tuition would be worthwhile.

Dental and vision insurance, reimbursed moving expenses, and club
and association memberships prove too costly for most smaller businesses.
Generally, a good medical, life, accident, and disability insurance program
satisfies salespeople's major needs for expense protection. Likewise, only
a few smaller businesses provide company cars or company credit cards as
fringe benefits for salespeople.

Complacency Plateau

Whatever their financial rewards, most salespeople eventually reach a
complacency plateau or comfort zone. Money is not a universal incentive
and does not motivate most salespeople beyond a certain level. When income taxes claim 38 percent of each additional commission dollar, or when
a salesperson has acquired the desired material possessions, or when the
children have graduated from college, or when there is a two-person family income, a salesperson questions the extra effort necessary to increase
orders each year. When a salesperson reaches this complacency level, other
rewards such as challenge, achievement, recognition, status, personal
growth, authority and freedom must become the motivators.

Annual Review

Every compensation plan represents a compromise between company objectives and salespeople's needs, and because these change continually, a
good compensation plan requires annual review. When changing your plan,
avoid loss of continuity or uniformity. For example, raising or lowering
commission rates or salary level maintains uniformity and continuity, but
suddenly changing from a 100 percent salary plan to a 100 percent commission plan destroys it. Your type of compensation plan attracts a particular type of salesperson. Change the direction too quickly and you most
likely will change the sales force, too.

Territorial Profit-and-Loss Statement

A smaller business requires reliable information on resource use and people productivity. The bottom line for each salesperson is the profitability
of his or her territory.

Once a year you should subtract from each salesperson's annual shipment dollars his or her salary, commission, bonus, field sales expenses, and fringe benefit costs. Then you subtract other direct sales expenses identified with customers in that territory, such as advertising, rebates, promotion, and freight. Finally, subtract the estimated manufacturing costs (labor, material, factory overhead) for the goods shipped into the territory. This will vary from one territory to the next depending on product mix and pricing. The result is dollars contributed by the territory to cover fixed selling, general, and administrative expenses. Such an analysis allows you to compare each territory's profitability in dollars and percent of sales, and, if appropriate, to adjust the compensation plan.

4

Sales Force Organization and Time and Territory Management

Have you ever calculated the total expense of a typical representative in your sales organization or the average cost of each sales call and order? The surprisingly high results of such calculations emphasize the importance of proper organization and full utilization of each salesperson and each territory. Only with proper sales force organization and proper time and territory management will salespeople economically make the optimum number of effective calls on the right customers and prospects.

You arrive at the cost of the typical experienced salesperson in your company by taking the annual compensation (salary plus commission plus bonus), say $40,000, adding to it the reimbursed or company-paid selling expenses (such as travel, car, entertainment, telephone, samples, and possibly showroom or clerical support), say $6,000, then adding the cost of fringe benefits (such as social security, unemployment taxes, company-paid insurance, possibly a retirement plan), say another $10,000. The $56,000 total then would equal the annual expense of keeping your typical sales representative in business. Often we think about a salesperson's cost only in terms of direct compensation.

Share with each of your salespeople the total cost of putting them on the road, their cost per day, per hour, per call, per sale, per new account. In our example, the cost per day, assuming 240 working days a year, is $233, or, assuming an eight-hour day, $29 per hour. If a salesperson opens one new account a week, the cost of a new account might be calculated at $1,120.

Divide the total, in this case $56,000, by the average number of sales calls your typical salesperson makes in a year. You calculate this figure by multiplying average calls per day, say five times average working days in a year, or 240, to arrive at 1,200 calls per year. In this example, the average cost per call would be $56,000 divided by 1,200, or $46.66. If obtaining an order generally requires five sales calls, the average selling cost per order becomes $233.

For some small businesses, direct selling expenses are a disproportionate and growing percentage of the sales dollar. Once you have arrived at the average selling cost per order, in our example $233, determine the average sales or revenue per order. Divide your annual revenues by the number of orders written in a year. Analyze average selling cost per order as a percentage of average revenue per order. Can you lower it? Compare average selling cost per order to average revenue per order for each salesperson. Some salespeople may be much more profitable than others. You must decide on whether to include orders that are mailed or phoned in.

A further refinement of these calculations might involve prorating the onetime cost of hiring a salesperson, say $4,000, and his or her training costs, say $5,000, and adding this sum to each year's total salesperson selling cost. Then you divide this higher number by sales calls per annum or subtract it from territory revenues.

Sales & Marketing Management magazine's 1990 Survey of Selling Costs shows that the median cost of a sales call for consumer companies rose from $118.46 in 1986 to $196.26 in 1989, for industrial companies from $178.96 to $224.87, and for service companies from $161.76 to $165.85.*

The Dartnell Corporation's 1989 Survey of Sales Force Compensation for 400 companies lists the data in Table 4-1 as interpreted by *Sales & Marketing Management*.

The Dartnell survey includes information from 400 companies employing a total of 55,000 salespeople. Thirty-nine percent of the respondents had annual sales under $5 million and 71 percent had annual sales under $25 million. For all 400 companies the cost of a sales call averaged $64.07, the number of calls per day averaged 4.1, and the number of calls to close averaged 3.6.

Another recent Dartnell survey shows that the average salesperson spends only 32 percent of his or her time in face-to-face selling, versus 19 percent in selling over the phone, 21 percent traveling between calls and waiting to sell accounts, 15 percent on administrative tasks such as paperwork, reports, and attending sales meetings, and 13 percent on collecting

*Reprinted by permission of *Sales & Marketing Management*. Copyright: Survey of Selling Costs, February 26, 1990.

Table 4-1. Sales call statistics and operating expenses.

Industry Group	Cost per Call	Number of Calls Needed to Close a Sale	Sales Force Costs as a % of Total Sales
Business Services	$ 46.00	4.6	19.3%
Chemicals	165.80	2.8	3.0
Communications	40.60	4.0	21.6
Construction	111.20	2.8	3.2
Electronics	133.30	3.9	12.0
Fabricated Metals	80.80	3.3	6.4
Food Products	131.60	4.8	9.6
Instruments	226.00	5.3	10.3
Insurance	53.00	3.4	15.6
Machinery	68.50	3.0	13.0
Misc. Manufacturing	85.90	2.8	13.2
Office Equipment	25.00	3.7	15.0
Printing/Publishing	70.10	4.5	8.3
Retail	25.00	3.3	23.5
Rubber/Plastics	248.20	4.7	2.8
Utilities	89.90	4.8	17.3
Wholesale (Consumer)	84.10	3.0	7.0
Wholesale (Industrial)	50.00	3.3	12.6
Average	$96.39	3.8	11.9%

Note: Industry groups reflect categories selected and reported by the Dartnell Corporation. The overall average has been calculated by *Sales & Marketing Management* based on data from eighteen industries listed.
Source: Sales Force Compensation, Dartnell's 25th Survey. Used with permission of the Dartnell Corporation and reprinted by permission of *Sales & Marketing Management.* Copyright: Survey of Selling Costs, February 26, 1990.

overdue payables, expediting orders, answering complaints, and other service matters.★ With costs per call increasing each year and "eyeball-to-eyeball" selling time limited, using a salesperson's time efficiently represents a potential competitive advantage for small businesses.

★From *Sales Force Compensation, Dartnell's 25th Survey Edition.* Used with permission of the Dartnell Corporation, Chicago, Ill. All rights reserved.

In a smaller business, human and financial resources are limited, and so you must obtain maximum results from your most important asset, your salespeople. Imagine the possible sales increases from one more call a day or one more sale a week. Imagine the cost of the 32 percent of a salesperson's time spent in the customer's presence. Thirty-two percent of a five-day, forty-hour week is thirteen hours, or about one and a half days.

Proper hiring, training, and compensation, discussed in previous chapters, represent an important aid in obtaining maximum results, as do proper motivation, communication, planning, and appraisal, which will be discussed in future chapters. Unless you organize your sales force correctly, structure territories effectively, and help salespeople to manage their time, you cannot maximize results. The goal is utilizing each salesperson to his or her full potential.

A sales manager's job is making heroes, not being one, which involves helping his or her people. All this requires time and thought when you have everyday pressures to generate sales, crises requiring immediate attention, and no one to assist you. But, as with correct hiring, training, and compensation, properly organizing your salespeople and their territories eventually decreases everyday pressures and crises.

Remember, business is a dynamic process. Therefore, question old methods of organization to make sure that you have not simply inherited and then perpetuated past errors—and each year, review customer and territory assignments.

Types of Organization

Your sales force can be organized by product, account/customer, geographic territory, function, some combination of these methods, or with no restrictions. Each method of organization has its strengths and weaknesses. The choice depends on your particular products, accounts, markets, sales force, and objectives. Choose whatever type of organization best meets customer needs and best uses your salespeople, one that maximizes revenues and minimizes expenses.

Product Line Organization

If your company offers a wide variety of dissimilar or unrelated products or services—especially if they are complex—or if your company's products or services are sold to totally different markets, you should consider a sales force organized by product line. A product-line sales organization allows each of the various markets and each of the diverse or complex product lines to receive a high degree of specialized attention. It is difficult for one salesperson to effectively sell drilling equipment to oil companies, shoes to department stores, and a data-processing service to small offices. The products are just too dissimilar.

A California electronics company with sales under $1 million manufactured power sources for laboratory lasers, professional-quality flashguns for photographers, and emergency lighting for buildings. From a technical standpoint, all these product lines used pulse to power electronics. From a manufacturing stand point, all these product lines used batteries. From a sales and marketing standpoint, however, these lines had little in common. The lasers were for laboratory use and were sold mainly to universities; the flashguns were for consumer use and sold to photographic stores; and the emergency lighting was for commercial use and sold to building contractors or managers.

The company employed three salespeople, each of whom sold all three product lines: one salesperson in Los Angeles, another in the San Francisco Bay area, and a third person in Sacramento, the state capital. The company offered excellent products, but could not push annual sales beyond $1 million. The sales manager, who also handled customers outside California, decided to reorganize the sales force by product line. The Sacramento person would cover all of California for emergency lighting, the San Francisco person all of California for lasers, and the Los Angeles person all of California for photographic equipment. Travel expenses tripled, but unit sales doubled in five years.

A men's belt company with $5 million in annual sales manufactured a line of better designer merchandise for department and specialty stores as well as a low-end private-label line for chain and discount stores. The company employed ten salespeople, organized geographically, who called on both department and specialty stores and chains and discounters. Some salespeople showed unit growth with chains/discounters, but declines with department/specialty stores. Other salespeople showed unit growth with department/specialty stores, but declines with chains/discounters. The same salesperson had a difficult time selling price to chains/discounters and brand name, quality, and service to department/specialty stores. This performance resulted in no growth for the company.

The sales manager reorganized the sales force by product line. The five best chain/discount store salespeople received larger territories, but just carried the private-label lower-end line. The five best department/

specialty store salespeople received larger territories, but just carried the designer-label better line. Territories overlapped, but customers did not; travel expenses doubled, but unit sales of both lines grew at 20 percent annually.

Organization of the sales force by product/service line does not always have positive results. An institutional cleaning service with annual revenues of under $1 million, but growing rapidly, had three salespeople, each calling on restaurants, factories, and hospitals in different parts of Dallas. The sales manager, who was also owner and president, felt that even more rapid growth would result from having one salesperson specialize in food services, another in commercial services, and the third in medical services. He reasoned that each type of customer had different needs, and a specialized salesperson could better meet those needs. He also reasoned that because no territory would exceed greater Dallas, there would be only nominal increases in travel expenses.

Under the new arrangement, growth rates slowed; both customers and salespeople expressed unhappiness. All three salespeople were calling on the same hospital purchasing agent: one to clean the halls, one to clean the operating rooms, and one to clean the kitchen. Both the food services and commercial cleaning salespeople called on the same factory and office building purchasing agents, causing similar overlap.

The sales manager thought that two salespeople calling on the same account would result in a larger share of the customer's business. Two salespeople would get more of the buyer's times and would more aggressively push their particular service. One salesperson might be satisfied to get $10,000 of business, but two or even three could do much better.

In this case, however, two or three salespeople from one company calling on the same buyer caused confusion and frustration on both ends. Purchasing agents resented spending extra time with multiple salespeople from the same company. Salespeople resented competing against each other for the same sales dollar.

As the three companies illustrate, a sales force organized by product line can increase effectiveness for businesses with diverse or complex products and services, or markets, because each product/service or each market segment receives a higher degree of specialized attention. However, this often results in greater travel expense, and sometimes requires you to add more salespeople. When more than one salesperson from a company calls on the same buyer or purchasing agent, confusion, resentment, and frustration can result. Within a sales force organized by product line, each salesperson is assigned a specific geographic area or customer list to call on.

Account/Customer Organization

If your company sells large quantities of products or services to a limited number of major customers, especially customers with many branches, you should consider a sales force organized by account. A sales force organized by account allows each major customer to receive a higher degree of specialized attention.

Eighty percent of a ladies' pantyhose mill's production was sold to Sears, Ward's, Penny's, and K Mart. The central buying offices chose programs twice a year, but computer-generated reorders were placed by individual stores or regional branches. The pantyhose company assigned one salesperson to handle the central buying office, all regional branches, and all individual stores for each chain. That person had the specialized knowledge, contacts, and experience necessary to produce optimum results.

Ninety percent of all nail-making machines in North America are purchased by various branches of Armco Steel Corp., Atlantic Steel Co., Bethlehem, Bostitch, Continental, Dominion Steel & Coal Corp., Keystone Steel & Wire, Mid-States Steel & Wire, Northwestern, U.S. Steel, C.F. and I. Corp., and Steel Company of Canada. Each machine costs about $50,000, resulting in total annual North American shipments of $5 million. Two companies compete in this market; both organize their two-person sales force by customer. One salesperson services the headquarters and all the branches of half the steel companies; the second salesperson performs the same task for the other half.

A local refuse-removal company in eastern Michigan, which specializes in recycling waste, has three sales/service representatives: one for General Motors plants, one for Ford plants, and one for Chrysler plants. Each representative knows the specific needs of each company.

As these three examples show, a sales force organized by customer proves best for businesses where a few key accounts or national accounts represent a large percentage of sales. However, as with a sales force organized by product, this often results in greater travel expenses than in one organized by geographic area. Within a sales force organized by product line, each salesperson might also be assigned specific customers to call on.

Geographic Territory Organization

If your company sells similar or closely related products or services to a large number of widely dispersed customers in the same industry, then you should consider a sales force organized by geographic territory. This means that salespeople sell all your products or services to any appropriate customers within their assigned territories. Most smaller businesses use this format because of its simplicity and low cost. Most smaller-business people don't even think about the alternatives.

The geographic organization of territories allows salespeople to cultivate local markets more intensely by becoming more familiar with local problems, people, and conditions. Also, a person living in the territory often finds a more receptive ear than an outsider would. Texans know how to handle Texans, and New Yorkers know how to handle New Yorkers. Similarly, salespeople living in a territory can provide better service at less cost because generally less travel is required

A small St. Louis company imports fine Italian, brand-name men's ties with exclusive sales rights to the U.S. market. Potentially, 15,000 department and specialty stores might purchase these ties. The company sells through twenty independent sales representatives, who also carry other non-conflicting lines and call on all department and men's specialty stores within certain nonoverlapping geographic territories.

A small Texas finance company purchased used computers from their current owners and leased them back, allowing the previous owner an option to buy when the lease expired. The company offered this one specialized service to any business owning a computer. Although customer industries varied, the service provided remained the same. The company chose to organize its sales force on the basis of nonoverlapping geographic areas because of the large number of widely dispersed customers and the narrowness of its service.

A bakery supply distributor offers 4,000 items to independent bakeries, restaurants, hotels, hospitals, yogurt shops, and grocery stores. The potential account base is immense. Salespeople often walk from one account to another. They are organized by geographic territory, but management is considering having market specialists.

Products and services sold door to door such as fire alarms, books, cable TV, cosmetics, home repairs, magazines, and political and religious solicitations involve the assignment of salespeople to nonoverlapping specific streets, neighborhoods, or towns. Similarly, route delivery salespeople (beer, bread, industrial fasteners) generally have exclusive geographic territories.

Functional Organization

If you offer a product that requires considerable service after the sale and different skills for selling than for servicing, consider a two-tiered sales organization with separate functions. A men's underwear company with a sales force of ten stopped growing when annual sales reached $5 million. The sales manager asked each salesperson why his or her sales had stopped increasing, and all replied that because they were so busy servicing current accounts they had no time to open new ones. The sales manager hired part-time salespeople to count stock and fill display fixtures for existing accounts. This left the full-time salespeople with enough time both to write reorders at existing customers and to open new accounts. Eventually this grew into a two-tiered sales force with different functions, one concentrating on new account development, and the other on account maintenance. The new account salespeople continued receiving a partial commission on customers turned over to the account maintenance sales force.

In a functional sales organization, customers sometimes dislike the change of salespeople, and salespeople sometimes dislike the change of customers. However, if your salespeople show superior account development skills but a lack of interest in retaining or maintaining accounts, try the two-tier approach. You can test it in one territory at a time.

No Restrictions and Combinations

If the methods described previously for organizing your sales force do not appear appropriate, consider having no restrictions. Salespeople who sell consumer services often operate without restrictions to products or services, accounts, or geographic territories.

A small Minneapolis concern selling real estate and oil tax shelters employs four salesmen who may sell any type shelter to any potential customer regardless of location. Independent insurance agencies allow their agents to write any type of policies without territorial limitations. Security brokers too may sell their services to anyone who cares to buy, and real estate salespeople generally do not have territories or customer limitations.

The most effective use of your sales force may involve combining elements of product, account, geographic territory, function, and no restrictions. Because of varying market structures, you may wish to use a different type of organization in different geographic areas or a different type of organization for different product lines. Remember, simple but flexible structures work best. Generally, smaller companies are more flexible than larger ones, allowing them more readily to use combinations. Use this flexibility to your advantage.

A running-shoe company with annual sales of $6 million organized salespeople by geographic territory in the Midwest, where it sold to small accounts. However, on the East and West Coast, where it primarily sold to regional chains, the sales force was organized by key accounts.

A specialty book publisher with revenues of $2 million employed one salaried full-time salesperson to call on the ten major bookstore chains, including B. Dalton, Kroch's and Brentano's, Crown Book, and Waldenbooks. However, it used commissioned sales representatives, who carried other nonconflicting lines, to call on the remainder of the trade, and organized them by geographic territory.

A sweater company with annual sales of $3 million employed two representatives in New York City—one for men's styles and one for women's. In Los Angeles it also employed two representatives—one for selling new accounts and one for servicing existing customers. In Chicago it employed one salesperson for department stores and another for specialty stores. In the rest of the country, salespeople sold all company products and performed all services for any account within their geographic territory.

In a smaller company your most important resource is the human resource, and your decisions concerning sales force organization must recognize this factor. If one of your salespeople has excellent contacts with certain major accounts, you may wish to assign him or her to these customers while organizing the rest of the sales force by geographic territory. If one of your salespeople has a very close relationship with a major customer, you may wish to have him or her sell all your products to that account while organizing the rest of the sales force by product line. If one of your good salespeople does well with smaller accounts but poorly with large, you may wish to place two salespeople in this territory rather than the usual one. The second person would call on large accounts, allowing the original salesperson to continue concentrating on the smaller ones. If one of your good salespeople cannot travel overnight, but your sales force is organized by widely spread key accounts, you may wish to build a geographic territory of nonkey accounts within a day's drive of this person's home.

The flexibility of a small business allows you to fully utilize the human resource by combining various types of sales force organizations.

Territory and Time Management

Once you have decided on the most effective means of organizing your sales force, you must determine the exact size or limits of each territory. A territory that is too small will not financially support a salesperson. A territory that is too large may be expensive to travel and will not maximize company sales.

To create territories that most effectively use salespeople's time and maximize company revenues, you should examine current and potential sales, current and potential customers, plus transportation systems, market clusters, and the salesperson's call capacity.

Once you have determined the exact size or limits of each territory, you must help salespeople to organize and schedule their time. Salespeople need to follow logical customer cluster routes, or they will spend too much time traveling and too little time with accounts. Effective salespeople must know how often to call on major accounts versus smaller ones; how often to call on prospects versus established business; how much time to devote to one product line versus another; and how much time to devote to service versus selling.

Proper time and territory management can increase company revenues by 10 percent to 20 percent with minimal increases in costs. Territory realignments and proper salesperson time allocation can make you a hero.

In most small firms, 70 percent of the business is written by 30 percent of the sales force. Often this results from territories of unequal potential. Realigning territories to create more equal potential increases total revenues.

In most small firms there is one salesperson who opens many new accounts but is weak in retention or penetration of existing customers, whereas another shows the opposite results. Proper time and territory management can even out this disparity.

Surveys report that the average salesperson spends under 40 percent of his or her time with customers. Proper time and territory management increases the number of calls a salesperson makes, lowers the cost per call, and increases the percent of time in the customer's presence.

Structuring Territories

Smaller-business sales managers often inherit the territory structure from their predecessors; or they may simply divide their market area into seven territories of equal physical size among seven salespeople; or just assign each salesperson to one of the seven largest cities in the total market area; or divide the market area into seven territories with equal past sales or an equal number of active accounts. Such arrangements do not most effectively use salespeople's time or maximize revenues.

For example, one company created territories that reached 100 miles in any direction from the salesperson's home. Another allowed salespeople to sell any potential customer within their home states. Yet another company established territories extending ten miles in either direction from certain parts of major highway systems. Still another divided the major city in its market into east, west, north, and south sides and gave each salesperson one area.

Because business is a dynamic process, you should reanalyze territories each year. Every year customers come and go, grow and decline. To create territories that most effectively use salespeople's time and maximize company revenues, you should examine each territory's current and potential sales, current and potential customers, the salesperson's call rate and contacts, and the territory's physical characteristics and highway system. Doing it once is not enough.

Current and Potential Sales

After reviewing current sales volume by territory, determine what statistics best indicate the market potential for your product/service and investigate the sources of these statistics. Once you obtain the information, use it to assist in establishing geographic or product line territories with a more equal potential or proper potential to meet your marketing objectives. Such information, however, does not prove terribly helpful for a sales force organized by major account.

Let's say you have recently been hired as sales manager for a men's hosiery company with annual sales of $3 million. The company currently employs ten sales representatives with the following territories and annual shipments: New England, $800,000; Greater New York, $500,000; Eastern Pennsylvania/Maryland/D.C., $300,000; Florida, $200,000; Texas, $200,000; Michigan, $200,000; Ohio, $200,000; Illinois, $200,000; Rocky Mountain States, $100,000; and California, $300,000. The ten salespeople live in Boston, New York City, Philadelphia, Miami, Dallas, Detroit, Cleveland, Chicago, Denver, and Los Angeles. Your quality line of branded hose is sold to department and specialty stores.

Current sales by territory indicate great unevenness in market share or market potential. Possibly some territories contain more experienced salespeople or have had no sales representation until recently. Certain states still have no representation.

You decide to analyze each territory's potential sales by referring to the most recent "Survey of Buying Power" published in *Sales & Marketing Management* magazine. You also have a copy of the *1990 Census User's*

Guide published by the Bureau of the Census, U.S. Government Printing Office, Washington, D.C.

Most better men's hose is purchased in department stores by people more than twenty years of age with incomes over $20,000. Therefore, you accumulate data by geographic area on population, average age, households, retail sales and buying power per household, families with annual incomes of $20,000 and over, annual dollars of retail sales, annual dollars of general merchandise sales, department store sales, and annual dollars of men's and boy's clothing (including hosiery) sold in department stores and in all stores. You look at current Effective Buying Income (EBI) and Buying Power Index (BPI) and at estimates of future EBI, BPI, and population growth. All this information is available at no charge by state, city, region, and county.

Effective Buying Income (EBI) consists of disposable personal income after taxes. Buying Power Index converts population, EBI, and retail sales into a measurement of a market's "ability to buy" expressed as a percentage of the national total. Thus you can easily compare one region, city, or county with another.

Based on these figures, you discover that the market potential of Greater New York City appears only slightly smaller than that of Chicago and Los Angeles combined, and so you consider adding a second person to the New York area. You also discover that northern California, including greater San Francisco, contains a market potential almost equal to either Michigan or Ohio, and so you consider having separate salespeople for northern California (San Francisco) and southern California (Los Angeles). These figures also reveal that greater St. Louis, Atlanta, and Minneapolis each contain a market potential almost equal to that of Cleveland and greater than that of the Rocky Mountain States. You therefore consider eliminating the Denver-based territory, combining Michigan and Ohio into one, and adding a salesperson for Georgia, Missouri, or Minnesota.

These figures also show that about a third of U.S. households live in the ten largest metropolitan areas, and that 65 percent of all U.S. families with annual incomes over $20,000 live in the forty largest metropolitan areas. This information starts you thinking about some longer-range changes in the sales force.

If your company sold home smoke alarms door to door and you wanted information on market potential or buying power in various areas, you would consult census figures on "Families with Incomes over $25,000" and "Owner-Occupied Housing Units Valued at $35,999 and Over." If your company leased ice-making machines to restaurants and you needed market potential information for various areas, you would consult the National Restaurant Association for statistics on the number of restaurants, their revenues, and number of employees in certain geographic areas. If your company sold a medical waste removal service to hospitals and you wanted information on market potential, you would consult the American Hospital Association for statistics on the number of hospitals, number of beds, number of employees, and dollars of annual revenues in certain geographic areas.

The amount of helpful, free market-evaluation information available from industry trade associations and trade publications, from national, state, and city governments, and from local Chambers of Commerce will surprise you. You are not the company economist, but general market statistics will help you create equitable territories containing the greatest potential. For every significant economic activity, there is an association that represents it, a government agency that monitors it, and a magazine that covers it. Obtaining statistical data is simply a matter of identifying the associations, government agencies, and publications in a specific field and getting the information directly from the source. There are a number of reference books that identify these sources: *Encyclopedia of Associations, National Trade and Professional Associations of the United States, Statistical Abstracts of the United States, The United States Government Manual, Guide to Special Issues and Indexes of Periodicals,* and *Standard Periodical Directory*.

Companies with several product lines may require a variety of statistics that indicate whether there is greater potential for one of their lines than for another in a specific territory. Management then must weigh the importance of each line in establishing its territories.

For companies with several territories in condensed geographic market areas, such as one city, statistics can be obtained by neighborhood or zip code. In this situation, the Yellow Pages also prove helpful. For example, the potential market by area for products/services sold to restaurants or hospitals in Chicago can be partially ascertained by looking under the appropriate listings in the Yellow Pages.

In addition to general buying power information, more specific market statistics may be available from government, industry, and civic organizations showing actual unit and dollar sales of your product/service for certain geographic territories. For example, industry sources can provide information on unit purchases of semiconductor devices, reed relays, horn antennas, robots, and may other items by state.

Sales and Marketing Management magazine also publishes a "Survey of U.S. Industrial and Commercial Buying Power." This survey lists by state and county the number of establishments by major SIC code, their shipments and receipts, and their percent of the U.S. total for their SIC code.

A commercial garbage removal company entering Orange County, California, wanted to establish four territories with equal potential sales. The sales manager needed statistics on the quantity of waste generated by thousands of businesses. After a great deal of frustration, she found that an areas tax base plus the number of employees and the county's development plans for construction correlated to the quantity of waste. She also obtained information on the number of competitor's trucks in each area and on the number of loads deposited at various landfills.

Current and Potential Customers

Analyzing an area's potential sales or buying power allows you to determine the general outline for each territory, but now you must fine-tune the focus, further refine the filter, by analyzing the number and type of actual and potential customers. Salespeople's results are limited by the number of visits they can make in a day, week, month, or year, and by the number of different type customers they can handle. The maximum number of accounts limits a territory's size. After a certain point, a salesperson does not have time to adequately service any more customers or to open any more new accounts.

Your analysis begins by identifying the number of actual and potential accounts in each area, and then classifying accounts as to sales potential and time or call frequency required to service them. Accounts and prospects requiring a monthly call might be classified as A customers, accounts requiring a call every other month as B customers, and every third month as C customers. Whether your company sells men's hosiery to retail stores, smoke alarms to home owners, ice machines to restaurants, or software to chemical companies, you can obtain information on current accounts in a territory from company records, and on potential accounts to be sold from reference books, trade publications, trade associations, and the Yellow Pages.

Next, you determine the number of days each salesperson works in a year and the number of calls possible each day and each year in that area. This is the salesperson's capacity, universe, number of shots, and varies with a territory's density, the type accounts there, and the salesperson's work habits. The New York City salesperson makes twice the number of calls as the Colorado salesperson. A salesperson operating in a territory with many small accounts or a lot of reorders may have a higher call rate per day than the salesperson in a territory in which several large customers with complicated reorders are concentrated. Generally, a salesperson's call rate will not change more than 10 percent unless telemarketing is employed or a sales support person is added. Salespeople who are backed up by a customer service representative, a telemarketer, or a sales administrator can increase their call rates dramatically. By talking or traveling with salespeople and by reading call reports and order copies, you can obtain information on the total calls possible per day, month, or year, and on the varying time/call frequency necessary for different types of accounts.

Last, you compare the annual number of calls possible for each salesperson with the annual number of calls and time required to service current and potential accounts in an area. When you factor this information with desired market share, the boundaries of a territory emerge. Territories become defined then by classifying accounts as to importance, sales potential, and necessary call frequency; then comparing current and potential accounts with desired market share, and the physical call limits of a salesperson.

Returning to the men's hosiery company, you obtain an active account list for each current territory by reviewing last year's invoices and each territory's customer analysis report. The customer analysis report lists customers by territory along with their orders or shipments in dollars or units by product line as compared with previous periods. The New England territory contains 185 specialty store and 5 department store accounts, Greater New York contains 7 department store accounts with fifty-five branches; the Pennsylvania/Maryland/D.C. territory contains 70 specialty stores and 5 department store accounts; the Florida territory contains 90 specialty store accounts; the Texas territory contains 40 specialty stores and 10 department store accounts; the Michigan territory contains one department store and 100 specialty store accounts; the Ohio territory contains 20 specialty store and 10 department store accounts; the Illinois territory contains 110 specialty store and 2 department store accounts; the Rocky Mountain territory contains 30 specialty store accounts; and the California territory contains 20 specialty store accounts and 3 department stores with forty branches.

After discussions with each salesperson, you realize that the New England representative can average five sales calls per day because his territory contains few department stores but many specialty stores located close to one another. Department stores require more time because the salesperson must count stock at each branch and then deliver the counts to a central buyer located at the main store, who writes an order. Specialty stores, although they also require stock counts at their single location, have smaller quantities, and the buyer resides at the store. Also, waiting time to see department store buyers exceeds that for seeing the specialty store buyer.

Moreover, while specialty stores require stock counting every eight weeks, department stores and their branches require it every four weeks. Therefore, 185 New England specialty stores necessitate 1,110 calls annually, and the 5 department stores, each with five branches, require 360 calls annually, for a total current customer annual call load of 1,470.

For the New England salesperson working 240 days a year and averaging five calls per day, the total potential annual calls would be 1,200. Obviously, no time exists for the New England salesperson to call on new accounts, and he or she may not even be able to fully serve some existing accounts. You arrive at average work days per year for a salesperson by deducting the time required for weekends, vacation, holidays, sick days, and sales meetings.

Next you examine the total number of potential hosiery accounts in New England by referring to *The Salesman's Guide to Mens & Boys Wear Buyers,* to the Yellow Pages for major market areas under "men's wear retail," and to the men's wear section of the National Retailers Association for the number of men's wear retailers. From this information you estimate that 3,000 potential specialty store customers exist in New England in addition to 50 department stores. This means you currently sell to 6 percent of the potential New England specialty stores and to 10 percent of the department stores. On a national basis, the company's dollar market share approximates 5 percent.

Although company market penetration of New England in terms of number of accounts exceeds national market share in terms of dollar sales, and although your salesperson has produced excellent results, he has no time to pursue new accounts and barely time to look after existing customers. You consider adding another salesperson in New England for certain areas like southern Connecticut, where current distribution appears weakest.

You repeat this analysis by ranking customers and prospects according to dollars of potential sales, by analyzing how large a sales volume one person can efficiently handle, and then by comparing this to the territory's total estimated sales figure and your desired market share. Where service is important, salespeople may be limited not only by the number of accounts but by the dollar volume of sales they can handle. The New England salesperson currently sells $800,000 worth of men's hose a year. The 185 specialty store customers produce $600,000 of this volume and have a potential for producing $800,000. The five department stores produce $200,000, and have a potential for $400,000. Past experience shows that a salesperson has difficulty handling more than $1 million in annual volume. Trade sources reveal that approximately $24 million worth of better men's hose are bought by retailers in New England, which means that your current dollar market share is 3.3 percent and that your potential dollar market share from existing accounts is 5 percent. Fifty more specialty stores and five more department stores with a potential volume of $700,000 can be identified as prime prospects in New England. This analysis confirms the previous one. Although your New England salesperson has produced excellent results, there is the potential for supporting another person in the territory.

The New York City salesperson, dealing with fifty-five department store branches and urban auto traffic, averages only three sales calls a day, or 720 a year. The seven department stores with fifty-five branches require 744 calls annually. Obviously, little time exists for the New York City salesperson to call on new accounts. From the same market sources as those used in New England, you learn that there are 5,000 potential specialty store customers in Greater New York plus fifty department stores with 500 branches. You decide to add another salesperson to call on specialty stores and on the department stores not already sold. Statistics on buying power and potential sales reinforce your decision.

This type of customer analysis shows that the potential number of accounts and dollars of sales in Texas may eventually require two people, and that a second person should be added now for northern California and northern Nevada combined. The number of accounts in the Rocky Mountain areas does not justify a salesperson, and travel expenses appear large. Again earlier statistics on buying power and market potential reinforce the decision concerning northern California and the Rocky Mountain states.

This type of customer analysis shows that Ohio contains too many potential accounts for one salesperson, and that all the current business clusters in the northern section. Illinois contains too many potential accounts for one salesperson, and all the business clusters around Chicago. Michigan does not contain enough potential accounts for one salesperson, and current market penetration is unlikely to grow. You therefore create a new territory composed of south and central Illinois, Indiana, and Ohio, and you add Milwaukee to the old Illinois territory, Detroit to the old Ohio territory, and northern Indiana to the new Michigan territory.

Although these examples deal with redefining existing territories, you use the same techniques to define the boundaries of new territories. With a new territory, however, you often have no actual sales volume or existing accounts and must base your analysis entirely on potential and prospects.

Using a customer analysis and a salesperson work load to define territories for key account selling proves easier than it does for geographic territories with no customer restrictions. You can expand or decrease the number of specific key accounts, depending on necessary call frequency and sales potential, more easily than you can change the physical boundaries of a territory.

Many industrial products have limited customer bases, which makes defining territories easier for the companies that sell those products. If your small business sells parabolic antennas to telephone companies, railroads, utilities, and the government for use in microwave communication systems, salespeople spend some time with all potential users. Generally, you know exactly which customers require how much time.

By contrast, companies offering a wide variety of products or services to many customers in different markets have a more complex task. Establishing territories based on the potential number of accounts or market potential proves difficult but not impossible for a waste disposal firm or distributors of diverse products such as bakery supplies, grinding wheels, or paper accessories. Management must assign a relative importance to each product line or customer group.

Figure 4-1 shows the format a salesperson can use to plan time allocation. Modify this sample planner to fit your particular products/services and market, then ask each of your salespeople to fill in the blanks and discuss the information. The results will allow you and your sales staff to evaluate territory boundaries more analytically.

A local garbage disposal company employing five salespeople asked each one to fill out this form. The salespeople were provided with a list of their active accounts, each account's monthly service fee, and the date on which the service contract expired. Depending on the size of an account, salespeople classified them as A, requiring four calls a year; B, requiring three calls a year; and C, requiring two calls a year. Each salesperson wrote in the number of A, B, and C accounts and multiplied each type of account by the required call frequency to arrive at the total number of required retention calls.

The sales manager established a goal of one new account per week. Experience showed that it took ten prospecting calls to open one new account. Some prospects showed no interest; others required several calls before they were willing to sign a contract. Because there are forty-eight working weeks in a year, a salesperson needed to make 480 prospecting calls to open one new account a week, or forty-eight new accounts a year.

The sales manager and salespeople checked call reports and found that nonselling service matters required twenty calls a week, or nine hundred

Figure 4-1. Sample salesperson's time allocation planner.

Total number of active accounts in this category	Number of retention calls required per year on each category of active account	Total calls per year in this category
A _____	×	
B _____	×	
C _____	×	

Total Accounts _____

Total annual required retention calls on active accounts	_____
Plus estimated number of annual calls on prospects (new account calls)	_____
Plus estimated number of annual nonselling service calls	_____
Total number of required annual calls	_____
Average number of calls per day	_____
Times work days per year	× _____
Total number of calls you can actually make in a year	_____
Difference between required annual calls and number of calls you can actually make in a year	_____

sixty a year. Customers often wanted to see a salesperson concerning container condition or placement or missed pickups.

The sales manager and salesperson then established how many calls the salesperson should make in a day, a month, and a year. They compared this figure with the required calls and, when necessary, made territory changes.

In two territories where revenues had stalled, they found that the salesperson could not possibly make the required number of retention calls on current active accounts, let alone open the new accounts with prospecting calls or respond to service issues. In one territory an inside customer service representative was assigned to contact some smaller accounts by phone. In the other territory, boundaries were changed so that the salesperson had fewer accounts, fewer retention calls, and more time for prospecting. The following year both territories grew by 15 percent in net revenues and added fifty new accounts.

In another territory revenues were increasing rapidly from a small base, but the analysis showed that the salesperson had to work only half a day to produce these results. His territory was expanded and dollars of revenue continued to increase. Another sales manager used this analysis to convince her boss that hiring an additional salesperson would pay for itself.

Using these analytical techniques to establish territory boundaries does not constitute an exact science, but it is a logical approach to improving salespeople's performance. And computer software programs exist to assist you in this task.

The Human Element

Your salespeople, their needs and contacts, also require serious consideration in setting territory boundaries. Flexibility represents a competitive advantage for smaller concerns, allowing you to temper the analytical approach to territories with important human considerations. Take into account where your salespeople live, their personalities, personal needs, likes and dislikes, and contacts. One salesperson may prefer a territory with smaller accounts; another might do better with majors.

A small concern offering imported gourmet food to restaurants and hotels in the West employed an excellent salesman in San Francisco. The salesman, an older bachelor, enjoyed skiing at Lake Tahoe once a month in the winter and gambling at Reno once a month in the summer. Over the years he had met socially most major hotel and restaurant managers in these two areas. When he requested that his territory be expanded to include Tahoe and Reno, management wisely agreed. The salesman had already established the contacts, and he made a trip to Nevada once a month anyway.

The Ohio salesman for a Midwest gear company had excellent contacts with the steel company buyers in Pittsburgh because he had covered Pennsylvania for his previous employer. The gear company added Pittsburgh to the Ohio territory.

The St. Louis saleswoman for a Midwest Christmas ornament distributor had a daughter attending college in Kansas City. She visited her daughter once a month, and asked if she could cover the entire state of Missouri. Her employer agreed.

The top salesman for a Midwest office supply company traveled the entire state of Minnesota. When family problems developed at home, his employer agreed to reduce his territory so that overnight stays would be unnecessary.

Personal relationships aside, some sales managers claim that they obtain better results by rotating salespeople every few years between territories. Practically, this can only be done in small geographic areas. These sales managers claim that this prevents salespeople from developing bad habits and geting into a rut. Salespeople then do their best to outdo their predecessors in the territory.

Many sales managers, however, find it difficult and unpleasant to sell a territory change to a salesperson. Salespeople particularly resent and resist territory reductions. Often your best salesperson, the superstar with the large ego, produces more business than he or she can service. You then reward that star performance by halving the territory that produced it!

You must sell the benefits of a territory reduction, such as less travel, more leisure time, more time for account development and prospecting. You must provide a temporary equitable allowance for possible reduced compensation, an override on the lost accounts or a draw. You must massage the salesperson's ego with a new title or lunch with the president. Make the salesperson feel important. Territory changes are a necessary way of life. Make it a challenge, not a penalty.

The way in which you reduce or increase a territory greatly influences how your salespeople will react to the change. Try and change accounts at the fringes. Try and change a mix of large and small accounts. Take into consideration how your salespeople travel the territory, their route analyses, and where they live.

Physical Characteristics and Highways

Although market information on buying power, potential sales, and number of possible accounts is generally available by county, zip code, city, state, or region, sales territory boundaries may not lend themselves to city, county, or state lines. Highway systems, rivers, bridges, subways, and mountains must be considered. Also, major market areas cross state lines.

For example, the highway system connecting Columbus, Dayton, and Cincinnati with Indianapolis is better and shorter than the highway system connecting Columbus, Dayton, and Cincinnati with northern Ohio. The greater Cincinnati trading area also includes counties in Kentucky and Indiana. Therefore, many companies create a territory that includes central and southern Ohio, central and southern Indiana, and northern Kentucky.

Similarly, highways and distances allow Springfield, Illinois, to be covered more easily from St. Louis than from Chicago. However, highways and distances allow Milwaukee, Wisconsin, easy access from Chicago.

When dividing the state of Florida into two territories, many companies establish an east and west coast division rather than a north-south division because the major cities are connected by highway systems running north and south along either coast. When dividing the island of Manhattan into two territories, experienced companies establish an East and West Side rather than an uptown and downtown division because the subway systems basically run up and down the island, not across.

Although Denver and Salt Lake City look close on a map, the Rocky Mountains cause many hours of driving between these two major Western markets. Most companies do not include them in the same territory. Similarly, because of mountains in the Northwest, Seattle and Portland generally form one territory, with eastern Oregon and Washington covered from western Idaho. Similarly, territories that include rivers must take into account where bridges are located.

Time Management

Based on current and potential sales and current and potential customers, your salespeople's work load limitations, contacts, and needs, and available transportation systems and distances between major market areas, you have established your territory boundaries. Now you must help your salespeople to plan their time within these territories. Time represents an important resource for salespeople. They must learn how to best utilize a finite amount of time within their specific geographic area.

Unless salespeople follow logical customer cluster routes, they will spend too much time traveling and too little time with accounts. Effective salespeople must know how often to call on major accounts versus smaller ones; how often to call on prospects versus established business; how much time to devote to one product line versus another; and how much time to devote to service versus selling. Effective salespeople must understand time wasters, the required number of daily calls, and how their time is actually spent.

I will bet you the price of this book that neither you nor your salespeople know precisely what percent of their time is spent eyeball to eyeball with customers. Ask your salespeople to log their time for one month. The results will surprise you and awaken them. This log will give you the basis for a discussion of time management.

Use anticipated duties from the job description as categories for the time log. The categories will vary from company to company. For example, ask salespeople to report what percent of their time, how many hours a month, a week, or a day are actually spent with customers versus hours spent traveling between accounts, waiting, on the phone, following up on orders, doing paperwork, at sales meetings, or in the office.

Decide how you want salespeople to allocate their time and which allocation produces the best results, compare this with their logs, and suggest corrective action. This analysis may indicate the need for more telemarketing or for a customer service person, sales administrator, or order expediter.

Route Analysis

Planning efficient travel routes optimizes salespeople's selling time. You help each salesperson to organize his or her travel so as to minimize the time between calls and maximize the time spent with customers and prospects. The smaller a territory, the easier it is to meet these objectives because less time and expense are required for travel.

During the initial home office training sessions or during a field visit, you mark a map of the territory with the locations of each current account and major prospect. You classify accounts and prospects by the frequency with which they must be seen. Factory or store branches requiring service are also classified and marked.

Next, you and the salesperson review this map and discuss the most efficient schedule and routes for meeting these call requirements. Look for clusters of accounts and prospects that can be seen in a day, with the first and last calls closest to home. The sales manager for a bakery supply distributor instructs salespeople to look right and left after making each call to see if there is a prospect within walking distance. To reduce expenses, schedule as few overnight trips as possible. Discuss efficient highway or public transportation systems for moving between accounts.

Some sales managers organize territories into four quadrants, sections, or slices. A salesperson spends a day per week or a week per month in each quadrant, working it in a clover-leaf pattern, or starting at the farthest point and working back, or working a line between two overnight stops. Usually one day a week is left for cleaning up unplanned events. Some sales managers further refine this technique by gridding each quadrant and assigning it one day of the week or month. Sales managers may also ask their salespeople to make all planned calls before 2:00 P.M. (prime selling time) and to use the time after 2:00 o'clock to react to customer calls, missed accounts, and other problems. In other words, act in the morning, react in the afternoon. Every product, service, company, and territory requires a customized approach because the problems, opportunities, needs, and customers are different.

Experienced salespeople don't enjoy being told how to organize their day. So present your map merely as an aid, and let them tell you how they plan to organize their schedule. Provide suggestions and information where you feel they are necessary to accomplish the desired goals.

Some sales managers feel that helping their people to schedule calls is not worthy of their time because it represents a skill possessed by every salesperson. But if your average sales call costs $47, as calculated previously, and if proper scheduling results in one more call a day, or 240 more calls a year per salesperson, then you might be increasing efficiency or lowering expense by $11,280 per salesperson. Considered in this light, scheduling deserves and needs your time and attention.

Even the best salespeople sometimes possess poor planning skills or have developed bad scheduling habits. As an objective voice from outside the territory, you can suggest changes.

One salesman for a small industrial chemical company had a large account that required a visit each Friday. The visit took only thirty minutes, but the trip required 90 minutes of driving in each direction. The salesman deadheaded 90 minutes each way because no established customers were located on the route. The sales manager suggested calling on a dozen major prospects en route to (and from) the important customer. Within a year, three of the prospects had become customers, and the salesman had income-producing stops to make each Friday on the way to and from his major customer.

A salesman for a small packaging company called exclusively on toy, gift, and Christmas ornament manufacturers located in four nearby buildings in New York City. He organized his schedule by floors within each building.

Call Frequency

With each salesperson, share your knowledge of the call frequency required by each account and prospect. Remember that large accounts and prospects do not always demand the most frequent calls, and that all accounts have different needs.

An office supply saleswoman felt it necessary to call on her ten largest accounts each week. She believed that they all wished to place orders that often, and so her weekly call represented a service the customer would appreciate. Her sales manager suggested she inquire about necessary call frequency with each of these ten majors. They appreciated her asking, and she discovered that five wished to continue weekly orders, three wished to order every other week, and two once a month. Their volume continued to grow, and her time was freed for other sales calls. The saleswoman then selected three small but growing accounts that might benefit from more frequent service. She called on them once every two weeks rather than once a month, and orders increased rapidly.

Again, the use of in-house customer service representatives, telemarketers, and sales administrators can change necessary call frequency. You should consider these alternatives.

Many sales managers use two sets of customer/prospect profile cards to assist them in scheduling customer calls. One set is filed alphabetically, the other by the date of the next customer/prospect visit. Each day the salesperson pulls the appropriate customer/prospect cards from the file and knows who to call on. Each card contains the customer's name, address, phone number, date of last visit, sales history, problems, needs, and personal information on the buyer. Some salespeople color code cards as to necessary call frequency.

Prospects vs. Established Business

With each salesperson, share your knowledge of how to allocate time as between prospects and established business. You should suggest a different allocation for matured territories with many established accounts than for a newer territory with only a few established customers. Growth occurs not only from opening new accounts but from properly cultivating existing ones.

The Cincinnati salesman for an abrasive grinding wheel distributor had two large accounts, each of which required 20 percent of his time. His sales manager suggested spending only 10 percent with one, because the company had 100 percent of its grinding wheel business, and increasing the time spent with the other to 30 percent, because the company had less than half of its possible business.

Outside of these two major customers, the salesman had only a few worthwhile accounts. The sales manager suggested splitting the remaining 60 percent of the salesman's time equally between current and prospective accounts.

The sales manger of a temporary personnel company tells her salespeople to make ten calls a day—five retention or penetration calls on current accounts, two service request calls on existing customers, and three cold or follow-up calls on prospects. This company wants each salesperson to open one new account each week. It takes approximately fifteen cold or prospect calls to open a new account. This sales manager buys lunch for any salesperson who has opened a new account, but suggests that salespeople don't eat lunch until after they have made three cold calls.

Service vs. Selling

With each salesperson, share your knowledge of the service versus selling time required for each customer, type of customer, or territory. What allocation produces the best results?

A small cosmetics company in Detroit manufactured and sold beauty and hair care aids to drug stores. Only one salesperson showed shipment increases under 20 percent a year. The sales manager discovered that this one salesperson spent 60 percent of her time filling in stock and setting up displays for customers as opposed to only 40 percent actually calling on buyers for reorders. He suggested she reverse the ratio, and soon her orders increased by over 20 percent annually.

One Product Line or Customer Group vs. Another

If your company sells more than one product line, you should share your knowledge with each salesperson on how to allocate time between lines. What allocation produces the best results? A small local pet food company manufactured dog and cat food for several southern states. In Texas, where the dog population surpasses the cat population, the sales manager instructed salespeople to allocate 60 percent to 70 percent of their time selling dog food. In Florida, where the cat population exceeds dogs, the sales manager instructed salespeople to allocate 60 percent to 70 percent of their time selling cat food.

For companies with different/distinct markets or customer groups, the sales manager should share his or her knowledge on how to allocate time between these markets or customer groups. The sales manager for a refuse removal company instructs her salespeople to call on construction sites between 7:00 and 10:00 A.M., on industrial firms from 10:00 A.M. to 3:00 P.M., and on restaurants from 3:00 to 6:00 P.M. The sales manager for a food distributor instructs his salespeople to call on bakeries from 6:00 to 9:00 A.M., on food service firms from 9:00 A.M. to 1:00 P.M., on restaurants from 1:00 to 3:00 P.M., and on yogurt/ice cream shops from 3:00 to 5:00 P.M. This time split produces good results and represents the time of day when the specific customer group will see salespeople.

Time Wasters and Time Traps

Figure 4-2 lists forty time-wasting activities or conditions that slow salespeople down. Give it to your salespeople and have them place an X next to those activities that are problems and then identify and rank the four most important. Discuss ways to overcome these time wasters with your salespeople. And it wouldn't hurt to do the time waster exercise yourself. You may have a case of memo-itis or be an inefficient do-it-yourselfer. Remember, it's as important for you to properly allocate your precious time as it is to teach others to manage theirs.

Working smart, or efficiently, is as important as working long and hard. You need to do both. Many salespeople attempt to disguise their ineffectiveness by appearing to work hard and long.

Be sure your salespeople plan their calls a week in advance and that they put their plans into writing. Who will they see and what do they wish to accomplish?

Be sure your salespeople don't call on unqualified leads that have not been properly screened, analyzed, evaluated, or updated. Selling time is too precious to squander.

Be sure your salespeople not only use the telephone to make appoint-

Figure 4-2. Forty time wasters affecting sales efficiency.

___ 1. Telephone calls

___ 2. Interruptions, drop-in visitors

___ 3. Meetings, scheduled or unscheduled

___ 4. Crises, "firefighting"

___ 5. Lack of objectives, deadlines, priorities

___ 6. Cluttered desk and office, personal disorganization

___ 7. Ineffective delegation

___ 8. Doing dull tasks

___ 9. Attempting too much at once

___ 10. Unrealistic time estimates

___ 11. Ineffective communication

___ 12. Inadequate training or development of subordinates

___ 13. Procrastination, indecision, daydreaming

___ 14. Inability to say "no"

___ 15. Leaving tasks unfinished, jumping from one task to another

___ 16. Involvement in too much detail, "doing it yourself"

___ 17. Inadequate staff or poor performance by staff

___ 18. Socializing, idle conversation

___ 19. Lack of self-discipline

___ 20. Constantly switching priorities

___ 21. Failure to listen

___ 22. Lack of feedback, inadequate information

___ 23. Conflict, personnel problems

___ 24. Worry, fear, anxiety

___ 25. Inadequate planning, failure to consider alternatives

___ 26. Waiting

___ 27. Memo-itis

___ 28. Poor memory

___ 29. Confusing activities with results

___ 30. Fatigue, boredom

___ 31. Blaming others

___ 32. Stress and tension

___ 33. Inadequate facilities or equipment

___ 34. Company policies

___ 35. Poor filing system

___ 36. Excess paperwork, mail, reports, reading matter

___ 37. Travel, commuting

___ 38. Pet projects or outside activities

___ 39. Impatience, haste

___ 40. Failure to do first things first

ments but to answer certain questions and write certain reorders. Salespeople often underutilize the phone. You can talk to a lot more customers each day by phone than in person.

Be sure salespeople understand what hours you want worked and how often you want them in the office. Does the day start at 7:00 or 9:00 A.M.? Does it end at 4:00 or 6:00 P.M.? Is lunch to be used for selling or relaxing? Does Friday end at 2:00 or 5:00?

Be sure your salespeople don't bury themselves in paperwork and then use that as an excuse for not selling. Analyze their paperwork load and help them to reduce it.

Be sure your salespeople prioritize their day, listing their tasks by importance. Salespeople have a tendency to do the easy work, which may not be the most important work, first.

Encourage your salespeople to set daily objectives and deadlines, to focus on results, and to develop alternatives. Encourage your salespeople to avoid procrastinating, to concentrate their efforts on one thing at a time, and to consider delegating by using available resources intelligently. Remind them of their schedules, but when unplanned events occur, encourage them to be flexible. Remind them that to maintain their priorities, they must occasionally say no to customers, fellow employees, and even you. Help them to anticipate problems and to develop contingency plans, to manage the continual flow of daily interruptions. Lack of persistence and poor communication can also be time wasters.

Planning Your Time

In addition to helping salespeople plan their time, you need to efficiently allocate *your* precious resource, time. For one month keep a time log. What percent of your time was spent training salespeople in the field, in front of customers, traveling, at sales meetings, on the phone answering questions or following up on orders, doing paperwork, at management meetings, or preparing bids, proposals, budgets, or plans? Make a list of your duties. Keep track of how you spend your time. Analyze whether a different allocation would produce better results, and if so, what action is required to produce that different allocation.

The objective of all this information is to have salespeople economically make the optimum number of effective calls on the right customers and prospects. The emphasis is on helping the salesperson work smarter, thus creating a more productive and efficient sales force. Do salespeople control their territories or do the territories control them? Knowledge is power and time is money.

5

Motivation

To fully capitalize on a salesperson's potential, you must motivate that salesperson. In a sense, you have led the horse to water; now you must make it drink.

In a smaller company you cannot offer your salespeople promotions for making that extra effort, and money alone does not always serve as an incentive once the salesperson has reached a certain level of comfort. This chapter deals largely with nonmonetary techniques for motivating your salesforce.

A small medical instrument company employed twelve salespeople. The New York City salesman had flunked out of college trying to pursue his father's career as a physician. He had grown up in sumptuous surroundings on Long Island and wanted to maintain that standard of living and social status for himself, his wife, and three children. Earning enough money to achieve this personal goal motivated him to work long, hard, and smart. The more he made, the more he needed.

By contrast, the Los Angeles salesman had been a history major in college, had no children, and his wife worked. He and his wife had grown up in a small town in Iowa. He was content to rent an apartment in Pasadena and was not terribly motivated by money.

The Chicago salesman was in his mid-fifties, had grown children and considerable savings. Ten years earlier he had worked long days to support his growing family. Now he was content to work a six-hour day.

The Dallas saleswoman, the only daughter of an oil company executive, worked like a demon and invested most of her money in real estate. She needed little more motivation than her paycheck.

As these examples illustrate, different salespeople have different aspirations and needs and so respond differently to identical stimuli. Your job is to find the particular stimuli that will light each salesperson's fire.

Therefore, you cannot motivate salespeople as a group; you must tackle motivation individual by individual.

Your success as a sales manager depends on the efforts of your salespeople and the results, and therefore on their motivation. Your job, after all, is getting work done through other people. Although you can't force a salesperson to be successful, you can learn to recognize people's motivational needs and problems and then to develop techniques for meeting those needs and solving those problems.

Your rank and power, used as a means of getting people to do what you want, will go only so far. And threats and punishments, though they may work on some people, tend to lose their effectiveness when used too often. Offering positive incentives produces better results.

Because a smaller business is more personal and more flexible than a larger one, the sales manager should find it easier to motivate people individually. Also, a sales manager needs to be less concerned with company politics, because the organization is smaller and has more energy to devote to the problems and motivations of his or her sales force.

Why be concerned with motivating salespeople? After all, our salespeople owe us a good day's work for a good day's pay, don't they? Motivating salespeople requires extra time and effort on the sales manager's part. Many sales managers consider motivation silly. My boss doesn't have to motivate me; why should I have to motivate the people working under me?

The answer is simple. Salespeople are an expensive and important human resource of your company. Motivated salespeople produce more dollars of revenue per dollar of expense. Motivated salespeople stay with you longer because they have less reason to leave, and this reduces the cost of turnover. Motivating salespeople is especially important in small companies because of the limited career ladders and sometimes limited remuneration that they offer.

Yes, you deserve a day's work for a day's pay, but motivated salespeople can give you a day and a half's work for a day's pay. Motivated salespeople are more confident and enthusiastic. Motivation converts salespeople's complacency into the elixir of enthusiasm. A motivated sales force costs no more than an unmotivated sales force.

The Motivational Process

To motivate salespeople, you must first understand the specific needs and desires driving individuals and then find the activities and rewards that satisfy those needs. Each salesperson has a particular package of needs and goals, and these are not necessarily rational. Most salespeople, for instance, need varying degrees of recognition, a sense of achievement, a feeling of usefulness, and consistent leadership. In addition, some salespeople have a strong need to belong; many others require job or financial security.

Needs create tensions, and to relieve these tensions salespeople engage in goal-directed, motivated behavior. When they achieve their goals, the tension is reduced. Other individuals and social groups influence peoples' needs and the goals they choose to satisfy these needs. A salesperson might desire certain positive results such as leisure, recognition, security, more money, or better use of time. Achieving these results will create peace of mind and prestige. Not achieving them leads to a sense of failure, humiliation, or rejection and creates anxiety and depression.

As sales manager, your job is both to locate the needs and to encourage the goal-directed actions that lead to the satisfaction of those needs. By using the individual's needs and goals, you thus motivate the salesperson to optimum performance. Of course, the results of this action also increase sales. And, eventually, salespeople obtain enough pleasure from their goal-directed activities to become self-motivated.

Once you have created an environment that encourages self-motivation, it is much easier to sell your ideas to the sales force, whether this involves correcting a salesperson's bad habits or suggesting some new direction. You can accomplish much of this on field trips by actually demonstrating the benefits of certain techniques or by pointing to the success of other salespeople who use them.

Generally, a smaller company presents a better opportunity for knowing the sales force than a larger one. During field visits, you can also develop personal relationships with your people and find out what they want from life. At dinner after the workday ends, or between calls in the car, involve them in some relaxed, self-revealing conversation. Although you are not the company psychologist, you need insight into those who work for you to create a proper working environment that promotes motivation and job satisfaction.

You will find that most salespeople desire success and enjoy working hard at something. Your job involves showing them how they can be successful by transferring more of their efforts into their selling.

A small Midwest office equipment company employed a Minneapolis salesman who produced great results when he worked, but he did not work often or hard enough. On a field visit, the sales manager was invited to the salesman's home for dinner. The sales manager noticed several old cars in the garage. At dinner the salesman spoke about his passion for fixing old cars, but complained about his lack of funds to buy spare parts.

The next day between calls, the sales manager asked how much money the parts required. He then showed the salesman that by selling one more machine a month he would generate sufficient commission income to pay for the parts.

That year, Minneapolis sales increased by one machine a month. In subsequent years, the sales manager set up a quota/bonus plan for the salesman. The bonus equaled the salesman's cash needs for auto parts, and the quota equaled the sales manager's needs for increased annual sales.

Motivation is an internal process of need satisfaction. You can't force salespeople to be motivated. But motivation, this internal process, is very much influenced by external factors, the most important of which is you, the boss. Think about how your motivation changes depending on your relationship with your boss.

In a smaller company, salespeople's needs, goals, and motivations can be classified as those related to praise and recognition; feelings of usefulness; challenge and achievement; authority and freedom; self-realization and fulfillment through personal growth; esteem and status; a sense of belonging; pleasant interpersonal relationships with management and peers; consistent, competent leadership; fair company policy and administration; job security and compensation. For a larger company this list would also include advancement.

These are the external factors that influence internal motivation. No one of these factors alone is terribly important, but taken together they create a powerful interrelated motivational force that requires a delicate, ever-changing balance.

These factors, needs, and goals not only motivate salespeople but any employee. Although this book deals with salespeople, you need to motivate all your employees using these techniques.

Recognition

Salespeople want to be noticed, praised, and appreciated for their performance, and as sales manager you should reinforce and reward positive results with such recognition. Recognition involves anything from a casual thank-you over the phone to a formal awards dinner. Salespeople seem to possess an insatiable appetite for recognition.

Salespeople must understand exactly which positive results will be rewarded with recognition: for example, more new accounts, more calls per day, better retention of existing business, selling price increases, increased net sales, or better collections. The required results and the form of recognition, for example, a plaque, membership in a sales club, or a prize, should be different for different salespeople. Moreover, you must create different levels of recognition for varying levels of performance. The salesperson who visits a customer on Saturday to handle a service complaint deserves your "Thank you." The salesperson who doubles his quarterly new account quota deserves to be nominated for salesperson of the month.

Also, lack of recognition, the silent treatment, can be a powerful tool. Make sure the person you choose not to recognize knows why.

Recognition becomes a more effective motivational tool when it is sincere, receives publicity, is recorded, and involves top management. Insincere praise has a negative effect on the recipient. Say it as if you mean it, or don't say it at all.

Where appropriate, as when someone has won a sales contest, publicize the recognition in the company newsletter or in a bulletin sent to all salespeople. If the recognition involves an award or civic involvement, consider sending press releases with pictures to the local papers. Community and small town newspapers need this type of material.

Where appropriate, record recognition with plaques, sales club memberships, certificates, or annual awards. For example, if a salesperson goes 50 percent over annual quota, issue a plaque or certificate inscribed with his or her name to commemorate the results.

You might establish a special club or honor society, the Circle of Excellence, say, or the President's Club, for any salespeople whose annual or cumulative volumes exceed a certain amount. Each year you might also give an award for the highest number of new accounts opened or the greatest percentage sales increase. Then have members of the honor society or sales club and winners of awards serve on an advisory council that reviews new products and services, sets agendas for sales meetings, and has dinner with the company president once a quarter. Members might also receive new business cards stating their membership in the Million Dollar Club, Circle of Excellence, or President's Club.

For a really superior performance, a congratulatory letter or phone call from the president proves very effective. Salespeople need to feel that someone at the top knows and cares, and in a smaller concern that particular someone is the president. The letter should be sent home so that it can be shared with the salesperson's spouse, and a copy of the letter placed in the employee's file. The cost is minimal, but the motivational effect is tremendous.

The sales manager for a local St. Louis greeting card company went to a sales seminar in New York. Company sales had stagnated, and salespeople were performing under their potential. During the seminar, the sales manager realized that she seldom praised or recognized her salespeople, either privately or publicly. She had an excellent combination compensation plan, with bonuses for outstanding performance, but she never said, "Thanks for a good job," or established formal awards for high performers. After talking with the company president, she created an entire recognition program with awards, publicity, honor clubs, contests, and management involvement. Depending on the territory, she recognized some salespeople for new accounts, some for dollar increases in shipments, and some for unit increases of a particular line.

Whenever the sales manager wanted to encourage a particular type of behavior, she would praise the salesperson who performed it. "Thank you, Carl, for servicing that major drug store even though you did not receive an order." "Susan, I received your call report and found it very helpful." "I saw that great order you sent in last week, George."

The sales manager inaugurated a salesperson of the month award. The criteria changed from month to month. The sales manager established criteria that fit her marketing/sales plan and that were important to the company's success: calls per day, new accounts per month, net revenue increases, percentage above quota, dollars of overdue accounts, gross margin contributions, list price maintenance. The salesperson who did the worst each month got to choose the criterion for the next month. Every fourth month the sales manager chose a winner based on extra effort, improved results, or some outstanding performance related to solving a problem. The goal was for everyone to be a winner at least once a year.

The salesperson of the month used a reserved parking place with gold lines, got a day off (with the sales manager covering the territory), had his or her picture hung in the reception room, and received a trophy that rotated each month among winners as well as a bouquet of flowers. In addition, the sales manager established a salesperson of the year award based on her criteria. Winners received a ring, a watch, a clock, or a pin commemorating the award and had their pictures hung in the reception room for the next twelve months. The salesperson of the month award was given at a weekly sales meeting. The salesperson of the year was awarded at the annual sales dinner. Larger companies often honor a salesperson of the month and year for each district or region, and these winners become finalists in the companywide program.

The sales manager also put a blackboard outside her office with each salesperson's name, their dollar sales to date for the week, and their cumulative sales for the year as a percent of quota. The salespeople's names were ranked by results, the highest producer appearing in the number one slot and the weakest producer in the bottom slot.

As a result of these many recognition programs, the St. Louis greeting card company doubled its sales in four years.

Feeling of Usefulness

Salespeople need to feel that their work serves a useful purpose and contributes significantly to the company's success and well-being. A salesperson's motivation can be destroyed overnight by a feeling of worthlessness. Training programs, management's attitudes, good communications, and the appreciation of their work and sensitivity to their problems all contribute to a sense of usefulness.

Although they hide it, many salespeople approach their jobs with feelings of insecurity and inferiority. They live with customer rejection every day. Their skills are intangible and difficult to describe, and nonselling coworkers, even family members, often don't respect or understand them.

Your investment of time and the company's investment of money in training or sales meetings help create a feeling of usefulness. During the initial training period and in periodic field visits and sales meetings, management should make it clear that the company could not exist without its salespeople. Without a sales force, there would be no orders, shipments, or revenues to employ anyone else. Management's positive attitude will in turn influence that of its nonselling employees, which will further reinforce the salespeople's sense of worth. Management's lead in recognizing the centrality of its sales force is particularly important in design-, engineering-, or operations-driven companies.

However, many manufacturing-, design-, engineering-, or operations- driven firms look at salespeople as a necessary evil: the turkeys and jokers with company cars and expense accounts. This attitude makes salespeople feel useless, worthless, and unmotivated.

Good communications, especially timeliness in responding to their efforts or to their particular problems, help make salespeople feel useful. For example, when a salesperson has invested effort in opening a new account or obtaining an order, respond to the situation with the attention it deserves. Don't let orders for new accounts lie on someone's desk for weeks before obtaining credit information. Such lack of action tells the salesperson that he or she is useless; it communicates the message that new accounts, and the salesperson's efforts, don't count.

For example, if an order arrives that cannot be shipped on time, or when you can't deliver the promised service, discuss it with the salesperson immediately. Don't wait until after the proposed shipping date has passed. Lack of communication in such instances totally demoralizes your sales staff.

When you raise prices, or a new competitor enters the market, let your salespeople know that you sympathize with the problems this causes them. Help them with your knowledge. Don't say, "That's part of your job, now get it done."

In-house customer service representatives and sales coordinators who provide sales support can help to motivate salespeople in the field. The message is "we care; you are important."

As sales manager, you should promptly answer all correspondence and phone calls from your people. Make sure they receive samples, catalogs, bulletins, and sales aids on time. When you wait days or weeks to answer a call or letter from your people, you place their usefulness in question. Always return salespeople's calls even if only to report, "I am very busy this afternoon but will call back tomorrow." How do you feel when your boss or one of your customers does not return your calls? Similarly, when a salesperson unexpectedly pops into your office and you are swamped, don't say, "I don't have time to see you," but rather, "I am busy right now, but let's set a time to talk tomorrow."

Some smaller companies, especially those using commission compensation and/or expense reimbursement, do not pay their salespeople promptly. They may send checks out late or defer payments until the following month. The message conveyed by such action is that the salesperson's work contributes little, and this quickly destroys motivation.

The Philadelphia salesman for a men's clothing company called on a number of major accounts who preferred to review his line at the company's New York showroom. The Philadelphia salesman asked his sales manager, who ran the New York showroom, if he could come to New York to work with these major accounts. The sales manager replied that this was not necessary, because he, the sales manager, would work with these accounts himself. The sales manager assured his salesman that all commissions on such sales would be credited to him. The sales manager felt the Philadelphia salesman had plenty to do calling on the many smaller retailers in his territory.

These major accounts did purchase clothing through the New York office, and the salesman did receive his commission, but he nevertheless continued to complain that he wanted to participate in the selling, even though he received a commission for putting forth no effort. Management refused to let him participate, and after two years the salesman joined a competitor. At his previous job, he had felt useless.

As sales manager, keep in mind that a salesperson must feel useful, must feel a sense of worth in relation to the company. Temper your words and actions to your knowledge of this need, and treat salespeople as mature professionals who are performing significant work.

Some small companies conduct climate surveys of salespeople, which ask for their opinion of their managers. A copy of one such survey appears in Chapter 6. What do you do to make your salespeople feel useful, important and worthwhile? Equally important, do some of your actions turn salespeople off?

Challenge and Achievement

Many salespeople thrive on the challenge of opening new accounts and increasing the volumes of existing ones. They possess a high need to achieve that exceeds any monetary rewards they may gain. Long after they have satisfied their financial needs, these achievers continue going the extra mile to do better.

Can you pick out the superstars in your organization, the 30 percent who produce 70 percent of your sales? The people with no complacency plateau or comfort level? Often we concentrate on motivating underperformers when in fact motivating the superstars could produce better results.

Generally, such high achievers enjoy taking personal responsibility for problem solving, are willing to take calculated risks, enjoy participating in management decisions, and need constant feedback on their performance. Because they are your best performers, you must continue to motivate them by providing outlets for their achievement-related needs. Assign such people difficult customers, possibly expand their territory, and let them participate in management decisions. These assignments motivate them, and their participation can benefit the company. One note of caution: These people will accept whatever challenge you assign them, so beware of overloading them.

A small Denver company erected towers for radio, telephone, and television transmission. Its California salesperson had an insatiable appetite for achievement and challenge. When its largest national customer threatened to take its business elsewhere, the sales manager asked the California salesperson to accompany him on a visit to the customer's national headquarters in Washington. Together they won the business back, and the salesman talked about his participation in this success for the next year.

When a Chicago insurance agency had an opportunity to bid on a large group program in Dallas, it sent its highest-achieving salesperson to make the presentation. He failed to obtain that business, but he enjoyed the opportunity, appreciated the recognition, and worked even harder on his return.

Because many high achievers enjoy participating in management decisions, you should develop vehicles for accommodating this need. For instance, invite these people to participate in the committees that set the agendas for sales meetings, approve new products or services, discuss field problems with management, or develop new sales techniques. Let them interview potential new hires, or help train them, or make presentations at sales meetings. Encourage them to make positive suggestions for change. Seek their advice. Let them know you consider their recommendations seriously. When you take a vacation, put them in charge. From this participation they gain a special sense of achievement and self-worth, and you get a job well done.

Reducing a high achiever's territory can severely damage his or her motivation. Such people need to perceive unlimited challenges and opportunities for achievement. Often they outrun their ability to service all the new accounts they open. But by reducing their territory, you are giving a message that can only be interpreted as, "Thanks for the great job; your reward is a demotion, a penalty."

A small children's pajama company in Tennessee was acquired by a large conglomerate in Atlanta. The pajama company's New York salesperson also covered Boston and Philadelphia. He worked six days a week, never took a vacation, and produced 25 percent of company sales. The conglomerate reduced his territory to New York City, so less traveling would be involved and so that Philadelphia and Boston could each have a resident salesperson. His salary remained at the same high level, making him the highest-paid person in the pajama company.

After six months he quit and went to work for a competitor. Because he sold every major account in New York, no challenge remained, and he lost interest in the job.

This unfortunate situation might have been avoided by giving the salesperson part of New Jersey or Connecticut, which were underdeveloped, or by giving him a title, such as national accounts sales manager or assistant sales manager, or by explaining the benefits of a smaller territory: less travel expense and more time off the road for customers and leisure.

High achievers want constant feedback on their results. Be sure these people receive weekly, if not daily, comparisons of their results to forecast, quota and previous year. They respond to and understand gross margin analysis and profit contribution numbers. Discuss this material with them.

A larger concern can offer the achiever advancement into management, for which he or she may or may not be qualified. A smaller concern cannot offer advancement, but through flexibility, it can offer challenging selling opportunities and participation in management decisions. In this situation, the smaller company approach often proves more satisfying for the high achiever; and so, properly handled, these people often prefer a smaller concern. What are you doing to motivate your superstars with a high need for challenge and achievement?

Freedom and Authority

Many salespeople prize the freedom and authority available to them through selling. They thrive on planning their own day, not going to an office, representing the company to a customer, and making their own decisions. Many salespeople even feel that they are in business for themselves and enjoy managing their own territories. This is why they chose a career in sales to begin with. Can you pick these people out in your organization?

To satisfy such people's needs, you can remove some of the controls, allowing them more freedom and authority. Also, you can allow them to work directly with customers on certain nonselling activities, hold them accountable for performance results, and issue them titles.

You might, for instance, let them make certain decisions on their own that previously had required your approval. As an example, if an account met volume and credit requirements, you might let the salesperson vary prices, terms, freight and advertising allowances within certain limits. They generally accept this new freedom by pricing at the higher end. If you normally require weekly route sheets and call reports from your salespeople, you might require them only biweekly from this person. As with the high achiever, you might assign this person more responsibility for forecasting monthly sales in his or her territory, calling on the management of major customers and prospects, or handling national accounts with headquarters in the territory.

Such a person often enjoys working directly with the customer on nonselling, service-related projects. Depending on the product or service, this might involve advertising, promotions, recycling, plant layout, safety issues, formulas, markups, perpetual inventories, estate planning, or displays. Allow this person the time and authority to get involved with these sorts of activities.

Salespeople with a high need for authority and freedom like to be held accountable for performance results, and generally enjoy the performance appraisal process. If they understand profitability, you can share information on each product line's margins and set goals relating to their territories' profits.

Salespeople of this type also like titles that suggest authority. Instead of being called a sales representative, they prefer titles such as national account manager, territory manager, account executive, marketing representative, sales associate, sales engineer, technical representative, sales counselor, sales coordinator, sales consultant, sales specialist, account representative, or market specialist. In that advancement opportunity is very limited in a smaller company, you can use a series of these titles to create a career path program indicating rank, seniority, and promotion within the sales force. Your salespeople might start as account representatives and, after several years of successful performance, move up to account executive, with the ultimate goal of being promoted to territory manager. These titles would appear on their calling cards. Discuss the issue of titles with your key salespeople. Their responses will surprise you.

The star salesperson for a small printer in Columbus, Ohio, was a chronic complainer who both annoyed the sales manager and disturbed the general morale. He openly criticized the company and his sales manager. Criticisms often started with, "If I were sales manager. . . ." At the root of the problem lay his frustration over lack of advancement opportunity into management. Because the printing company depended on this star salesman's results, the sales manager decided to turn the salesman's need for authority into a positive rather than a negative motivational factor.

During lunch at the local country club, the sales manager assigned the star performer responsibility for a national account currently handled by the company president and at the same time gave him the title of national accounts sales manager. He also granted him authority to quote prices on stock jobs and to assist customers in designing forms. The salesman's complaining tapered off, and his job satisfaction improved.

The salesperson with a high need for authority and freedom is often the superstar with a high need for challenge and achievement. All the needs and goals discussed in this chapter are interrelated.

Self-Realization and Fulfillment Through Personal Growth

Most salespeople require personal growth for self-realization and fulfillment. They want to feel that they are more effective, more skilled at selling today than they were two years ago or ten years ago. This need is especially strong in salespeople over forty or in those who have been with the company for more than ten years.

Continual training helps to satisfy this need and can take many forms, including sales meetings, field visits, workshops, seminars, industry conferences, and trade shows. Trained salespeople produce more sales not only because of improved knowledge but also because of improved motivation.

Most salespeople like a certain amount of change, if only to avoid "being in a rut." Your responsibility as sales manager is to create an environment conducive to productive change and personal growth so your salespeople don't get burned out.

The sales manager of a successful company selling highway safety devices to various government agencies detected growing dissatisfaction among his three best salespeople. All three individuals were well compensated, received adequate recognition, and were allowed considerable authority, and each had been with the company more than fifteen years and was over fifty. Their dissatisfaction puzzled the sales manager until he realized that these three salespeople had stopped growing personally, that they felt burned out and had developed bad self-images.

The sales manager decided to send one salesman to a conference in Washington on highway safety; another to a marketing association three-day seminar on selling municipal customers; and the third to view a new European safety system being installed in Mexico City. The next two years he repeated this type of experience, but rotated each salesperson's activity. The salesmen learned, grew, and a feeling of self-realization and fulfillment replaced that of dissatisfaction.

The sales manager for a small giftware company had a plateaued salesperson who had represented the company for ten years. Paul had long been an above-average performer, had handled the largest territory in terms of dollar sales, and was respected and liked by customers and prospects. But ever since his two children's graduation from college and his wife's promotion at her firm, Paul's attitude and performance had been disappointing. His calls per day fell along with his number of new accounts and total sales dollars.

The final blow came when Paul started losing a significant number of accounts because of a price increase. To make matters worse, the sales manager and Paul had become personal friends. She could not live with the situation but wanted to avoid terminating Paul, who had just reached fifty. If you haven't had this problem, you will. Only the names will change.

Calling Paul into her office, the sales manager explained how she perceived the problem. She then asked Paul what his goals were, what he would do to solve the problem, and, if their roles were reversed, what action he would take. Together they came up with a specific remedial plan and the time frame for its execution. She reminded Paul of his excellent past performance, but they both agreed that Paul was unmotivated and felt left behind, that he had a bruised ego that needed pumping.

They looked at a number of alternatives: changing the territory, giving Paul some special projects, making him an inside customer service representative, putting him in charge of trade shows and a national account, using him for training new people.

The sales manager gave Paul a title, sent him to several seminars, let him represent the company at trade shows, and assigned specific performance goals. They met every two weeks for five months and even discussed the possibility of termination. At one meeting his wife was present; at another they watched a video on motivation. Slowly Paul started to feel better and once again became an above-average performer.

Many sales managers would prefer to complain about the Pauls in their departments than to confront the issues squarely. Unfortunately, the problem only gets worse unless you take the bull by the horns and actually offer to help the unmotivated salesperson.

Esteem, Status, and Respect

Most salespeople want the esteem of their fellow salespeople and of other company employees, management, customers, friends, and family. This helps build their self-esteem. For some, esteem comes in the shape of praise, recognition, or money. For others it is associated with status within the organization and is represented by a job title, still others need more direct expressions of esteem.

Little items such as impressive calling cards help establish self-esteem and status every day. When an auto parts distributor stopped issuing embossed calling cards to his salespeople and substituted cheaper offset cards to save money, several of his salespeople paid for the printing of the old personalized embossed cards out of their own pockets.

A successful salesman of small steel products did a great deal of customer entertaining with his wife at company expense. They wined and dined customers twice a week, played golf with many, and even took a few on vacations. When industry sales declined because of a recession, the sales manager cut back on these entertainment expenses. The salesman asked for the expense allowance to be continued even if it meant a decrease in his salary. The life-style made available by the expense account was critical to this man's status in the company and to his personal self-esteem.

The salesperson with a high need for esteem and status requires special treatment. Your budget permitting, consider satisfying this person with a special privilege such as a company credit card, subscriptions to trade publications, better car, first choice on vacation time, airline or hotel room upgrades, bigger desk, automobile phone, membership in a private club, entertainment allowance, or fancy calling card. Most important, as sales manager, you should enhance every salesperson's esteem through your respect.

Sense of Belonging

Many salespeople have a strong need to belong, which they express through club and church memberships, strong family ties, community involvement, and, of course, participation in their work organization. Within the work organization, any group activities, such as sales meetings, conferences, contests, social events, and training seminars, can satisfy this need to belong. If the sales force lives within a day's drive of your office, scheduling frequent group activities is more practical than if they live far away. If the sales force sells out of one central office, the everyday personal social contact creates the sense of belonging. In addition, the sales manager's field visits remind salespeople that they belong to an organization. Satisfying the need to belong for a national field sales force spread from Boston to Los Angeles proves the most difficult, yet because these people are physically separated from each other their need is the greatest. A salesperson who works far from the home office can get very lonely.

Sales bulletins and newsletters, which contain news of other salespeople or other employees, remind salespeople that they belong to an organization. Both personal news (concerning births, new houses, birthdays,

anniversaries of employment, vacations, illness, and retirement) and business news (concerning contests, competition, customers, programs, products, services, promotions, quotas, results, and new accounts) prove
effective. Have salespeople contribute articles and information. Have a
contest to name your newsletter. Make it warm and folksy. Many small
firms use the newsletter to report on each salesperson's results. Salespeople
are ranked by their percent of quota or percent increase over last year. No
one wants to be in the bottom third.

Once or twice a year, resources permitting, a well-planned sales meeting
can provide a productive means of communication, motivation, and training. The sales meeting is of particular importance because it offers a prime
opportunity for one-to-one human interaction within the sales force and
between management and the sales organization. Many small companies
or regional offices with local salespeople hold monthly or even weekly
sales meetings. All this satisfies a salesperson's need to belong.

Also, in a smaller company the sales manager's and president's
expressions of concern for salespeople's well-being create a feeling of belonging. Congratulate your salespeople on happy events such as a birth,
graduation, or marriage. Express your sympathies when someone in a
salesperson's family becomes ill or dies. Remember how you felt when
your boss expressed these concerns. People never forget it, which creates
bonding and loyalty.

The president of a small bakery supply company sends and personally
signs birthday cards to all employees. The sales manager of a small garbage disposal company has a birthday cake and brief party for his people.
A giftware company gives salespeople a day off on their birthday. Many
companies have similar programs to celebrate anniversaries of employment. A wholesale seed company sends flowers to its people on the anni-
versary of their employment. Many companies send birthday cards to
employees' children and spouses. The cost is nominal, the motivational
results excellent.

The sales manager of a small processed meat company visited each of
sixteen field sales representatives twice a year. The first question salespeople asked concerned news of their colleagues in other territories. The company could afford only one national sales meeting a year, but the sales
manager sensed a strong feeling for or need for belonging. He decided to
have shorter, less expensive regional sales meetings six months after each
national meeting. Then between regional meetings he sent videotapes on
selling skills and product knowledge to the salespeople. Each month the
tapes were rotated.

He also asked his secretary to write a newsletter for the sales force.

Each salesperson submitted information. Each month salespeople received a bouquet with one carnation for every new account opened. A nice spirit developed, and the sales force seemed even more willing to put forth that extra effort.

Interpersonal Relationships With Management and Peers

Pleasant personal relationships with management and peers represent a positive motivational force for salespeople and also foster a feeling of belonging. Unpleasant relationships represent a negative motivational force, which reduces a salesperson's productivity.

The Los Angeles representative of a small West Coast gear company did a satisfactory selling job in his territory, but he had a personality clash with the sales manager. The sales manager was an authoritarian, high-powered generalist, and the salesperson a low-key, detail man. The sales manager recognized their difference in styles as a problem, and knew that his salesman would do better if their relationship improved.

Over the next few months, the sales manager showed more flexibility toward, and applied less pressure on, the Los Angeles salesman. He also provided this salesman with more detailed information on his territory. The relationship improved, and so did sales in that area.

A Detroit office furniture company employed five excellent salespeople for the greater metropolitan area. One of the people annoyed the other four to the point where sales were affected. This member of the sales organization always had the right answers, told his colleagues what to do, and how to do it, monopolized sales meetings, and bragged a great deal. His ideas were right, everyone else's wrong. He was a superstar with a giant ego. He constantly told the sales manager how to do her job, and seldom listened to her suggestions. You've probably met this person.

The sales manager realized that this dissident salesman's problem probably stemmed from lack of self-esteem and self-discipline. One day at lunch, the sales manager expressed her respect for the salesman's performance, skills, and judgment, but noted that the salesman must also respect his colleague's opinions. She explained that he was becoming a problem. She asked a number of questions to stimulate self-analysis and discussion. "What do you feel is causing the problem?" "What would you do if you were sales manager?" "What are your career goals?" She mentioned that he was a role model for younger salespeople.

At that meeting she discovered he wanted her job and had time on his hands. They agreed on a program: He would make certain presentations at sales meetings, attend several workshops or seminars, take responsibility for several large inactive accounts, represent the company at several trade shows, read a book on getting along with people, and each month they would meet to discuss progress toward their goal. The sales manager also stated very firmly that unless his behavior improved, other less pleasant action would be necessary. Thereafter, the two had many discussions concerning this matter, and finally the problem subsided. As a result, the performance of all five people improved.

Leadership and Motivation

Salespeople require consistent, motivated, and competent leadership in order to maintain their own motivation. A sales force is seldom more motivated or competent than its sales manager.

Successful sales managers vary greatly in style from autocratic to democratic, from sales- or task-oriented to employee-oriented, from persuasive to consultive. However, successful sales managers do have three common traits. They realize that their job is getting work done through other people; their styles, techniques, and policies are consistent; and they believe in what they are doing. This belief creates strong personal motivation, which they communicate to their sales force.

The sales manager for a Christmas ornament company asked his salespeople to call on certain specific retail accounts. If they didn't call on the accounts within ten days, the sales manager would make an appointment to see the retailer. Soon the sales manager was calling on more accounts and the sales force fewer. As a result, company sales declined. This sales manager had failed to realize that his job depended on getting work done through other people.

When the United States surgeon general issued his initial warning on smoking, an entrepreneur started marketing no-tobacco lettuce leaf cigarettes. The sales manager for this new product continued smoking his old brand, and this contributed to his sales force's lack of motivation. Sales managers must believe in what they are doing.

The sales manager for a regional soft-drink company told the sales force not to call on restaurants, because of credit problems; then, the next month, he introduced a special-size bottle just for that market. One week this sales manager would use persuasion to implement policy, the next week, threats. During the soft-drink company's busiest month, August, he took a three-week vacation. The salespeople responded by losing their motivation. This sales manager was not competent, consistent, or motivated.

You may wish to ask your salespeople to evaluate you as a sales manager. Every year give them a one-page anonymous questionnaire that asks them to evaluate your abilities as a leader, communicator, trainer, policy maker, and organizer; you can also ask for suggestions for improvement. At the least, evaluate yourself quarterly asking the following questions:

1. How motivated do I appear to the sales force? Do I believe in what I am doing?
2. Am I consistent in my style of management and my techniques/ policies?
3. Do I attempt to get work done through other people or just do it myself?
4. How much time do I spend training salespeople?
5. Do salespeople have difficulty understanding what I want from them?
6. How often do salespeople turn over in my division?
7. Is each salesperson showing net revenue increases?
8. Are the salespeople self-motivated or must I always prod them?
9. What percent of my time do I spend each month on administrative duties? personal selling? time with salespeople? other responsibilities?

Company Policy and Administration

Company policies and administration that promote an open, constructive, and relaxed environment and embody trust, faith, consistency, and fairness will promote job satisfaction and positive motivation. Likewise, company policies and administration that promote inefficiency, ineffectiveness, and frustration within the organization and do not embody trust, consistency, and fairness will cause job dissatisfaction and damage salespeople's motivation.

For example, a company policy that prohibits salespeople from calling the factory to check on delivery dates or outstanding customer balances can create frustration and job dissatisfaction. A less rigid policy that allowed salespeople to call once a week would satisfy both management's need to limit the time and expense involved and the sales force's need for information.

A company policy that prohibits salespeople from making collect calls to the sales manager or using the 800 number can cause frustration and unhappiness. A company policy that asked people to pay for every other call would allow them to share the cost, which is more equitable. The latter policy embodies trust but prevents salespeople from abusing a privilege.

An administrative policy requiring the company president to review each order can unnecessarily delay order processing and thus shipping by four or five days. Such a policy might cause job dissatisfaction and damage salespeople's motivation. A more moderate policy requiring presidential review only of new-account orders would be less likely to damage either salespeople's morale or delivery schedules.

A credit policy prohibiting additional sales to any account that pays invoices late, no matter what the reason, might cause frustration and unhappiness in the sales force and seriously damage motivation. A credit policy notifying the salesperson of any account in arrears and prohibiting shipments only if payments are over thirty days late twice in a row would be less damaging.

A company policy establishing certain national house accounts on which salespeople receive no income certainly dulls motivation. A policy that splits national accounts among a number of salespeople, who then share the income, would improve motivation.

In one small family-owned company, salespeople were not allowed to park in the company lot and the president/owner opened all incoming mail and occasionally listened to phone conversations. Sales force turnover was 50 percent a year.

Job Security and Compensation

A salesperson who feels underpaid or on the verge of termination will not put forth that extra effort you are looking for. In fact, all other motivational techniques fail when salespeople sense that their jobs are threatened or believe that their remuneration, including expense reimbursements and fringe benefits, is inadequate.

A St. Louis securities firm employed seven brokers to handle its "retail" business with individual investors. When the firm's major partner passed away, the brokers (salespeople) became concerned about their jobs. Unnerved by persistent rumors concerning the firm's imminent liquidation or sale, they became much less aggressive in pursuing new business. To offset this concern, the other partners increased the brokers' commissions, called them account executives, and held weekly sales meetings—all to no avail. Only after a year did the brokers realize that their fears were unfounded and once again start producing additional business.

A small company selling housewares door to door employed five excellent salespeople. During the 1990 slowdown, sales dropped slightly and expenses increased significantly. The sales manager announced that one of the five would have to be terminated. The final decision was to be made in four weeks. During that four weeks sales dropped dramatically, and continued dropping subsequently for the remaining four people. Feeling insecure about their future, none of the salespeople could get very motivated.

Once you threaten salespeople with termination or put them on probation, the probability of improvement narrows. Occasionally you must do this, but at the same time look for a replacement.

In 1990 a specialty shoe importer lowered its sales force's commission rate from 10 percent to 6 percent because inflation and exchange rates had raised the price of its line by 40 percent. The sales manager never fully explained the reason for lowering the commission rate to his people. Even though their dollars of commission income rose slightly, because dollars of sales increased over 40 percent, the salespeople failed to produce that extra effort. They felt underpaid.

A temporary employment agency hired a top salesperson at a salary considerably lower than his most recent position had paid. The salesperson arrived at work late, left early, showed little interest in his job, and had to be terminated. He obviously felt underpaid and was not motivated.

Sales Contests/Incentive Plans

Sales contests provide fast and frequent reinforcement to a salesperson's needs for recognition, achievement, fulfillment, status, belonging, and additional compensation. As such, they represent a powerful tool for improving sales force motivation and increasing sales.

Sales contests prove most helpful in meeting specific, short-term objectives, such as smoothing out seasonal sales dips, bringing attention to a good product or service that has been neglected, launching a new product, increasing the number of active accounts, or stimulating upgrades and conversions. Sales contests can also be used to revive enthusiasm for meeting longer-term goals, such as improved collections, lower expenses, higher number of cold calls, higher dollar volume, higher number of orders, higher average order size, new prospects, account retention, increased use of displays, and revival of inactive accounts.

In all cases, these contests attempt to elicit an extra "beyond the normal" effort from the sales force by generating enthusiasm and excitement. Selling can become boring and discouraging. A well-thought out contest generates a continuing momentum even after it has ended because salespeople have experienced the satisfaction of higher sales and earnings. Also, a good incentive program can assist in creating good working habits that will make the sales force more productive on a continuing basis.

Poorly conceived sales contests, by contrast, can lower morale, reduce sales, and lead to resignations. For example, don't use a sales contest to revive an inferior or obsolete product or service that has seen its day. Don't use a sales contest if you can't deliver the product or service being sold. Don't use a sales contest when you already control over 70 percent of the market for that product or service. In all three cases, salespeople become frustrated rather than motivated. During contests, salespeople have been known to overstock customers, to move orders from one period to another, and even to cheat. You must realize this and set up safeguards.

Contests lose their ability to excite and motivate when they are used too frequently or when the same contest is repeated. Generally, one to three different contests a year satisfy the sales force's appetite.

There are three basic types of incentive plans: (1) contests in which salespeople compete directly against one another, resulting in prizes going to a winner and several runners-up; (2) contests in which salespeople are divided into teams by region or product line, and each team competes against the others for prizes; and (3) contests in which salespeople win prizes by meeting or exceeding certain individual goals.

Direct Competition

Direct competition plans offering prizes to one winner and several runners-up do not motivate or involve the entire sales force. At the beginning, half the participants decide that they don't have a chance to win because the cards are stacked against them, and so they do not get involved in the contest.

For example, if the contest rewards the three salespeople who open the most new accounts in April, many salespeople immediately lose interest because they know that their territory does not contain the potential new accounts that another salesperson's territory does. Then, halfway through the contest, when it becomes evident which three people will win, all but the winners give up. The losers are left unmotivated and with a feeling that management does not care about them.

A contest that does not involve the entire sales force will not achieve its motivational or specific performance goals. Active participation by the entire sales organization is vital. Direct competition proves especially inappropriate for small sales forces because the same person always wins. In a small sales force cooperation is often more important than competition.

Teams

Team competition plans offering a prize to be shared by the winning group involve more people than direct competition plans but are not calculated to rouse your star performers. The stars feel that the group dilutes their individual efforts and results. When the star performer produces, he or she wants the spotlight. Therefore, in group contests, the stars, who may produce most of your sales volume, generally perform under their potential. You can partially offset this by making your star performers team captains.

Team contests do create good group spirit, cooperation, and positive peer pressure. More experienced salespeople help and advise less experienced team members in achieving desired goals. Also, no team member wants the responsibility for causing the team's loss. Therefore, all team members exert some extra effort.

Team contests do not produce resentment against individual winners, because a group wins, but they can produce general resentment unless each team has an equal chance to win. When improving group spirit is more important than motivating star performers, consider using a group incentive program. Team contests, however, are inappropriate for small sales forces, which lack the numbers to form teams.

Individual Goals

Contests in which salespeople win prizes by meeting or exceeding certain individual goals produce the best results. In these, salespeople do not compete against each other, but rather against an individual target. Everyone becomes interested and involved and participates because everyone can win prizes.

If the contest's objective is opening new accounts in April, then you as sales manager set a goal or quota for each salesperson. These individual objectives should reflect each territory's potential, which thus gives everyone an equal opportunity to win by leveling the playing field. A territory with a hundred potential new accounts might carry a quota of ten, while a territory with fifty potential new accounts might have a quota of five. You can obtain information on potential new accounts from the reference material used to design territories and from field trips. Before setting the quota, discuss your reasoning with the involved salesperson to make sure he or she accepts the quota as realistic, attainable, and fair.

Any salesperson who achieves 80 percent of his or her goal should receive a prize, but a salesperson achieving 120 percent of quota should receive a more valuable prize. Prizes for reaching various percentage levels of quota are the same for each salesperson regardless of territory or quota size.

For example, if the salesperson with a quota of ten new accounts opens eight, he or she receives the same prize as the salesperson with a quota of five new accounts who opens four. Both achieved 80 percent of quota. Similarly, the salesperson with a quota of ten new accounts who opens twelve receives the same prize as the salesperson with a quota of five new accounts who opens six. Both achieved 120 percent of quota.

Individual goals incentive plans bear a striking resemblance to the quota/bonus form of compensation discussed in Chapter 3. However, the quota/bonus form of compensation rewards superior performance spanning six months or a year with considerable money, whereas the individual goals contest rewards superior performance spanning one to three months with noncash prizes. The sales contest provides a more immediate reward for superior performance. Also, while bonus plans might reward one salesperson for new accounts and another for dollar sales increase, sales contests reward all salespeople for one type of performance. In addition, winners of sales contests receive publicity, no matter how many reach their objectives, while quota/bonus compensation rewards remain private information.

A variation of this individual goal plan involves a point system. A salesperson receives points for achieving 80 percent of his or her target in the sales contest, and receives an increasing number of points as the percentage of or over target increases. When the contest ends, the salesperson uses these points to buy prizes.

Another variation involves adding overall winners to the individual goal plan. For example, the three people who achieve the largest percentage gain over quota receive a prize in addition to their other awards. Everyone continues to have individual goals and individual awards, but you add additional awards for overall winners. This creates some element of direct competition among salespeople and provides an added incentive for star performers.

Setting targets for these individual goal plans can be time-consuming because past sales records require studying and each salesperson requires a meeting. Administration of these contests is also time-consuming considering that just about everyone wins something. In a smaller concern, setting targets and administration of the program falls on the sales manager, who is already short of time. However, the results generally justify the extra time required. Individual goal plans prove especially suitable for small sales forces in that they can be used with any number of people, even one lone salesperson.

Objectives

Regardless of which plan you use—direct competition, teams, or individual goals—properly handled sales contests require objectives, budgets, time frames, appropriate prizes, adequate promotion, and simple, clearly explained rules.

A sales contest without specific short-term objectives, and some more general longer-term goals as well, wastes time and money, which a smaller business especially can ill afford. Generally, sales contests without specific objectives fail. Company policy mandating at least one sales contest a year hardly qualifies as an objective. You need a reason for such a project, and the reason must support your basic marketing plan.

The objectives of a sales contest might include increased sales of a particular product, upgrades to more service, increased overall unit or dollar sales during a certain period, conversions to a particular raw material, increased order size, increased number of customers, improved collections, reduced selling expenses, better use of selling aids, better retention of present accounts, or more prospecting. Using the specific objectives, you assign each activity a time frame and each territory a goal. For example, how many additional units of a particular product, how many additional dollars of sales, or what percentage increase in sales do you want from each salesperson during the contest period? How many new customers do you want each salesperson to add? If improved collections are a goal, how many days' accounts receivable do you want in each territory? If reduced selling expenses are a goal, how many dollars or what percentage decrease do you want from each salesperson?

All sales contests should have as long-range goals the reinforcement of salespeoples' motivational needs for recognition, achievement, fulfillment, status, belonging, and additional compensation. The contests should also seek to generate continuing momentum by establishing good work habits and exposing salespeople to higher income levels. An incentive plan's objectives naturally influence your choice among the three types of plans.

Budgets

Sales contests and incentive programs are especially suited to the needs of smaller concerns with limited financial and human resources, because, if properly structured, they can increase sales and profits from existing personnel with minimum increases in overhead. To achieve this, you must understand the economics of your objectives and have a budget. A small business can ill afford to pay out more in prizes than it reaps in additional profits.

Here you will require the assistance of the company president, controller, or accountant. For example, if the contest increases sales by 5 percent, or $100,000, how much additional profits will be generated before contest costs? Look at the profit potential for the best possible, worst possible, and most probable sales results.

Next decide, with the help of your president, controller, or accountant, what percentage of the increased profits should pay for the contest costs. If a $100,000 sales increase produces a $10,000 profit before taxes, your colleagues might budget 33 percent, or $3,300, for contest expenses. A more successful contest generates greater sales and profits, but if you use an individual quota plan it also results in greater prize expenses. You must also take into account that a contest affects both current and future sales and profits, and that there are motivational benefits that cannot be measured in dollars.

Let's assume that the most probable result of your individual quota contest is a 5 percent, or $100,000, sales increase, resulting in a $10,000 pretax profit increase, and thus creating a $3,300 budget for the program. First, you deduct from the $3,300 the sum of $500 for out-of-pocket promotional costs. This covers extra phone calls, mailing expenses, and certain promotional literature, and leaves you with $2,800 to purchase prizes for your four salespeople.

Now you work backwards, assigning each salesperson a portion of the $100,000 increase appropriate to the contest's objectives and to the potential of his or her territory. This portion, whether $15,000, $20,000, $30,000, or $35,000, becomes related to his or her quota. If they all reach quota, the cost of their prizes would be $2,800 divided by 4, or $700 each. If one, several, or all exceed quota, you increase the $700 on a prorated basis. If they miss quota, you decrease the $700 on a prorated basis. These numbers then become your budget.

Contests and incentive plans that do not produce immediate sales or profit increases are more difficult to budget. If the contest's objectives involve more prospecting or improving collections, it is difficult to measure the immediate impact on sales or profits. In such instances you use the same techniques, but must place a value on the longer-range benefits.

Time Frame

Sales contests that go on too long or are held too often lose their effectiveness because participants lose their enthusiasm and interest. Contests should be looked on as temporary schemes to elicit extra effort in a particular area.

Sales contests lasting from one to two months usually prove most effective. Generally, one to three contests a year will provide enough extra motivation for a sales force. According to ECS/A Wyatt Data Services Company, for companies that use contests the average number per year is three.*

Contests lasting less than a month do not allow salespeople sufficient time to become involved or to translate their enthusiasm into results. The minimum time span for a contest would be that required to perform the necessary tasks. For example, if a contest involves increasing dollar sales to achieve certain goals, you must allow enough time for the salespeople to contact all their important customers. If a contest involves opening new accounts, you must allow enough time for proper prospecting, appointment setting, and callbacks.

To maintain interest and enthusiasm, longer contests require more substantial prizes than those appropriate for short contests. You may obtain good results by offering a free dinner for two at a French restaurant to any salesperson who reduces his or her territory's overdue accounts receivable by 10 percent in the next thirty days. However, such a prize would not generate sufficient enthusiasm for a contest lasting ninety days that involved opening a substantial number of new accounts. By comparison, to whip up enthusiasm for the ninety-day contest, you might have to offer a free weekend on the town at a local hotel.

Prizes

You can best motivate salespeople by offering luxurious, exotic, fascinating prizes that they normally would not purchase for themselves, in other

*From the *1990/91 Sales & Marketing Personnel Report* (Ft. Lee, N.J.: ECS/A Wyatt Data Services Company).

words, prizes that capture the imagination. Cash, therefore, is not the best contest award, and would also interfere with your regular compensation plan. Prizes such as limo service, pamper centers, flowers or fruits of the month work better than cash.

If your budget is $200, dinner for two at a fine restaurant along with theater or sporting event tickets might provide an appropriate prize. If your budget is $600, a weekend for two on the town or a compact disc player might prove an appropriate prize. If your budget is $1,500, a videotape recorder, home computer, quadraphonic sound system, or fine camera or a weekend for two in New York, San Francisco, or New Orleans might provide an appropriate prize.

Always offer a choice, because one type of prize is seldom acceptable to all the participants, yet you want all participants motivated to win a prize. For example, some salespeople do enough traveling during the week and would prefer a prize for the house rather than another trip.

Prizes such as maid service, baby sitting, days off, entertainment, lottery tickets, golf fees, or tennis lessons that benefit both the participant and spouse work well. This produces a little extra pressure at home to perform well and a little extra prestige for winning. Also, prizes such as home computers, car phones, car wash coupons, auto accessories, and telephone answering machines that a salesperson can use on the job are very appropriate.

The Internal Revenue Service considers the cash value or cost of most prizes as taxable income to the recipient. However, some prizes valued under $400 might not be taxable to the employee if considered a gift. You should consult your company's financial officer for details, and inform your sales force.

In addition to prizes, you might also consider issuing inexpensive certificates and plaques. These represent a lasting form of recognition, and recognition represents an important motivational force.

Prizes need not be expensive to be effective. One sales manager takes over each winner's territory during an extra day off. Another gives winners an upgrade on their hotel rooms at sales meetings or on leased company cars. Another awards golf lessons and green fees. Another cooks dinner for the winners and their spouse or significant other.

Think about buying prizes from or through your customers to obtain discounts and make friends. A refuse removal company services many hotels and restaurants. If you sell through retail stores, think about awarding gift certificates.

The sales manager for a temporary help service ran out of new ideas for contests, so he established a mystery prize. All winners and their spouses

or significant others attended the awards luncheon. The sales manager announced that the prize was a choice of gift certificates at several local stores,
and winners had the afternoon off to go shopping.

In the 1989 survey of employee motivation practices conducted by
Incentive magazine, 59 percent of the companies contacted still use cash as
awards, 46 percent use selected merchandise, 36 percent plaques or jew-
elry, 22 percent travel, 25 percent merchandise catalogs, and 10 percent
honorary titles.* Because many companies use more than one type of award,
depending on the particular contest or incentive plan, or give salespeople
their choice of awards, numbers total more than 100 percent. In a similar
survey conducted by the Dartnell Corporation as part of its Sales Force
Compensation report, 50 percent of the 400 companies contacted use travel
awards, 65 percent cash, 30 percent merchandise, and 68 percent recognition.†

The 1990/91 Sales & Marketing Personnel Report (ECS/A Wyatt Data
Services Company) showed that 57 percent of the 200 companies contacted still use cash awards, 33 percent merchandise, 61 percent trips with
spouse, and 13 percent a trip without spouse.‡ The 1989/1990 TPF&C
Sales Compensation Survey of 160 Fortune 1000 firms reports that consumer product companies award trips 63 percent of the time, cash 47 percent, and recognition 80 percent; industrial products and process component
companies award trips 28 percent of the time, cash 25 percent, and recognition 46 percent; and service companies award trips 59 percent of the
time, cash 45 percent, and recognition 55 percent.§

Promotion

Like the product or service you sell, a successful sales contest requires
creativity, merchandising, and promotion. A sales contest must capture
the salesperson's imagination by injecting some pizzazz, drama, and ad-
venture into the everyday corporate routine. Make the sales contest fun.

If possible, announce the contest at a sales meeting, where you can
personally sell it to the group and answer questions. Prepare an innovative
promotional piece, clearly explaining the rules and describing or picturing

*Reprinted by permission of *Sales & Marketing Management*. Copyright: Survey of
Selling Costs, February 26, 1990.
†From *Sales Force Compensation, Dartnell's 25th Survey Edition*. Used with permis-
sion of the Dartnell Corporation, Chicago, Ill. All rights reserved.
‡From *Sales & Marketing Personnel Report*, ECS.
§From 1989/1990 Sales Compensation Survey, TPF&C, a Towers Perrin Com-
pany, Chicago, Ill.

the prizes. If a sales meeting is not practical, mail the promotional piece to each salesperson with a covering letter, and follow up with a telephone call. Sales contests require personal enthusiastic selling by the sales manager to excite the participants.

Create an appropriate name and theme for your sales contest, one that relates to the prizes or objective. If most prizes are home entertainment devices, you might call it "Electronic Whirl." If most prizes are trips to Florida, you might call it "Sunny Skies." If the objective is to sell recycling, you might call it "Waste Reduction."

Even properly organized individual goal sales contests that start out well can begin losing salespeoples' interest at midpoint. To maintain their interest, issue weekly bulletins on results, write personal congratulatory letters to the leaders, and remind all salespeople of the prizes involved.

If possible, end the contest with a dinner announcing the results. If this is not possible, issue a bulletin with the results. You and the president should write congratulatory letters to all prize recipients. Remember that a sales contest not only achieves certain specific company objectives and awards prizes to participants, but also reinforces salespeoples' needs for recognition, achievement, fulfillment, status, and belonging. A good sales contest boosts personal morale and pride in the company.

Rules

Many contests fail because participants do not understand the rules. Therefore, keep the rules as simple as possible, and ask for individual feedback to ensure that salespeople have a complete understanding. Make certain that everyone knows the opening and closing dates; which achievements are sought by the company; by what date products/services have to be sold or shipped; what products/services, customers, expenses, or accounts receivable are included; how sales, expenses, or new accounts are reported and validated; the basis for awards; how and when prizes will be awarded; and what assistance the company will provide salespeople in the contest. For example, are contest results based on orders or shipments? What about a customer's credit? Will reactivated inactive accounts be counted as new accounts? Must orders be written on the company order form but signed by the customer? One very successful contest lost its impact because winners expected their prizes in August but did not receive them until November.

Using this chapter as a guide put together a sales contest/incentive program for your people. The results will please you.

6

Communication Skills and Techniques

In order to hire, train, compensate, organize, motivate, and evaluate a sales force, you must be able to communicate with your salespeople. We spend 70 percent to 80 percent of our waking hours communicating. Often a sales manager communicates well with customers and with bosses, but not with the sales force. Many sales managers lack the understanding, sensitivity, and skills required for good communication with their subordinates. Significant differences exist between selling and managing those who do the selling. Your job is getting work done through other people and that requires good communication. A saleswoman once told me that her sales manager talked well but communicated poorly.

Managing salespeople involves influencing their thoughts and causing actions. Therefore, communication means not only explaining but also persuading and changing.

Often companies with a small number of employees, especially family-owned and family-managed concerns, have greater communication problems than companies with a large number of employees. Good communication does not depend on the number of people involved, but on the skills, techniques, commitment, concern, and sensitivity of those people. In many smaller companies a negative attitude toward communicating prevails: "Since everyone will find out sooner or later, why waste time telling them?" Moreover, in a small organization, people may become more essential by monopolizing information than they would by passing it along. Good communication involves open doors and open minds. Knowledge/information is power and needs to be shared.

Effective communication is essential not only within the sales organization of a smaller business but also among all levels of sales, production, and accounting. At a small paper products company in Cincinnati the plant continued manufacturing an item that had been discontinued six months earlier simply because sales and manufacturing did not talk. In another instance, accounting continued to send paychecks to a salesperson who had quit months before because the sales manager had failed to notify the payroll department. As these examples illustrate, a breakdown in communications can prove more expensive than a breakdown in machinery.

Managing a successful small business, particularly an effective sales program, is very difficult *with* good communication; without good communication, it is impossible. When management, beginning with the chief executive officer, communicates well, other employees find good communication easier. Good communication starts at the top and is contagious. However, I have observed that the higher you go in an organization, the more barriers there are to good communication, and therefore the more difficult it becomes to communicate.

To communicate effectively, a sales manager must understand the skills, techniques, sensitivities, and human dynamics involved, such as feedback, perception, initiation of action through commands and persuasion, organization and clarity of expression, simplicity, the role of personal prejudice and of informal or unconscious communication, listening, and measuring results. To communicate effectively, a sales manager must also establish regular channels of communication with the sales force, such as route sheets, call reports, customer analysis, product analysis, commission statements, expense reports, orders, sales forecasts, expense budgets, performance appraisals, phone calls, bulletins, letters, audiotapes, manuals, catalogs, sales meetings, individual meetings, staff meetings, training sessions, and bulletin boards.

Communication is a physical and psychological process that uses a common system of sounds, symbols, and behaviors to create mutual understanding so that people can interact effectively. Communication is a transfer of ideas and information, an attempt to become understood.

Feedback and Perception

All communication involves a sender and a receiver trying to achieve a commonness of meaning. This is not achieved until the sender receives feedback that his or her message was received by the recipient in its intended form. When communicating with a salesperson, do you ask for feedback to ensure that he or she understands and accepts the meaning of your message? Do you give feedback to ensure that you have understood the meaning of his or her message?

For example, the sales manager of a ladies' dress company told his five salespeople "not to call on discounters any more." Three months later, one salesperson was still selling to discounters because she had thought the sales manager meant not to open any new discount store accounts. Another salesperson stopped selling to both chain and discount stores because he considered chain stores as discounters. Another salesperson thought she could continue selling to discount stores through the current season.

The sales manager should have asked each salesperson for specific feedback to ensure proper understanding of the message. For example, "What discount stores are you currently selling to?" "When will you see them next to inform them of this policy change?"

When you communicate with salespeople, they may receive a message different from the one you intended, or you may receive a message different from the one they intended, because their experience, desires, and expectations differ from yours. You should convey messages in terms of the recipient's perceptions, and you should receive messages with a sensitivity for the sender's perceptions. This necessitates being specific, dealing with issues, stating facts, and using terms, expressions, and analogies that the hearer can readily understand. When communicating with salespeople, use language that is part of their daily experience—language that they themselves would use. Avoid overly strong emotional statements, which increase misunderstanding.

Remember that words have different meanings to different people, and that an expression common to you may not be common to your sales force. This hold especially true for technical terms, clichés, abbreviations, initials, and "businessese." Many sales managers build a mystique around their trade by using buzz words and jargon, and this results in poor communication. Also, certain words or phrases have hidden emotional meanings that can produce friendly or hostile feelings. For example, "house accounts," "paperwork," "expense account" all produce negative feelings in many salespeople. A female salesperson might react badly if you referred to her as a salesman. A good communicator knows and is sensitive to the audience and chooses words carefully. A good communicator also listens with a sensitivity for the sender's perception of words.

One sales manager told a trainee that all shipments were "FOB Factory, 2% 10 days EOM net 60." The trainee had previously been employed as a sales clerk in a retail store. When the sales manager questioned the trainee's orders calling for his employer to pay freight, the trainee explained that his understanding of "FOB Factory" was that the vendor/

shipper paid freight to the customer's factory, not the opposite. When the trainee's customers started paying invoices late, the sales manager discovered that his new salesman thought "2% 10 days EOM net 60" meant sixty days after the ten days EOM (end of month), not sixty days from invoice date.

This sales manager spoke accounting and shipping language to an inexperienced salesperson. The sales manager should have said, "On all shipments, customers pay all freight charges from our factory to theirs, which we call 'FOB Factory.' Invoices must be paid sixty days after the goods are shipped, but a 2 percent discount can be taken on invoices paid within ten days after the month in which goods are shipped. We call these payment terms '2% 10 days EOM net 60.'" Then the sales manager might have asked for feedback by saying, "If an order is shipped on April 15, when must it be paid to take the discount, and when must it be paid before it becomes delinquent?"

People hear what they expect and desire to hear, which is not necessarily the sender's intended meaning. Therefore, to communicate effectively, you must understand what the recipient expects and desires to hear as well as his or her experience and perceptions. This enables you to express your message accordingly so as to achieve your desired meaning. Similarly, as a listener you must understand the sender's expectations, desires, experience, and perceptions to accurately interpret the intended meaning of the message.

In July a sales manager told a salesman whose sales had declined, "I will have to reduce your salary 10 percent unless sales improve." The salesperson, expecting orders to increase in the fourth quarter, a major shipping period, thought he had until the end of the year to show improvement. The sales manager, expecting the salesperson's orders to decline in the third quarter, and wanting to reduce expenses, had decided that he would make the decision in October. The salesperson's orders did decline in the third quarter, which resulted in a salary cut. The salesperson quit because he had expected and believed he had a longer time period in which to improve results. The sales manager lost a valuable employee simply because he did not realize the two had different expectations and perceptions of the time period involved.

In July the sales manager should have said, "I will have to reduce your salary 10 percent unless sales increase above $10,000 a week by October 1. Do you think that is fair?" A discussion would have followed, which might have led to a compromise date; but in any case the salesperson would have completely understood the sales manager's message.

The sales manager for a sweater company told his sales force that "all off-price orders for promotions must be limited to 20 percent of a customer's purchases." The sales manager's goal involved reducing off-price volume, thus improving profits. He wished to restrict any off-price promotional orders to 20 percent of that item's regular-price unit volume the previous twelve months. The salespeople's goal involved maximizing orders, thus improving their commission income. They interpreted the sales manager's message to mean that off-price promotional orders could not exceed 20 percent of the account's *total expected* dollar volume for the next twelve months. This misunderstanding resulted in the sales manager continually scaling back off-price promotional orders written by his sales force, which upset customers. The sales force and the sales manager had different expectations and perceptions of "off-price orders for promotions" and of "20 percent of a customer's purchases." These different expectations and perceptions led to a misunderstanding that caused embarrassment, waste, and bad feelings.

The sales manager should have said, "Off-price orders for promotions must be limited to 20 percent of a customer's regular-price unit purchases of that item for the past twelve months. Now, please look at the shipments for your largest accounts, and let's discuss their allowable quantities for their next promotion." Asking for this feedback would have established whether the salespeople had received the correct message.

Initiating Action

Much of what you communicate is intended to initiate action or change on the part of the recipient. Initiating action or change involves persuasion and selling. You sell a particular action by giving a reason for it, and the reason must promise a desired result for the listener.

Initiating action or change also necessitates "I messages" and direct commands. Many sales managers assume that their salespeople know what is expected of them. If they "think" the desired action, they believe that the sales force can read their minds and somehow perceive it. You must verbally communicate demands to initiate change or action, not just think them.

Sales managers often try to initiate action by making a report or a suggestion when what they really intend is to issue a demand. Then they complain that no one listens to or follows instructions. If you want route sheets on your desk by noon each Friday, do not tell the sales force, "I review route sheets each Friday afternoon, so I can discuss them with each salesperson Monday morning." You are reporting or describing an event and will be lucky to receive route sheets from half the sales force. Instead, issue a direct command/demand by saying, "You must have your route sheet on my desk by Friday noon, or I will call you Saturday." Then (for feedback) ask, "What day will you mail it?"

If you want to meet with a salesperson Monday morning, don't say, "We better have a meeting Monday," and then wonder why he or she does not show up. You are making a suggestion, not issuing a command/demand. Instead say, "I want to discuss several of your accounts. Please be in my office Monday morning at 8:30 for a meeting. Is an 8:30 meeting convenient?" You are giving an "I message," describing what you want, how you feel, and what effect certain action has on you and the organization.

To initiate action, you must make demands that produce desirable results for the listener, demands that persuade by appealing to his or her motivation. If you make demands that go against the listener's motivations, aspirations, self-image, or values, they will be resisted. The fewer demands you make in each communication, the more likely you will achieve the desired action. Messages with too many demands weaken the communication's effectiveness.

You can persuade the Ohio salesperson, who lives in Cleveland, to make more trips to Cincinnati and Columbus by reminding him that more trips should result in more orders, which in turn will result in more commission income. You do not tell him to make more trips to Toledo and Pittsburgh while discussing Cincinnati and Columbus. Make one demand for action at a time, and point out the personal benefits.

You could persuade the Illinois salesperson to call on more prospects by noting that such action might help him win a prize in the new-account sales contest. You would have difficulty persuading him to take a booth at the Chicago trade show, because he will not get credit for orders from customers outside Illinois.

You can convince the California salesperson to accept a realignment in her territory by selling the possible benefits—less travel between accounts, fewer overnights, lower expenses, more time to open new accounts and expand existing ones, in the long run, less work, more leisure, and greater income.

You convince the New York salesman to lead a discussion at the sales meeting by appealing to his need for recognition and achievement. You convince the same person to call on the Navy Exchange buying office in Brooklyn by arranging a lunch date with the company president to discuss the meeting.

Your Michigan salesman is sixty-eight and plans to retire in two years.

He works only three days a week, but has the good health to work five. You remind him that working five days a week will increase his income; but money no longer motivates him. You cannot threaten early retirement because his wife is the president's sister. As a last resort, you write a special bulletin to the entire sales force praising the Michigan salesman's record and years with the company. You note that his sales have risen each year he has been with the company. Suddenly he starts working five days a week to maintain his record of unbroken sales gains.

Organization and Clarity of Expression

Whatever you wish to communicate, think it through first, control your emotions, keep it simple, be direct, be specific, be logical, and use visual aids wherever appropriate. Many failures in communication stem from not knowing exactly what idea, information, demand, or instruction we wish to express. Many failures in communication stem from not organizing our thoughts before we speak. We retain 10 percent of what we read, 20 percent of what we hear, 30 percent of what we see, and 50 percent of what we both hear and see.

The sales manager of a specialty steel distributor in Atlanta discovered that his star salesman wanted his job and was "bad mouthing" him to the other salespeople. This sales manager had a dilemma because he did not plan to vacate his job and could not afford to lose his star performer. Initially, the sales manager responded by getting angry and verbally attacking the salesman rather than by analyzing the problem.

Eventually, the sales manager discussed the problem with his boss, the company president. They decided that the sales manager should communicate the following message to his star salesman: (1) The salesman was a valuable, appreciated member of the company organization. (2) The sales manager's job was not available. (3) The salesman's responsibilities would be enlarged to include handling certain national accounts, as well as helping to plan sales meetings, new products, advertising, and contests. (4) The salesman would be promoted to national accounts sales manager, but he would still report to his present boss, the general sales manager.

The sales manager arranged a meeting with his star performer to discuss the four points. The sales manager clearly and calmly presented the program, stressing the benefits for the listener. He spoke to the problem rather than attacking the person. This time the sales manager had thought out and organized exactly what he intended to communicate.

When customers of a small Omaha industrial fastener company started complaining to the sales manager about late deliveries, he called the warehouse manager. The warehouse manager complained that three salespeople were writing their orders incorrectly, which necessitated time-consuming rewriting at the warehouse, thus delaying shipments. The sales manager immediately called the first salesman and expressed anger at his stupidity, because correct order writing had been explained many times. The sales manager attacked the person, not the problem.

When the sales manager called the second salesman, his anger had subsided. He said, "Customers have complained about poor deliveries, and the warehouse manager says this results from your incorrectly writing orders." The salesman replied, "Be specific; what have I done wrong?" The sales manager replied, "Your handwriting is sloppy, customers' addresses are incorrect, you wrote quantities in the wrong column, data-processing codes do not have all the digits, quantities by page are not totaled, and product descriptions carry incorrect abbreviations. Refer to the sales manual and straighten this out." The sales manager had answered the question, but he still had not thought through and organized exactly what he wanted to express.

By the time the sales manager called the third salesman, he had thought through the problem and organized his message. He said, "Your customers are complaining about poor deliveries, which may cost you some business unless you take the following corrective action in order writing: (1) Ask all customers for their correct billing and shipping address. (2) Place quantities only in column six, and total them for each item and page. (3) All data-processing codes must use seven digits including zeros. (4) Abbreviate product descriptions by using the first two letters of each word. (5) Print or typewrite each order." The sales manager continued, "I am returning several incorrectly written orders. Please rewrite them correctly and mail them back to me by Monday." The first and second salesmen continued to write faulty orders; the third salesman did not. Eventually the sales manager wrote a bulletin on order writing, and discussed it at the next sales meeting.

Attempt to organize your written and verbal communications in a simple, concise way. More words do not necessarily make communication clearer.

The sales manager for a small specialty chemical company sent out the following bulletin to all salespeople:

> Many of you have requested that the company have a sales meeting this spring. Although the cost of the meeting will be high, we feel the benefits will be greater.

In searching for a central theme or focal point, we considered "opening new accounts," "handling objections," "organizing time," and "new product development." After much thought, we decided on the latter.

You may drive or take a train or bus to the meeting. The opening night dinner begins at 7:00 p.m.

We debated whether to have the meeting at a resort or in a city and whether to have it in the Midwest or on the East or West Coast. We finally decided to have it at Stouffer's on Fountain Square in Cincinnati because of the factory location and good transportation.

We finally decided to have a three-day meeting rather than two or four. The meeting begins on April 3rd and ends on April 5th.

After receiving this bulletin, every salesperson called the sales manager in confusion with questions and comments. A clearer message could have been sent by simply saying:

There will be a spring sales meeting at the Fountain Square Stouffer's in Cincinnati, beginning with an opening dinner at 7:00 p.m. on Friday, April 3, and ending at 5:00 p.m. on Sunday, April 5. Arrange your own transportation, but inform me of the details by March 15. The meeting will concentrate on new product information.

Often charts, diagrams, and photographs communicate messages better than words. Always consider using visual aids. For example, the sales manager for a small San Francisco specialty food purveyor was able to condense a three-page written explanation of a sales contest into a one-page memo accompanied by pictures of prizes and graphs explaining the performance necessary to win prizes.

Personal Prejudice and Informal Communication

Our personal prejudices are very precious to us and we relinquish them reluctantly, if at all. As sales manager, you don't have to like all your salespeople, but you do have to communicate with them all. Recognize that you have negative personal feelings about certain people and that this influences your ability to communicate with them effectively. Also, recognize that you may express these negative feelings unconsciously through nonverbal means of communication. It is safest and fairest to deal with issues and facts rather than with personalities and opinions.

The sales manager for a local truck-leasing company inherited a salesperson who continually complained about business, his family, his customers, and his employer. The salesman, however, had excellent contacts with the purchasing agents of major customers and wrote substantial business. The sales manager couldn't stand talking with this salesman. He communicated with him only by mail, and only when absolutely essential. As a result, the salesman always performed under his potential, and the complaining grew worse.

Sales managers may dislike individual salespeople for many reasons: the way they dress, the money they earn, their complaining, their lack of performance, their bragging, or their lack of maturity. You should be aware that these prejudices are not abnormal, but you must deal with them in order to communicate with all your salespeople.

And be aware that your nonverbal "silent language" may express negative personal feelings as strongly as words. Your eye contact (or lack of it), physical touch, tone of voice, body posture, facial expression, and gestures all convey strong messages to subordinates. You probably have experienced the "silent treatment" from a cold and uncommunicative boss. On the other hand, eye contact can communicate concern, warmth, and understanding to the recipient.

The sales manager for a small insurance agency employed a salesperson who resisted any sort of change. The sales manager dealt with this by personally explaining and selling all desired changes. During their meetings, the sales manager never looked the salesperson in the eye and always sat with his arms folded. He used long pauses with deep breaths to answer questions. The message of dislike, though expressed indirectly, came across strongly to the salesperson. The sales manager might more easily have achieved his goal of selling change if he had recognized and better controlled his nonverbal communication.

Listening

Good communication has two sides, talking and listening. No matter what your position—salesperson, sales manager, president, purchasing agent, or foreman—good listening skills are essential to communication. Proper listening involves showing interest, not acting judgmental, watching body language, concentrating on and thinking about the sender's intended message, perceptions, and expectations, and then giving feedback to the sender to confirm the intended meaning. Ten keys to good listening are suggested in Figure 6-1. Good listening involves sensing, interpreting, evaluating, and responding but not interrupting the sender. We can speak only 140 words per minute, but we can understand 500 words per minute, which leads to interrupting the speaker. Often we think and understand ideas faster than the speaker is able to send them. When a sales manager listens properly and sensitively to a salesperson, it communicates a sense of recognition and worth. Seek first to understand, then to be understood. We communicate by telling, asking, and listening. Most of us are better at the former than the latter. How good at listening are you? Figure 6-2 gives you a chance to test yourself.

The sales manager for a commercial laundry in St. Louis asked his salespeople to increase their calls on hospitals and uniform rental companies, which they did. The salespeople reported back to the sales manager that hospitals required one-day service rather than the three-day service currently offered to other customers. Also, uniform rental concerns required a specific type of folding not currently offered by the laundry. The sales manager heard this, but he did not really listen.

Had he listened, two alternatives would have emerged: either offer one-day service to hospitals, and/or special folding to rental concerns, or don't have the sales force waste any more of its time calling on these types of prospects. Instead, he offered no changes in the service, but he insisted that salespeople continue their fruitless calls on these type accounts.

The sales manager for a door-to-door cosmetic company asked her best salesperson why she was not selling the newest natural shampoo. She replied that customers objected to the ingredients. The sales manager pointed out that the ingredients were finer than those used by competitors. Had the sales manager been listening, concentrating, thinking, and aware of the salesperson's perceptions, she would have realized that the salesperson's problem involved selling the product's chemistry rather than its benefits, more beautiful hair. The problem was not the product, but the presentation; and the sales manager should have noted this to the saleswoman.

The sales manager for a paper recycling company received an urgent call from his best salesman: Unless the company increased his salary by 25 percent, he would resign. The sales manager asked why. The salesman replied that he had received an offer from a competitor at the higher salary level. The sales manager asked what other advantages the competitor offered, and then listened very carefully to the reply. It became obvious that

(*Text continued on page 185.*)

Figure 6-1. Ten keys to effective listening.

These keys are a positive guideline to better listening. In fact, they are at the heart of developing better listening habits that could last a lifetime.

10 Keys to Effective Listening	The Bad Listener	The Good Listener
1. Find areas of mutual interest	Tunes out dry subject	Opportunitizes; asks "what's in it for me?"
2. Judge content, not delivery	Tunes out if delivery is poor	Judges content, skips over delivery errors
3. Hold your fire	Tends to enter into argument	Doesn't judge until comprehension complete
4. Listen for ideas	Listens for facts	Listens for central themes
5. Be flexible	Takes intensive notes using only one system	Takes fewer notes. Uses 4–5 different systems, depending on speaker
6. Work at listening	Shows no energy output; fakes attention	Works hard, exhibits active body state
7. Resist distractions	Is easily distracted	Fights or avoids distractions, knows how to concentrate
8. Exercise your mind	Resists difficult expository material; seeks light, recreational material	Uses heavier material as exercise for the mind
9. Keep your mind open	Reacts to emotional words	Interprets color words; does not get hung up on them
10. Capitalize on fact that thought is faster than speech	Tends to daydream with slow speakers	Challenges, anticipates, mentally summarizes, weighs the evidence, listens between the lines to tone of voice

Figure 6-2. Listener's quiz.

Part A

Few virtues are more prized and less practiced than good listening. This checklist will help you gauge your own listening habits. Try to answer each question objectively.

When taking part in an interview or group meeting, do you	Usually	Sometimes	Seldom
1. Prepare yourself physically by sitting facing the speaker and by making sure that you can hear?	_____	_____	_____
2. Watch the speaker as well as listen to him/her?	_____	_____	_____
3. Decide from the speaker's appearance and delivery whether what he/she has to say is worthwhile?	_____	_____	_____
4. Listen primarily for ideas and underlying feelings?	_____	_____	_____
5. Determine your own bias, if any, and try to allow for it?	_____	_____	_____
6. Keep your mind on what the speaker is saying?	_____	_____	_____
7. Interrupt immediately if you hear a statement you feel is wrong?	_____	_____	_____
8. Make sure before answering that you've taken in the other person's point of view?	_____	_____	_____
9. Try to have the last word?	_____	_____	_____
10. Make a conscious effort to evaluate the logic and credibility of what you hear?	_____	_____	_____

Score yourself as follows: Questions 1,2,4,5,6,8,10—10 points for "usually," 5 for "sometimes," 0 for "seldom." Questions 3,7,9—0 points for "usually," 5 for "sometimes," 10 for "seldom."

If your score is below 70, you have developed some bad listening habits; if 70–85, you listen well but could still improve; if 90 or above, you're an excellent listener.

Part B

How well do you listen?
(A personal profile)

Here are three quizzes by which you can rate yourself as a listener. There are no correct or incorrect answers. Your responses, however, will extend your understanding of yourself as a listener and highlight areas in which improvement might be welcome . . . to you and to those around you.

Quiz 1

A. Circle the terms that best describes you as a listener.

Superior Excellent Above Average Average

Below Average Poor Terrible

B. On a scale of 0–100 (100 = highest), how would you rate yourself as a listener?

_____
(0–100)

Quiz 2

How do you think the following people would rate you as a listener? (0–100)

Your best friend   _____

Your boss   _____

Business colleague   _____

(Continued)

Figure 6-2. *(Continued.)*

| Job subordinate | _____ |
| Your spouse | _____ |

Quiz 3

As a listener, how often do you find yourself engaging in these 10 bad listening habits? First, check the appropriate columns. Then tabulate your score using the key below.

Listening Habit	Frequency					Score
	Almost Always	Usually	Some-times	Sel-dom	Almost Never	
1. Calling the subject uninteresting						
2. Criticizing the speaker's delivery or mannerisms						
3. Getting overstimu-lated by some-thing the speaker says						
4. Listening primar-ily for facts						
5. Trying to outline everything						
6. Faking attention to the speaker						
7. Allowing distrac-tions to interfere						

8. Avoiding difficult
   material

---

9. Letting emotion-
   laden words
   arouse personal
   antagonism

---

10. Daydreaming

KEY   Total ____
                                                    Score

For every "Almost Always" checked, give yourself a score of 2
For every "Usually" checked, give yourself a score of 4
For every "Sometimes" checked, give yourself a score of 6
For every "Seldom" checked, give yourself a score of 8
For every "Almost Never" checked, give yourself a score of 10

the salesman was flattered by the offer, and that the higher salary was contingent on performance. The salesman wanted recognition and the chance for more money.

The sales manager responded by changing the salesman's compensation from straight salary to salary plus commission, which created an opportunity for greater earnings, and by changing the salesman's title from sales representative to district sales manager. The salesman stayed with his current employer, and both benefited.

Communication Climate

Understanding the barriers to effective communication helps us to communicate better. Communication can be interfered with by environmental, psychological, and physiological factors. Respect and trust between participants builds good communication. Bias, prejudice, language and cultural differences, pressure, fear of failure, lack of knowledge, strong egos, preconceived ideas, differences in power, rank, and status, lack of attention, body language, and intimidation all interfere with communication. Dealing with issues rather than personalities, dealing with facts rather than opinions helps overcome some of these barriers.

Communication techniques such as feedback, perception, use of commands, organization, simplicity, clarity, nonverbal communication, and good listening work best in organizations with a supportive communication climate. To determine whether you as a sales manager contribute to making the communication climate in your company a supportive one, ask yourself the following questions:

1. Do you encourage flexibility, experimentation, and creativity in your salespeople?
2. Do you attempt to understand and listen to salespeople's problems and respect their feelings and values?
3. Do you respect salespeople or make them feel inferior by controlling them through status?
4. Is your communication honest and free from hidden agendas?
5. Are you critical, judgmental, and unwilling to accept explanations from subordinates?
6. Do you direct in an authoritarian manner and attempt to change other people?
7. Do you manipulate salespeople by misinterpreting, twisting, and distorting what they say?
8. Do you remain aloof from salespeople's personal problems and conflicts?
9. Do you make salespeople feel inadequate by closely overseeing their work and reminding them who is in charge?
10. Are you opinionated and unwilling to admit mistakes?

And to find out how your salespeople evaluate the communication environment at your company, ask them to participate in the survey shown in Figure 6-3. The salesperson climate survey, shown in Figure 6-4, also asks for their feedback on other issues. The survey questionnaires are not to be signed by the salespeople taking them and the results are to be tabulated by a neutral party. These surveys demonstrate your interest in the salespeople, and therefore have an important motivational effect on them. Be sure and respond to the surveys' findings and, where appropriate, take corrective action.

Figure 6-3. Communication climate inventory.

Instructions: The statements below relate to how you and your manager communicate on the job. There are no right or wrong answers. Read the statement on the left about you or your manager and decide whether you Strongly Agree (SA), Agree (A), are Uncertain (U), Disagree (D), or Strongly Disagree (SD). Once you have decided, circle the number under your choice.

	SA	A	U	D	SD
1. My manager criticizes my work without allowing me to explain.	1	2	3	4	5
2. My manager allows me as much creativity as possible in my job.	1	2	3	4	5
3. My manager always judges the actions of his or her subordinates.	1	2	3	4	5
4. My manager allows flexibility on the job.	1	2	3	4	5
5. My manager criticizes my work in the presence of others.	1	2	3	4	5
6. My manager is willing to try new ideas and to accept other points of view.	1	2	3	4	5
7. My manager believes that he or she must control how I do my work.	1	2	3	4	5
8. My manager understands the problems that I encounter in my job.	1	2	3	4	5
9. My manager is always trying to change other people's attitudes and behavior to suit his or her own.	1	2	3	4	5
10. My manager respects my feelings and values.	1	2	3	4	5
11. My manager always needs to be in charge of the situation.	1	2	3	4	5
12. My manager listens to my problems with interest.	1	2	3	4	5
13. My manager tries to manipulate subordinates to get what he or she wants or to make himself or herself look good.	1	2	3	4	5

(Continued)

Figure 6-3. *(Continued.)*

	SA	A	U	D	SD
14. My manager does not try to make me feel inferior.	1	2	3	4	5
15. I have to be careful when talking to my manager to avoid being misinterpreted.	1	2	3	4	5
16. My manager participates in meetings with employees without projecting his or her higher status or power.	1	2	3	4	5
17. I seldom say what is really on my mind because it might be twisted and distorted by my manager.	1	2	3	4	5
18. My manager treats me with respect.	1	2	3	4	5
19. My manager seldom becomes involved in employee conflicts.	1	2	3	4	5
20. My manager does not have hidden motives when dealing with me.	1	2	3	4	5
21. My manager is not interested in employee problems.	1	2	3	4	5
22. I feel that I can be honest and straightforward with my manager.	1	2	3	4	5
23. My manager rarely offers moral support during a personal crisis.	1	2	3	4	5
24. I feel that I can express my opinions and ideas honestly to my manager.	1	2	3	4	5
25. My manager tries to make me feel inadequate.	1	2	3	4	5
26. My manager defines problems so that they can be understood but does not insist that his or her subordinates agree.	1	2	3	4	5
27. My manager makes it clear that he or she is in charge.	1	2	3	4	5
28. I feel free to talk to my manager.	1	2	3	4	5
29. My manager believes that if a job is to be done right, he or she must oversee it or do it.	1	2	3	4	5
30. My manager defines problems and makes his or her subordinates aware of them.	1	2	3	4	5

31. My manager cannot admit that he or she makes mistakes.   1 2 3 4 5

32. My manager tries to describe situations fairly without labeling them as good or bad.   1 2 3 4 5

33. My manager is opinionated; it is useless for me to voice an opposing point of view.   1 2 3 4 5

34. My manager presents his or her feelings and perceptions without implying that a similar response is expected from me.   1 2 3 4 5

35. My manager thinks that he or she is always right   1 2 3 4 5

36. My manager attempts to explain situations clearly and without personal bias.   1 2 3 4 5

Communication Climate Inventory Scoring and Interpretation

Instructions: Place the numbers that you assigned to each statement in the appropriate blanks. Now add them together to determine a subtotal for each climate descriptor. Place the subtotals in the proper blanks and add your scores. Place an "X" in the graph to indicate what your perception is of your organization or department's communication climate. Some descriptions of the terms follow. You may wish to discuss with others their perceptions and interpretations.

Defensive Scores

Evaluation	*Neutrality*	*Control*
Question 1 ___	Question 19 ___	Question 7 ___
Question 3 ___	Question 21 ___	Question 9 ___
Question 5 ___	Question 23 ___	Question 11 ___
Subtotal ___	Subtotal ___	Subtotal ___

Superiority	*Strategy*	*Certainty*
Question 25 ___	Question 13 ___	Question 31 ___
Question 27 ___	Question 15 ___	Question 33 ___
Question 29 ___	Question 17 ___	Question 35 ___
Subtotal ___	Subtotal ___	Subtotal ___

(Continued)

Figure 6-3. *(Continued.)*

Subtotals for Defensive Scores

Evaluation   _____

Control   _____

Strategy   _____

Neutrality   _____

Superiority   _____

Certainty   _____

    Total   _____

| 18 | 25 | 30 | 35 | 40 | 45 | 50 | 55 | 60 | 65 | 70 | 75 | 80 | 85 | 90 |

| Defensive | | Defensive to Neutral | Neutral to Supportive | | Supportive |

Supportive Scores

Provisionalism

Question 2 ____
Question 4 ____
Question 6 ____
Subtotal ____

Empathy

Question 8 ____
Question 10 ____
Question 12 ____
Subtotal ____

Spontaneity

Question 20 ____
Question 22 ____
Question 24 ____
Subtotal ____

Problem Orientation

Question 26 ____
Question 28 ____
Question 30 ____
Subtotal ____

Equality	*Description*
Question 14 ___	Question 32 ___
Question 16 ___	Question 34 ___
Question 18 ___	Question 36 ___
Subtotal ___	Subtotal ___

Subtotals for Supportive Scores

Provisionalism   _____

Empathy   _____

Equality   _____

Spontaneity   _____

Problem Orientation   _____

Description   _____

    Total   _____

| 18 | 25 | 30 | 35 | 40 | 45 | 50 | 55 | 60 | 65 | 70 | 75 | 80 | 85 | 90 |

Supportive	Neutral to Supportive	Defensive to Neutral	Defensive

Figure 6-4. Salesperson climate survey.

Circle one answer for each question.

1. What is the level of your overall satisfaction with your position as a
    salesperson?

1	2	3	4
Very	Somewhat	Mostly	Completely
Dissatisfied	Dissatisfied	Satisfied	Satisfied

2. To what degree do you feel motivated to perform the responsibilities
    of a salesperson?

1	2	3	4
Very	Somewhat	Mostly	Completely
Unmotivated	Unmotivated	Motivated	Motivated

3. Are you satisfied with top management's appreciation of your job?

1	2	3	4
Very	Somewhat	Mostly	Completely
Dissatisfied	Dissatisfied	Satisfied	Satisfied

4. Are you satisfied with your manager's perception of the importance
    of your position?

1	2	3	4
Very	Somewhat	Mostly	Completely
Dissatisfied	Dissatisfied	Satisfied	Satisfied

5. Are you satisfied that your sales training needs are being met?

1	2	3	4
Very	Somewhat	Mostly	Completely
Dissatisfied	Dissatisfied	Satisfied	Satisfied

6. Are you satisfied that your product knowledge training needs are
    being met?

1	2	3	4
Very	Somewhat	Mostly	Completely
Dissatisfied	Dissatisfied	Satisfied	Satisfied

7. Are you satisfied with the level of your understanding of your sales goals?

1	2	3	4
Very Dissatisfied	Somewhat Dissatisfied	Mostly Satisfied	Completely Satisfied

8. Are you satisfied with management's responsiveness to employee ideas as to company policy and performance?

1	2	3	4
Very Dissatisfied	Somewhat Dissatisfied	Mostly Satisfied	Completely Satisfied

9. To what degree does your relationship with your sales manager support the accomplishment of your sales goals?

1	2	3	4
Not at All	Somewhat	Mostly	Completely

10. What is the level of importance of your compensation package in motivating you to greater accomplishments?

1	2	3	4
Very Unimportant	Not Important	Somewhat Important	Very Important

11. Your current compensation package is structured properly.

1	2	3	4
Completely Disagree	Moctly Disagree	Mostly Agree	Completely Agree

12. Employee policies are for the most part clearly articulated and fair.

1	2	3	4
Completely Disagree	Mostly Disagree	Mostly Agree	Completely Agree

13. Customer policies are for the most part clearly articulated and fair.

1	2	3	4
Completely Diagree	Mostly Disagree	Mostly Agree	Completely Agree

(Continued)

Figure 6-4. *(Continued.)*

---

14. The sales staff is cooperative and works with a team spirit.

1	2	3	4
Completely	Mostly	Mostly	Completely
Disagree	Disagree	Agree	Agree

Do you have any ideas for improvement?:

_____

_____

15. What is the level of effective communication between you and the following?:

Sales Manager	1	2	3	4
Customer Service	1	2	3	4
Credit Department	1	2	3	4
Inside Sales Support	1	2	3	4
Company Management	1	2	3	4

	Very Ineffective	Frequently Ineffective	Frequently Ineffective	Very Effective

16. How can your company help you to be more effective and more productive in the future?

_____

_____

17. What constructive criticism would you make of the selling function?

_____

_____

18. How can communications be improved?

_____

_____

7

Communication Channels: Reports, Analyses, and Sales Meetings

The major channels of communication include route sheets, call reports, customer analysis, commission statements, expense reports, orders, service agreements, bids, proposals, product analysis, sales forecasts, expense budgets, performance appraisals, phone calls, bulletins, letters, tapes, manuals, catalogs, sales meetings, individual meetings, staff meetings, training sessions, and bulletin boards. Through these channels, information, instructions, and demands are communicated.

Route Sheets and Call Reports

Typically, sales managers ask their salespeople to submit weekly route sheets and call reports. The route sheet lists the people and companies the salesperson *plans* to visit in the *coming* week and what he or she *plans* to accomplish. The call report lists the concerns he or she *actually* visited in the *past* week and what in fact was accomplished. These reports, if kept simple and submitted promptly, provide you with useful information from the marketplace. You must devote time to reading these reports, but at the same time realize that they may not be equally helpful to all salespeople. These two reports help most salespeople to allocate their time and measure results, while also communicating this information to management. Without a call plan, they can waste time and money by not using the most efficient travel routes or correct call frequency. The unplanned day or week are major time wasters.

The effectiveness of both reports depends on simplicity, timeliness, and responsiveness. Neither the salesperson nor the manager can afford to waste time on nonproductive paperwork. Some route sheets and call reports require unnecessary and burdensome details. A manager needs to know simply which customers his or her salespeople plan to see each day; whether they were seen; what the visit's objectives and accomplishments were; and any special information. Special information includes significant changes in the customer's buying habits, financial condition, staff, or attitude, and any significant changes in competitor activities or in the performance of your product/service.

As an example, a day on the route sheet might read, "March 12, Cabot Machinery, Montpelier, Vt. Obtain fill-in order for 50 gallons of cleaning fluid. Van Horne Engine Co., Burlington, Vt. Hope to open this new account with our metal cutting fluid." The same day on a call report might read, "March 12, Cabot Machinery, Montpelier, Vt. Wrote a $1,750 order for cleaning fluid. Purchasing agent being transferred to a new position. Met the new buyer, Dick Lang. Van Horne Engine Co., Burlington, Vt. Saw purchasing agent, Alex Gregoris. Likes our product, but sees no reason to change from present supplier, Henkle Chemical, which just lowered its prices."

Route sheets and call reports keep you informed and allow you to help salespeople to economically make the optimum number of effective calls on the right customers and prospects. Call reports also provide you with useful information from the marketplace on competitors, customers, and your product or service's performance, which you in turn can pass on to other salespeople. To be most helpful, route sheets and call reports should be submitted promptly each weekend. The information they contain proves most useful when fresh.

Salespeople should send each call report to their sales manager and also retain a copy for themselves. The call reports become their diary, the ship's log. They can then refer to them in future for customer information, frequency of visits, and order writing results, and use them in conjunction with the prospect/customer profile cards they maintain. The prospect/customer profile cards help salespeople to organize their time and contain pertinent information about each customer. Each customer/prospect card contains names, telephone numbers, addresses, personal information on the decision makers, plus notes on the account's history, needs, problems, and call frequency. Because these cards are organized both alphabetically and by date of next visit, they also provide information for the route sheets.

Often in smaller businesses, route sheets and call reports provide an exercise for salespeople but are not read by management. The salespeople speak to management through these reports. Responsive management must listen and reply, using these reports as a means of communication and control. The sales force's attitude toward writing route sheets and call reports generally reflects management's attitude toward reading them. If you respond to the significant information provided in call reports, most salespeople will faithfully submit them. If you don't read and use the reports, don't ask for them. Unread route sheets and call reports are a time waster and demotivator for salespeople.

The Human Element

You must build your reporting and communication function around the people you have. You must show flexibility by exempting certain salespeople from the requirement to submit weekly route sheets and/or call reports. Not all salespeople in your organization will benefit equally from submitting these reports. For example, the individual who sells and services only one major account has little reason to submit this information. The major men's shirt supplier for Broadway Department Stores in Los Angeles employs a salesman who spends all his time servicing their 28 branches. His activity and performance can best be monitored by reviewing the orders he submits.

Also, some salespeople produce outstanding volumes of business but cannot tolerate any paperwork beyond writing orders. In such an instance, do not argue with success; be flexible, monitor performance and field intelligence by weekly phone calls, or compromise on biweekly call reports.

A legendary ladies' sportswear salesman wrote his route sheets on the backs of match covers while relaxing on Friday evenings. Each night at dinner he wrote a daily call report on a paper table napkin. As long as he remained top salesman in the industry, management never complained about his reports. Detailed reporting is no substitute for success.

Also, sometimes superorganized salespeople obtain little benefit from submitting a formal route sheet. They have their own system, which better answers their needs.

However, average organizers and nonsuperstar salespeople, who comprise 80 percent of most sales organizations, do benefit from route sheets and call reports; and even if they object, you must insist on prompt weekly reporting to improve results. Some salespeople with strong needs for freedom and independence look on written reports as symbols of repression. They may also view these reports as an invasion of their privacy, as an attempt to find out if they are working or where they are every day, in short as a means of spying on them.

To overcome their objections and start receiving these reports regularly, you must persuade such salespeople that the reports will help them improve results. During a field visit, review the reports to make certain they understand their simplicity. During field visits and phone conversations, make helpful suggestions based on the information contained in the reports. This assures salespeople that you read and use the information.

When a small giftware firm introduced route sheets and call reports, salespeople threatened a palace revolt. Each week using the call reports and route sheets, the sales manager pointed out how each salesperson could increase his or her results by making a cold call between customer visits, by offering another product to an existing account, or by making more appointments. At the end of six months, salespeople were suggesting additional information to include on these reports.

Occasionally, salespeople do not submit reports regularly because of their embarrassment over their penmanship or poor spelling. Assure them that you do not grade the reports. Again, show them how they can improve results by using information in the reports. Compliment them on their performance as noted in the reports.

Some salespeople don't submit route sheets and call reports when they contain negative information, for example, a week with few calls or few orders. Let them know that you need records of disappointing as well as successful periods in order to help them improve their future results.

Route sheets and call reports require the sales force to maintain and submit certain information helpful to management. For effective communication, management must also collect and submit information of help to the sales force, such as sales reports. Many smaller businesses neglect to do this because of the cost and effort involved. But it is easier to ask the sales force for reports if you are providing them with data in return. In addition, these reports help salespeople to increase their business, and customers likewise need this information.

As discussed in Chapter 10, this information is readily available from orders or invoices and can be computer-generated. Don't use the excuse that the computer can't do it. More appropriately said is that management won't do it.

Customer Analysis

Every month, three months, six months, or year, depending on the selling cycle, your accounting department should produce a customer analysis. The customer analysis shows shipments and/or orders in units and dollars for the period and year to date by product/service for each customer, organized by territory, as compared with the previous year and possibly with the quota or forecast. For example, if your company sells men's hosiery and issues a quarterly customer analysis, the columns across the top would read:

Minnesota Territory

Current Year				Previous Year				Forecast			
Shipments This Quarter		Shipments Year to Date		Shipments This Quarter		Shipments Year to Date		Shipments This Quarter		Shipments Year to Date	
Dozens	Dollars	Dozens	Dollars	Dozens	Dollars	Dozens	Dollars	Dozens	Dollars	Dozens	Dollars

The columns down the side would read:

Nathan's Clothing Store
Style 112 - Orlon Crew Sock
Style 845 - Nylon Dress Hi Rise
Style 1050 - Wool Anklet
Total Store

Jack's Department Store
Style 1240 - White Athletic Hose
Style 66 - Cotton Dress Anklet
Style 99 - Argyle Mid-Length
Total Store

Every account in each salesperson's territory would be listed with total dozen and dollar sales accumulated for the entire territory. For example, if your company sold printing, the monthly customer analysis format might read:

Northwest Side Territory

| | Current Year | | | | Previous Year | | | | Forecast | | | |
| | Orders This Month | | Orders Year to Date | | Orders This Month | | Orders Year to Date | | Orders This Month | | Orders Year to Date | |
	Units	Dollars	Units	Dollars	Units	Dollars	Units	Dollars	Units	Dollars	Units	Dollars

Omaha Symphony
Orchestra
Programs
Fund-Raising Brochures
Annual Report
      Total Account

Union Pacific Railroad
Office Forms
Employee Magazine
Menus
      Total Account

Each salesperson receives the customer analysis only for his or her territory. The sales manager receives the customer analysis for all territories. If possible, sales by model, style, service, product, or product group should also be totaled and compared for the entire territory.

The customer analysis allows each salesperson and also the sales manager to compare this year's results with last year's results and with what has been projected, and then to use this information to prepare next year's sales forecast and to evaluate performance. The customer analysis provides a basis for productive discussion between the sales manager and the sales force. The sales manager might remark to the Ohio salesperson, "I see your sales are up in northern Ohio but down elsewhere. How often do you travel to Cincinnati, Dayton, and Columbus?" The salesperson might reply, "I still travel there once a month, but unemployment continues high in southern Ohio and business is weak."

When the salesperson calls on Nathan's Clothing Store, he or she can point out to the proprietor that their sales of crew socks this year are up, but that sales of nylon dress hose are down. When Jack's Department Store wants an off-price promotion on argyles, the salesperson can refer to the customer analysis for information on total unit purchases the previous year.

Capable salespeople thrive on this type of information. They want details on their performance so that they can set future goals to improve it. Similarly, capable sales managers need this information so that they can evaluate salespeople's performance and help them to improve. Customers respect and want to deal with vendors who can provide them with this type of information. The customer analysis becomes a competitive advantage in the marketplace. Not accumulating this type of information puts you at a competitive disadvantage.

The customer analysis is as important to good sales management as the profit-and-loss statement is to good financial management. Whether you use an in-house computer or employ a data-processing service bureau to keep track of invoices and inventory, you or the service can use the same information to print a customer analysis. Even a billing machine or personal computer that processes invoices can be programmed to produce the customer analysis. In both cases, the additional cost is nominal compared with the valuable information created.

Commission Statements

If you compensate salespeople with any form of commission, you must provide them with the monthly invoice information as to how you calculated the commission earned. The commission statement should list invoice numbers, amounts, and applicable commission rates to arrive at a total equal to the commission earned.

Commission statements can also compare the commission earned and total dollar sales for this month and year to date with last year's and with the forecast. It easy to calculate, they can compare total dollar sales by product line or customer type for this month and year to date with last year's and with the forecast. All this information can be quickly accumulated through data processing from the same invoices used to calculate commission earned.

Commission statements can also report on the number of new accounts opened and the number of total accounts sold during a period. Commission statements are the report every salesperson reads.

For example, as in Figure 7-1, the mens' hosiery commission statement might include information on monthly and year-to-date dollar sales compared with the previous year for branded versus unbranded business; or for crew socks, athletic hose, and dress hose; or for department stores versus specialty stores. The second page of the commission statement would list all the current-month invoices by number and date, showing the customer and dollar total, applicable commission rate, and resulting commis-

(*Text continued on p. 204.*)

Figure 7-1. Commission statement comparing monthly, year-to-date, and previous year's sales for type of merchandise and type of store.

Minnesota Territory

	Shipments			Commissions			Forecast		
	Current Month	Previous Total	Year to Date	Current Month	Previous Total	Year to Date	Current Month	Previous Total	Year to Date
Branded									
Department Stores									
Dress Hose									
Athletic									
Casual Hose									
Total Department Stores									
Branded									
Specialty Stores									
Dress Hose									
Athletic Hose									
Casual Hose									
Total Specialty Stores									
Unbranded									
Chain Stores									
Discount Stores									
Total Unbranded									
Grand Total Territory									
Number of New Accounts									
Number of Active Accounts									

Previous Year

	Shipments			Commissions			Forecast		
	Current Month	Previous Total	Year to Date	Current Month	Previous Total	Year to Date	Current Month	Previous Total	Year to Date
Branded Department Stores									
Dress Hose									
Athletic									
Casual Hose									
Total Department Stores									
Branded Specialty Stores									
Dress Hose									
Athletic Hose									
Casual Hose									
Total Specialty Stores									
Unbranded									
Chain Stores									
Discount Stores									
Total Unbranded									
Grand Total Territory									
Number of New Accounts									
Number of Active Accounts									

sion dollars due. Total dollars of sales and commissions on the addendum must naturally jibe with these same figures on each salesperson's commission statement.

Figure 7-2 shows a printing company commission statement, including information on monthly and year-to-date dollar sales and commissions compared with the previous year for magazines, office forms, books, and annual reports.

Again, good salespeople thrive on comparative information because they enjoy measuring themselves and planning for improvement. Good sales management thrives on comparative information because it is a means of measuring sales force performance and provides a basis for discussion with individual salespeople.

Expense Reports

If your company reimburses salespeople for certain travel, telephone, entertainment, and clerical expenses, their expense reports will provide you with valuable information about their activities. Under such a plan, salespeople submit weekly invoices or receipts for motel rooms, telephone calls, auto mileage, tolls, meals, airline tickets, and/or secretarial expenses. They record and total these items by day on an expense report along with the names of each city visited and each person entertained. Standard expense report forms are available at most office supply stores. The expense reports and receipts supplement information given on the call reports in addition to verifying expenditures and acting as a basis for cost control and reimbursement. In a smaller company, the sales manager should review all expense reports.

For example, by reviewing monthly long-distance telephone invoices, a sales manager knows what customers were called and how often. The telephone represents an important sales tool, and monthly bills reveal how effectively this sales tool is being utilized. Monthly telephone bills also show how often a salesperson called the factory, warehouse, or home office. An excess of such calls may indicate a problem requiring your investigation.

Expense reports also quickly tell you how much time a salesperson devotes to each part of the territory. By reviewing a salesperson's expense reports for a six-month period, you can tabulate how many days he or she spent in each city.

Similarly, you can review which customers or prospects were entertained. Did the salesperson entertain the same purchasing agent, possibly

(*Text continued on p. 206.*)

Figure 7-2. Sample printing company commission statement comparing monthly, year-to-date, and previous year's sales for different products.

Northwest Side Territory

	Shipments			Commissions			Forecast		
	Current Month	Previous Total	Year to Date	Current Month	Previous Total	Year to Date	Current Month	Previous Total	Year to Date
Magazines									
Office Forms									
Books									
Annual Reports									
Other									
Total Territory									
Number of New Accounts									
Number of Active Accounts									

(Continued)

Figure 7-2. (Continued.)

	Shipments			Previous Year Commissions			Forecast		
	Current Month	Previous Total	Year to Date	Current Month	Previous Total	Year to Date	Current Month	Previous Total	Year to Date
Magazines									
Office Forms									
Books									
Annual Reports									
Other									
Total Territory									
Number of New Accounts									
Number of Active Accounts									

Page 2

Dollar Commission Due

Invoice #	Date	Customer	Amount	Rate	Dollars
2260	10/06	Union Pacific	$8,460	5%	$423.
2316	10/10	Omaha Symphony	$4,612	5%	$230.
2409	10/15	Mutual Savings	$6,644	5%	$332.

a close personal friend, on each visit? Or were different customers and prospects entertained?

Orders

In a smaller company, the sales manager should receive and review copies of all orders. This is the moment of truth. Route sheets tell you what a salesperson intends to accomplish, call reports tell you about accomplishments, the customer analysis and commission statements summarize and compare results, and expense reports contain related cost information. But orders provide the most immediate hard information on a sales force, its market, and its results.

By reviewing orders, a sales manager keeps his or her hand on the pulse of the business. For example, last week's call report from the Georgia salesperson promised a large order from a major customer in Macon, but it hasn't arrived yet. Such inconsistencies deserve an inquiry. Why does a large order from a small customer contain last year's prices? A large order from California calls for containers that may be in short supply, requiring a memo to the plant manager.

Orders indicate that one new product is selling more than all the other new products combined. This information should prompt a call to production control. This information should also cause the sales manager to question whether the sales force understands the other new products.

Customers in one territory submit orders directly to the company rather than through the salesperson. Is the salesperson actually calling on these customers? Are customers circumventing the salesperson because they don't care to deal with him or her?

Product Analysis

As sales manager, you require certain sales information not necessarily produced by or shared directly with the sales force. On a weekly or monthly basis you need to know for the entire company cumulative orders, sales, or shipments in units and dollars totaled by product, product group, style, model, or service as compared with the previous year's sales and forecast. This is the product analysis.

For example, the hosiery company product analysis might read:

	Current Year Shipments				Previous Year Shipments				Forecast Shipments			
	This Month		Year to Date		This Month		Year to Date		This Month		Year to Date	
	Dozens	Dollars	Dozens	Dollars	Dozens	Dollars	Dozens	Dollars	Dozens	Dollars	Dozens	Dollars
Style 112 Orlon crew sock												
Style 115 Cotton athletic sock												
Style 845 Nylon dress anklet												
Style 945 Nylon dress hi rise												
Style 1050 Wool dress anklet												
Style 1150 Wool dress high rise												
Style 99 Argyle												
Style 250 Cotton dress anklet												
Style 350 Cotton dress hi rise												
Total Company												

Whether you require this information on orders, shipments, or both depends on your particular industry. Such comparative information on orders or shipments by product or service allows you to measure total company performance, spot trends, and forecast future sales. Why are total company orlon crew sock unit sales 10 percent lower than last year, while wool anklets are 15 percent ahead? Why are dollar orders for annual reports down 20 percent this year, while orders for magazines have risen 14 percent? Did you change the commission rate on certain products? Did the company open a major new account or lose a major existing customer? Did you realign territory boundaries? Have you lost or gained any salespeople? What corrective action should you communicate to the sales force?

Sales Forecasts, Sales Plans, Expense Budgets, Performance Appraisals

The next chapter deals in detail with sales forecasts, sales plans, expense budgets, and performance appraisals. These four activities require the sales manager and each salesperson to agree on future goals and a plan of action for reaching these objectives, and to compare actual performance to these plans or goals, suggesting corrective action when necessary. At least once a year, possibly once a quarter, you meet with each salesperson to discuss future anticipated sales, plus the specific activities and costs necessary to generate these sales. At least once a quarter, you meet with each salesperson to discuss how actual sales, costs, skills, knowledge, and activities compared to the anticipated levels discussed at previous meetings. As you will observe in the next chapter, the sales forecast, sales plan, expense budget, and performance appraisal process are critical for communication between sales manager and sales force.

Talking to the Field Force

Phone Calls

Regular weekly or biweekly fifteen-minute telephone calls from the sales manager to the field people are an inexpensive, personal and effective means of communication. If the salespeople live nearby, a fifteen-minute individual meeting can replace the phone call. The time, day of week, and length of conversation, whether conducted in person or by phone, should be decided beforehand and adhered to.

Before the meeting or call, the sales manager should carefully prepare a list of items for discussion, including suggested action to improve results. Route sheets, call reports, customer analysis, commission statements, expense reports, orders, product analysis, sales forecasts, sales plans, expense budgets, and performance appraisals all provide information that can become the basis for discussion. The sales manager might remark, "Gene, according to your call and expense reports, you visit Premier Hardware once a week and take the buyer to lunch. Do you feel its volume or potential justifies that much attention?" Gene might reply, "Probably not." The sales manager would then say, "I agree, so please concentrate more on Central Supply, which, according to your route sheets, is unhappy with its present vendor. I suggest you call both Premier and Central twice a month. What is the buyer's name at Central?"

Or the sales manager might remark, "Alex, I see that Atlas Chemical did not order any dyes last week. Is there a problem?" Alex might reply, "Yes, the purchasing agent has been promoted and replaced by a trainee." The sales manager could respond, "That sounds like a potential problem, Alex. Please set up a date for you and me to visit the plant manager."

Or the sales manager might remark, "Amy, your commission statement shows a 20 percent improvement in shipments so far this year, and I see from the customer analysis that you have both opened new accounts and expanded existing ones. Keep up the great work."

During the weekly discussions, the sales manager should listen to his or her people's needs and respond to them. If a salesperson reports that "deliveries arrive late," you should offer an explanation, or promise to follow up at the factory. If a salesperson requests your help in opening a "fat" prospect, make arrangements for an appointment with the buyer. If a salesperson has suddenly run out of catalogs, price lists, or order forms, immediately mail out the required material.

Bulletins and Letters

You don't always need the personal touch that the telephone affords. For instance, to communicate certain information applicable to the entire sales force, such as information on prices, policies, procedures, sales meetings, sales contests, and product changes, bulletins are the most efficient means. Copies of advertisements, press releases, or publicity are also best transmitted via bulletins so that all parties can have a permanent copy.

When you want to communicate certain types of information to one salesperson but still desire a permanent copy, letters are most appropriate. For example, after a field visit, you may wish to summarize for future reference what action was agreed to (customers to be seen, programs to be offered, closing techniques to be used, and so on). Certainly when hiring a new salesperson, territory boundaries and compensation require to be spelled out in writing; and any disciplinary action to be taken also requires a letter.

Tapes, Manuals, and Catalogs

Information that does not require immediate response or feedback lends itself to communication by way of video- or audiotapes, manuals, and catalogs. For example, detailed information on new products or selling techniques can be effectively communicated by video- or audiotape. The sales manual presents basic training material and thus becomes a salesperson's permanent reference book. Catalogs keep salespeople informed on changing product information such as price, packing, colors, ingredients, and construction.

Some companies send a half-hour audiotape to each salesperson once a month with suggestions for improving sales. The tapes carry the same initial message for everyone, but then present individual suggestions in the last ten minutes. Salespeople can listen to tapes while driving from one call to the next.

Generally, a new salesperson receives the sales manual after his or her initial training. A manual might cover correct order-writing procedures, advertising and freight policy, company history and organization, and reporting requirements. You can add and delete information from the manual by sending your salespeople new pages and asking them to destroy obsolete ones.

Generally, you issue a new catalog every time a selling season changes. Catalogs benefit both customers and salespeople. Often they show pictures of the new products. A catalog gives detailed product/service information on components, ingredients, characteristics, variations, price, terms, availability, and benefits.

Controlling Paperwork and Communication

Reports can become so institutionalized, complex, and inflexible that they take on a life of their own. Instead of being a means of communication, the report becomes an end in itself. One report often generates another. The activity of writing and submitting a report can become more important than the proposed result of communication. Information and communication are not synonymous.

The format of route sheets, call reports, customer and product analysis, commission statements, expense reports, and bulletins should be reviewed once a year. Sometimes these reports can be simplified; sometimes two reports can be combined into one.

Also once a year you should examine all the reports you receive and submit as well as all the reports the sales force receives and submits. Ask yourself: Who reads this report? How is the information used? Is the reason for creating the report still valid? Does the report help the salesperson or the sales manager to do a better job? Can the report be simplified or incorporated into another report? Based on your answers to these questions, you may wish to take action.

One notorious sales manager collected all these reports once a year and weighed them. If they weighed over three pounds, he began eliminating.

Regardless of the form—telephone calls, meetings, or reports—communication involves time and money. In some sales organizations, time and money are wasted on excessive, unnecessary communication. As sales manager, you don't have to know everything your salespeople do, and they don't need all the information available to you. Routine matters do not require notification, but exceptions do.

For example, when a customer who normally orders monthly fails to do so, you need to ask the salesperson for an explanation. When a customer who normally orders monthly continues to do so, no communication on this matter is required.

Sales Meetings

Periodic, well-planned sales meetings provide a productive format for communication, motivation, and training. The basic purposes of a sales meeting are (1) to provide continuing training to sales personnel; (2) to offer a forum for the sharing of problems and successes by salespeople and management; (3) to make salespeople feel useful, important, and part of something larger; (4) to give salespeople recognition for their achievements or motivation through peer pressure to perform; (5) to allow salespeople personally to meet management; (6) to give management a chance to disseminate policy to the sales force; (7) and to provide an opportunity for management to visit salespeople with minimum travel.

Contrary to popular belief, being a field salesperson is a lonely job full of disappointments and rejections. The sales meeting helps to assure salespeople that someone cares. They arrive dusty and tired from the commercial battlefield, and, with luck and intelligent planning, leave refreshed, enthusiastic, and ready for new challenges.

Sales meetings strongly influence salespeople's image of the company, which they pass on to customers. It is therefore very important that they leave feeling up. Have you ever had an unsuccessful sales meeting? What effect did it have on your short-term sales?

To justify the cost, time, and energy involved, the specific objectives of your sales meeting must be well thought out. These objectives must reinforce your marketing plan. Holding a meeting because you had one last week, last month, or last year does not constitute a justifiable objective. You need a more concrete reason. Decide in advance what you specifically hope to achieve and then carefully plan toward those goals. The objectives might include introducing a new product or service; alleviating tensions between the sales force and management; explaining a sales contest, forecast form, appraisal form, or new compensation plan; convincing the sales force that the company can stay in business; analyzing the competition; opening new accounts; retaining or expanding old accounts; improving collections; improving selling techniques; obtaining leads; managing time better; defining new territory boundaries; safety; or legal issues.

Open-ended sales meetings don't work. If you don't have an objective, don't have a sales meeting. Many sales managers have weekly or even daily sales meetings to review each person's results. In my opinion, this is better done in individual meetings. Ask salespeople what they would like to discuss at their sales meetings. They know what is needed.

Sometimes even with proper objectives these functions become stale and monotonous. At that point everyone needs a rest. If you feel the meetings no longer achieve their goals, change the format, or stop convening them for a while.

Many sales managers strongly dislike sales meetings because there they can't control the salespeople, who outnumber them. Also, they must listen to salespeople's complaints and accept criticism in front of the entire group. A good sales manager, however, will be sensitive to complaints and criticisms and welcome them because they generally contain important messages. A properly managed sales meeting minimizes these problems and should be both productive and enjoyable for all those involved.

Frequency

When the entire sales force resides locally and overnight accommodations are not necessary, meetings can be held frequently, but for short periods of time. For example, meetings could be held on the first Saturday of every other month, or the last Friday afternoon of each month, or every Monday morning. For local sales forces, sales meetings should be held no more frequently than once a week, no less frequently than once a month, and should last two to six hours. If most customers can't be seen Friday afternoons, have your meetings then. If each week you offer new services, have a meeting on Monday mornings.

When the sales force lives a plane trip away, economy necessitates less frequent but longer meetings. In such instances, two to three-day gatherings once or twice a year, or possibly every other year, generally provide the best use of time and money.

Annual, semiannual, or biennial sales meetings requiring several days should be scheduled during slack periods or at the start of a selling cycle. You don't want to remove a salesperson from his or her territory during a peak selling period. For example, many menswear manufacturers and book publishers schedule sales meetings in early December, because at this time retailers are too busy to see salespeople, and January begins a new wholesale selling season.

Costs

The cost of gathering ten or twenty national salespeople together for two or three days has risen astronomically and can strain the sales budget of a growing business. You can reduce the travel expenses of such a group by holding a series of regional meetings rather than one national meeting. Management can also lower costs by not inviting all salespeople to each meeting. For example, you can have two meetings annually, each with half the sales force, and each time a different mix of people. You might include more experienced salespeople in one group and less experienced in another.

The choice of city and meeting place also affects costs. For instance, it is less expensive for a Midwestern sales force to meet in a central location, such as Chicago or Nashville, which is serviced by reduced-fare airlines, than in Florida or California. It is less expensive to stay and dine at a suburban motel in Chicago than at a downtown hotel. Often, weekend hotel rates and Sunday return air fares can save the company money. Often an airline will discount tickets if everyone uses one carrier.

According to *Sales and Marketing Management* magazine's 1990 Survey of Selling Costs, the average per-person, per-diem cost of lodging, meals, and meeting rooms at a sales meeting is $150. This does not include transportation, guest speakers, or audio-visual aids. The cost varies from a high of $264 in New York City to a low of $111 in Omaha.*

If the entire sales force resides within a few hours' drive of your office, the sales meetings can be held there, and attendees can return home the same evening. Lunch can be ordered in, and dinner arranged for at a local restaurant. Such a meeting would involve minimal costs.

Format and Agenda

Sales meetings can consist of formal group meetings, formal individual meetings, informal social gatherings, official social functions, or some combination of these. Participants should receive an agenda before they arrive, so that everyone will know where to be, when to be there, what material is going to be covered, and what preparation is necessary. The agenda might state that once a formal group meeting has begun, you will lock the doors until break time. This eliminates a tendency for people to straggle in and thus to interrupt the gathering. Actually, once you initiate the locked-door policy, no one arrives late.

A typical annual national sales meeting agenda is shown in Figure 7-3. A typical weekly local sales meeting agenda is shown in Figure 7-4.

*Reprinted by permission of *Sales & Marketing Management*. Copyright: Survey of Selling Costs, February 26, 1990.

Formal Group Meetings

Whether you conduct three-day sales meetings twice a year, one-day sales meetings six times a year, half-day sales meetings monthly, or two-hour meetings weekly, you should allocate from 60 percent to 80 percent of your time to all formal group matters. The company president and other top management should attend some of these formal group meetings.

In these sessions, management introduces and everyone discusses subjects such as new or problematic products, services, or programs, opening new accounts, account retention, price increases, collections, company policies and organization, selling techniques, overcoming objections, time management, obtaining qualified leads and appointments, sales promotions, advertising, competition, sales contests, compensation plans, evaluation forms, and forecast and budget procedures. The subject matter must be applicable to the entire group and capable of being meaningfully presented in the time allotted. For example, a discussion of individual customers would not involve the entire group and would therefore be an inappropriate subject. The topic should be discussed at individual meetings. Likewise, selling in general represents too broad a topic, whereas selling benefits, or opening new accounts, or qualifying leads could be handled in ninety minutes.

Problem Areas

Sales meetings fail when administrative matters receive more time than selling matters, when one or more salespeople dominate the meeting, when trivial matters encroach on more important subjects, when management threatens and criticizes salespeople rather than training them, or when it lectures rather than discusses, when participants do not share a similar level of proficiency, when there is no agenda, and when the meeting takes too long.

Do not devote more than 25 percent of a meeting to administrative matters such as proper order-writing, credit and collection, sales reports, expense reports, or putting enough postage on order envelopes.

Do not allow any salesperson, whether it be a superstar or a laggard, to turn your meeting into a personal speaking platform. Remind these people that you have scheduled individual meetings to discuss individual problems. Also, involve people who have not participated by asking

Figure 7-3.   Sample annual national sales meeting agenda.

Friday, December 3

6:00	Cocktail hour in Suite 201
7:00	Dinner in private dining room B
8:30	Welcoming address by president

Saturday, December 4—Suite 201

8:00– 9:30	Discussion of new products, their prospective customers, and sales presentation—Sales Manager
9:30– 9:45	Break
9:45–10:15	Credit information needed for new accounts—Credit Manager
10:15–11:30	Techniques for opening new accounts, presenting benefits, and overcoming objections—Salesperson
11:30–11:45	Break
11:45–12:15	Discussion of complaints and criticisms

The doors to Suite 201 will be locked from 8:00 to 9:30 and from 9:45 to 11:30. So please be punctual.

12:30– 2:00	Lunch in main dining room
2:00– 5:00	Individual meetings in Room 150
	Recreation schedule to be announced
6:00– 7:00	Cocktail hour in Suite 201
7:00	Dinner in private dining room C
8:30	State-of-the-company address by president
9:00	Award presentations

Sunday December 5—Suite 201

8:00– 9:30	Competitive advantages of machines #72, #84, #96 presented by Forman, Rosenblatt, and Turner (Salespeople)

9:30–10:00	Quality Control—V.P. Manufacturing
10:00–10:15	Break
10:15–10:45	Explanation of new sales contest—Sales Manager
10:45–11:45	Time management—Sales Manager
11:45–12:00	Break
12:00–12:30	Discussion of complaints and criticisms
12:45– 2:00	Lunch in main dining room
2:00– 5:00	Individual meetings in Room 150
	Recreation
5:30–	Bus to airport

them questions. You must run the meeting, and not let the meeting run you.

Do not let the discussion digress into unimportant aspects of important matters. When a salesperson notes that the welding seam in your new ultrasonic cleaning tank rises one-half inch rather than one-quarter inch, remind this person that the new tank degreases customer components at half the cost in half the time of any competitive product.

Criticize in private, praise in public. Some sales managers feel obligated to start a sales meeting by telling their salespeople how bad they are. This is a real turn-off and not the purpose of the meeting. You are blaming both the strong and the weak performers and at the same time limiting the meeting's training and motivational benefits. Instead, start the meeting by asking a salesperson to share a success story.

Many sales managers dislike sales meetings because in this setting the sales force outnumbers them and may use it as a vehicle for criticism and complaints about the company. A good sales manager will nevertheless be sensitive to complaints and criticisms because they often contain important messages for you to understand. Although a continual negative barrage can ruin a sales meeting, you benefit by devoting a limited segment of time to complaints and criticisms that concern the entire group.

Group meetings can also lose their effectiveness when all participants do not share a similar level of proficiency. Mixing the most experienced salespeople with the least experienced, training the strong performers with the weak, can dilute the results. For certain subjects, you can remedy this problem by forming subgroups at the sales meeting.

Figure 7-4.   Sample weekly local sales meeting agenda.

Sales Meeting

Friday, December 3, at 1:00 P.M.

Second Floor Conference Room

Agenda

1:00–2:00	Overcoming Objections—Salesperson
2:00–3:00	Opening New Accounts—Salesperson
3:00–4:00	Competitive Advantage—Salesperson
4:00–5:00	Time Management—Sales Manager
5:00–6:00	Social hour—Pizza and Soda

Making It Interesting

Sales meetings can be made more interesting by group discussion, by having salespeople present certain subjects themselves, by telling success stories, by having competitors' products available for inspection, by inviting upper management or a friendly customer to address the meeting, or by including a factory visit, vendor presentation, skits, role playing, films, videotapes, or brainstorming as part of the activities. Also, you should devote at least some time to a presentation and discussion of company functions outside of selling, and allow time for any complaints or criticisms that involve companywide issues.

Organize the agenda so that a portion of each sales meeting is devoted to product knowledge, selling skills, current issues, administration, customers, competition, and management skills. Plan your sales meetings four months in advance even if you hold them every four weeks.

Because most salespeople are not classroom types, the best way to involve them and to hold their attention is through individual participation. Therefore, certain portions of the program should include presentations by the salespeople themselves. The person who opened the most new accounts could have fifteen minutes on the agenda to share his or her techniques. Another salesperson might lead a discussion on phone solicitation or time management. Product presentations can be organized so that different salespeople present different features and benefits. Be sure to review the appropriate material with the salesperson before his or her presentation. Remember, salespeople learn best through provocative group discussion, through sharing problems and information, not through lecture-type presentations by management. They believe each other alot more readily than they believe you. Encourage all sales people to participate in the discussion by asking questions.

The sales manager of a software firm asked her salespeople to submit the ten most common objections to opening a new account or expanding an existing one. Before the sales meeting she consolidated all the lists and removed duplications. At the sales meeting each person received a list of these objections, and one by one they discussed how to overcome them. After ninety minutes of sharing their knowledge everyone had gained more confidence. A role play ended this meeting.

Try beginning your sales meeting by having a salesperson tell a success story involving opening a difficult new account, saving a problem customer, adding an additional service to a major customer, or beating out your major competitor. Before long, your salespeople will be competing to tell their success stories in front of their peers.

Having competitors' products, product lines, service brochures, or service agreements at the meeting generates a lively and informative discussion. You might assign each salesperson one competitive product or service to analyze for the group. In such a discussion, be sure the sales force understands both your competitive strengths and weaknesses. Just concentrating on strengths does not prepare a salesperson for the realities of the marketplace.

Competitive grids are used in training sales people in competitive advantage. This approach is also applicable to sales meetings. For example, a bakery supply company devoted one sales meeting to competitors and competitive issues relating to frozen brownie mixes. The sales manager asked the salespeople to name the company's five major competitors, which were then listed across the top of the blackboard. Down the left-hand side, the sales manager wrote the salespeople's list of competitive issues: price, pack size, minimum order, delivery time, freeze/thaw cycle, shelf life, packaging concept, ingredients, breadth of line, specialized knowledge, major users, competitor's financial stability, image, salesperson's characteristics, and credit terms. Then the sales manager led a provocative discussion of how each competitor compared with her company on each competitive issue.

Inviting a friendly customer to address the meeting for thirty minutes on how he or she views your company, its products/services, and its sales force can be enlightening. You might invite customers from different industries to discuss what they look for in a vendor and what turns them on or off in a salesperson. You might then have your salespeople ask the customer questions. This approach allows salespeople to receive the customer's candid point of view in a neutral environment. Generally the customer feels complimented.

Films, videotapes, or guest speakers discussing such topics as selling techniques, motivation, collections, good listening, time management, or prospecting can spice up your meetings. Dartnell Publishing, Video Arts, Xerox Learning Systems, American Media Inc., Training Store, and Films Inc. all rent and sell films and videotapes. And most local telephone companies offer free guest speakers for sales meetings.

Use other members of your company's management team. For instance, invite the credit manager or controller to talk about collections, the manufacturing or operations manager to discuss quality, your boss to talk about pricing, and a supplier to talk about features and benefits. Outside speakers can offer a different slant.

If you hold the sales meeting near your main office or manufacturing facility, take the sales force on a tour and introduce them to key operating people. Salespeople find it easier to sell a product or service if they understand more about operations. Also, the order and billing people or customer service people find it easier to deal with salespeople they have met.

Take your salespeople to visit vendor facilities. A furniture retailer took her salespeople to visit a different company supplier each month.

Skits and role playing that enact customer–salesperson interchanges can be a powerful learning technique at sales meetings. One salesperson takes the role of the customer while the other plays him or herself. Use a script to describe the particulars of the situation. For example, you have neglected to call on this account regularly, or the purchasing agent has recently been approached by a particular competitor. Pick two people who will take the task seriously, and allow them to rehearse. Use a tape recorder or video camera, and occasionally stop the action. Then after the role play or during the playback, ask for analysis and comments from the group.

Salespeople dislike role playing, but it is the best way to simulate an actual sales situation. Furthermore, when salespeople know role play is part of the agenda, their attention level increases. Use self-graded multiple-choice tests at the end of each presentation so salespeople know what they actually learned versus what they were expected to learn.

With a group of senior salespeople, brainstorming can produce productive results. You see an unfilled need in the marketplace for a small nondestructive animal trap that can catch squirrels and other pests without injury, but will not attract pets such as cats. You ask your salespeople if they perceive the same need. If so, how would they design such a product, sell it, price it, and name it? Out of the group discussion and interaction will emerge not only some creative ideas but also a feeling of usefulness among the participants.

At each meeting, devote some time to a presentation and discussion of company functions outside of selling. For example, allow the credit manager and/or vice president of manufacturing an opportunity to exchange information and problems with the people who sell the product. The credit manager might discuss the information needed from the sales force to evaluate the financial status of a new account. Possibly the salespeople might complain about their lack of information concerning existing accounts that pay late. Similarly, the vice president of manufacturing might talk about improved quality control, while the sales force might confront him about poor deliveries.

At the end of each meeting, allow time for any complaints or criticisms that involve companywide issues such as late paychecks, poor deliveries, price increases, poor quality, lack of communication, return policy, or freight and advertising allowances. Complaints and criticisms that involve individual issues should be discussed later at the individual meetings.

Individual issues would include such items as customer credit problems, territory boundaries, or the handling of a particular account. Salespeople need a forum in which to express their frustrations, and if they know their "day in court" will arrive the rest of the meeting will be more productive.

Listen to, be sensitive to, and learn from their complaints and criticisms. Answer them, disagreeing where appropriate and promising remedial action if called for. Salespeople represent your link to customers and the marketplace. They should understand why certain things can't be done, such as overnight shipments; and you should understand why certain things must be done, such as eliminating back orders.

An upbeat way to end a sales meeting is by recognizing certain salespeople for their outstanding performance or by presenting awards. You might present the salesperson-of-the-month award, announce contest results, present a bonus check, or thank a salesperson in front of the group for opening a major new account. Often at multiday national sales meetings, this is done at an awards dinner.

Formal Individual Meetings

At annual or semiannual national sales force meetings, after the formal group meetings from 8:00 to 12:30 and a break for lunch, salespeople and management should meet individually for an hour in the afternoon. Here you may share concerns that do not affect the entire group.

You may meet with the salesperson alone in your room or office, or also ask the president to attend. Have a list of items you wish to discuss, and don't let the meeting digress into trivia or small talk. These meetings represent an important opportunity for a one-to-one interchange.

At such an individual meeting you may wish to discuss the change in personnel at a customer's or a prospect's company that requires a visit. You may have brought for discussion expense reports, call reports, or a customer analysis containing puzzling information. The salesperson may wish to discuss fears that a competitor has added more service people in the territory.

Do not use these individual conferences at sales meetings for formal compensation reviews or formal performance evaluations. Such procedures require more than an hour and considerable preparation, and they conflict with the learning/social atmosphere of a sales meeting. Compensation reviews and performance evaluations deserve separate handling in a different setting.

After weekly or monthly local sales force meetings, you may wish to have one or two individual meetings, time permitting. With a local sales force individual meetings can be arranged any time.

Informal Social Gatherings

Salespeople probably learn more from casual conversations with each other than they do in formal gatherings. So at annual or semiannual national sales force meetings, afternoons (between formal individual meetings) and evenings should allow opportunities for socializing. When salespeople get together, they do not discuss sports or politics; they discuss their jobs. "Who did you sell what, and how"? Although order sizes inflate by a third, the participants share valuable information. Maintaining a casual atmosphere even with tight scheduling promotes socializing.

Even in its most social moments, the gathering revolves around shoptalk, and for this reason, not to mention the additional costs involved, sales meetings work best without spouses. Also, some spouses resent and feel uncomfortable in the commercial atmosphere of a sales meeting.

After weekly or monthly local sales force meetings, occasionally invite the participants to lunch, dinner, golf, bowling, or a social hour. Even local sales forces benefit from the opportunity to socialize.

Official Social Gatherings

Official gatherings range from casual breakfasts or lunches to a more formal dinner at which speeches are made and awards presented.

Generally, at a multiday national meeting, the participants arrive in time for an opening dinner at which acquaintances are renewed, management delivers a welcoming address, and everyone unwinds. During dinner on the second evening, the president presents a state-of-the-company address, and this becomes another opportunity for management and sales force to socialize. The state-of-the-company address gives some insight into the "big picture," enlightening the sales force as to overall corporate performance and plans for the future.

A sales force that knows management on a personal basis becomes more involved. "I had dinner with the president of my company. He is a pleasant fellow, and certainly has his hands full." A management that knows the sales organization on a personal basis has more empathy. The company president might comment, "After spending several evenings with the sales force, I more fully appreciate their problems in reopening accounts we have lost because of late shipments. The salespeople are a noisy bunch, but they work hard at a difficult job."

After dinner on the second evening, the company president presents awards for outstanding performance and prizes to winners of the sales contests. Outstanding performers should be officially recognized by management in front of their peers. If possible, have an employee take photographs of these events, and mail copies to the participants.

Several times a year after local sales force meetings, invite participants to a formal social gathering, usually lunch or dinner, with upper management. The benefits and format are the same as those for national sales meetings.

Hopefully, everyone returns home from the sales meeting with renewed vigor and pleasant feelings. The sales force has learned, participated, and enjoyed. The company has said, "Thank you for doing a fine job" by attending to their needs, and showing them a good time. A successful sales meeting is a celebration that strongly influences the salespeoples' image of their company, which they pass on to your customers.

Even though larger competitors may offer superior advancement opportunities, greater compensation, and more comprehensive benefits, a smaller business can attract and retain effective salespeople through compassion and good communication. Many salespeople even prefer the flexibility and personal interaction to be found in a smaller organization. The sales meeting is of particular importance because it offers a prime, but often overlooked, opportunity for one-to-one human interaction between the sales organization and management.

8

Sales Forecasts, Sales Plans, and Budgets

A salesperson must not only plan each week with route sheets and measure that week's results with call reports and orders, but also, with the help of management, he or she must establish sales objectives, action plans for reaching those objectives, and expense goals for an entire quarter, season, or year. At the end of each season, quarter, or year, management then compares actual results against these objectives, goals, and plans, and rewards successful performers appropriately.

The sum of these individual sales objectives, after certain adjustments by management, becomes the company sales forecast. The combination of these individual sales plans, after management review, becomes the company sales plan, the action necessary to generate the sales forecast. The sum of these individual expense goals, after certain adjustments and additions, becomes the company sales expense budget, that is, the selling costs necessary to generate the sales forecast.

Sales forecasts, sales plans, expense budgets, and employee appraisals allow smaller companies to better utilize their limited human and financial resources and thus to better compete with larger concerns. An effective sales/marketing program starts with a financial plan and concludes with appraisal/evaluation of individual performance. Good management requires planning followed by comparisons of planned to actual results. Good salespeople expect objectives and periodic appraisals.

A business of any size requires a sales forecast in order to schedule purchases, employment, and production; establish inventory levels; estimate cash receipts for paying bills; borrow money; set quotas; and evaluate individual performance. A business of any size requires a sales plan in order to break the sales forecast down into bite-sized chunks and to agree on the specific action necessary to accomplish the sales goals. A business of any size requires a selling-expense budget in order to analyze the cost of obtaining sales; estimate cash disbursements for meeting payroll and payable obligations; borrow money; set individual cost goals; and evaluate individual performance.

A sales manager can best control a widely dispersed sales organization through individual objectives and goals, because in such an organization each salesperson has a different skill level and faces unique problems and opportunities in a territory with a unique set of customers. However, such objectives and goals will prove useless unless you periodically compare them with actual performance and employ rewards or corrective action where necessary.

Forecasting sales planning, budgeting, setting objectives, and appraising and evaluating take place between one and four times a year. Therefore, these worthwhile processes do not require a great deal of your time.

Many smaller businesses prepare no sales forecast, sales plan, or expense budget, and engage in no employee appraisal process. These companies are flying blind in a blizzard without aid of navigational instruments. Many small-business sales managers dislike sales forecasts, sales plans, expense budgets, and appraisals because they either misunderstand or mistrust the mechanics and because they also fear the results. When a sales manager's forecast, plan, or budget turns out to be incorrect, it reflects on his or her ability and performance. When you evaluate the performance of one of your salespeople, you also evaluate your own; a salesperson's performance reflects your ability as a manager. A sales force is no better than its management. Many sales managers feel more comfortable avoiding these risks. Also, in a performance appraisal managers may feel uncomfortable criticizing a subordinate and handling the inevitable argument that follows.

Sales Forecasts

The sales forecast process involves asking your people in the field to forecast sales in their individual territories. This is called the bubble-up or bottom-up forecasting technique. This participation get them involved or committed.

Format and Process

Thirty to ninety days before the start of your company's accounting year, you send each salesperson, agent, representative, or distributor who sells your product or service a forecast form for his or her territory. On this form you ask the sales force to forecast orders by month or quarter for each customer or industry as well as for each product/service/style, or product/service/style group. You may ask for this information in terms of dollars or units or both. Request information that the sales force finds easiest to work with and that proves most helpful in meeting the forecast's objectives. If the sales force thinks in terms of dollar sales per customer and if the objective of your sales forecast is cash flow projections, not inventory control, then ask each salesperson to forecast dollar sales per appropriate period by customer. Don't ask for unit sales by product/service.

If your company takes orders for future rather than immediate delivery, then the salesperson must identify what months orders are to be shipped in. If 90 percent of all orders are shipped within forty-five days, you can use a standard factor to translate orders into shipments. Similarly, you can translate any unit forecasts into dollars using standards or averages.

For example, the sales manager of a small ice cream manufacturer in Boston employs the following form:

Dollar sales forecast by quarter

	First	Second	Third	Fourth	Total
Grocery Stores					
Restaurants					
Drug Stores					
Vending Services					
Municipal					
Ball Parks					
Other					
Total					

On the other hand, the publisher of a monthly trade magazine asks sales representatives to submit the following unit product line information:

Space sales forecast by issue in column inches

	Jan.	Feb.	Mar.	Apr.	May	June	July	Aug.	Sep.	Oct.	Nov.	Dec.	Total
Classified													
Covers													
Page 1–20													
Page 21–40													
Page 41–60													
Total													

If your industry has selling seasons, as the apparel industry does, you may ask for a forecast by season rather than by month or quarter. You may also ask salespeople to update their forecasts each month or quarter to reflect the changing dynamics of the marketplace.

To prepare these forecasts, the sales force needs the various reports on past actual performance discussed in Chapter 7. If you want monthly order forecasts in dollars and units by customer and product, then you must supply each salesperson with a customer analysis containing the actual information for previous years. Without the actual results, a salesperson has no reference to build from. Without the actual results from the forecast period, the salesperson has no way of comparing actual performance against his or her forecast. So use a format for your forecast that reflects the way you report actual sales.

When territory boundaries are realigned, territorial forecasts by the responsible salesperson become more difficult. The salesperson does not have access to comparable historic information. If possible, move the historic results for the customers from the old territory to the new. If this is not possible, make assumptions.

At the same time as you ask your sales force to forecast orders by territory, you prepare a preliminary total company forecast using a similar format, whether it be in terms of dollars, customers, product lines, months, quarters, or seasons. Once your preliminary forecast is finished, you compare it with the sum of the preliminary individual territory forecasts prepared by each salesperson. You then discuss each individual territory forecast with the appropriate salesperson, suggesting and agreeing on certain changes.

Finally, you combine the adjusted individual territorial and total company forecasts into a completed version.

In preparing your preliminary companywide forecast and in reviewing each salesperson's preliminary territorial forecast, you must take into account past and present sales and trends; changes within the company such as a new product/service, higher prices, or the retirement of a salesperson; and changes outside the company such as the loss of a major customer, a new competitor, changes in demand, or a recession.

Past and Present Sales and Trends

Start your companywide preliminary sales forecast by reviewing past and present actual sales and trends. To forecast accurately, you require access to the appropriate historical information. If you are going to forecast orders by product or product line, or by major service or major customer, in units or dollars, by month or quarter, you must begin by reviewing these same figures for the current and past years. Do you expect orders to increase, decrease, or stay the same, and why? You may wish to analyze trends for total company sales, for product lines, or for customer groups. You may wish to use weighted or moving averages.

In preparing a preliminary 1992 company sales forecast for the Boston ice cream manufacturer, the sales manager relied on the following historical information given in Table 8-1.

First, the sales manager looked at average trends in the total annual sales figures. From 1988 to 1991 (three years) total company sales increased $550,000 (78 percent), from $700,000 to $1,250,000, or an average of $183,333 or 26 percent annually. As the first footnote indicates, higher prices per gallon accounted for 25 percent of this dollar increase. Therefore, average unit growth per year was about 18 percent. Assuming a 3 percent price increase per gallon in 1992 and projecting a continuation of the 1988–1991 18 percent unit growth rate, the sales manager forecasts a possible 21 percent dollar increase in 1992 sales, from $1,250,000 to $1,512,000.

In forecasting 1993 sales, the sales manager might use a trend projection that includes 1988–1992 actual results, or he might delete 1988 and continue with figures only for the past four years. Averages computed by removing the oldest period and adding the newest are called moving averages.

Next, the sales manager examined the dollar and percentage increase for each individual year since 1988. In 1989, total dollar sales increased $200,000, or 29 percent; in 1990, $225,000, or 25 percent, in 1991, $125,000,

Table 8-1. An ice cream manufacturer's actual dollar sales by year (in thousands).

	1991*	1990	1989	1988
Grocery Stores	$ 610	$ 580	$ 530	$ 480
Restaurants	161	168	160	75
Drug Stores	142	135	123	110
Vending Services	74	35	10	—
Municipalities	112	112	38	—
Ball Parks	106	52	—	—
Other	45	43	39	35
Total	$1,250	$1,125	$ 900	$ 700

Note: Average selling price per gallon rose 10% in 1989 and 1990, and 5% in 1991.
*An estimate based on actual sales January–October 1991.

or 11 percent. Adjusted for inflation, the increase in average selling price, total unit sales rose 19 percent in 1989, 15 percent in 1990, and 6 percent in 1991. So, although the unit growth rate after inflation has averaged 18 percent since 1988, year-to-year sales are growing at a rapidly decreasing rate. Assuming a 3 percent price increase per gallon in 1992, and project- ing a continuation of the decreasing rate of unit growth, the sales manager forecasted a possible 1992 sales figure of $1,250,000, just equal to 1991. In such a forecast, the sales manager assigned more importance to the current 1991 results than to 1990 or 1989.

Finally, the sales manager examined the trend for each customer group. Since 1988, grocery store sales, which represented about half of total com- pany volume for 1991, have shown virtually no unit growth, and a dollar growth equal only to the price increases. Restaurant sales, which repre- sented 13 percent of 1991 total company volume, doubled in 1989, but have actually declined in units since then. Since 1988, drug store sales, which represented 11 percent of 1991 total company volume, have shown virtually no unit growth, and dollar growth equal only to price increases. Sales to vending machine operators started in 1989, tripled in 1990, dou- bled in 1991, and now represent 6 percent of total company dollar volume. Sales to municipalities started in 1989, almost tripled in 1990, but leveled off in 1991, and now represent 9 percent of total company dollar volume. Sales to collegiate and professional baseball and football parks began in

1990, doubled in 1991 and now represent 8 percent of total company dollar volume. "Other" sales, which represented 4 percent of 1991 total company volume, have shown dollar growth only equal to price increases since 1988. Based on these customer group trends and a 3 percent price increase, the sales manager forecasts the following 1992 dollar sales: grocery stores, $620,000; restaurants, $160,000; drug stores, $150,000; vending services, $110,000; municipalities, $115,000; ball parks, $125,000; other, $45,000, for a total of $1,325,000.

Based on total company and customer group past and present sales trends, the sales manager has projected three 1992 dollar sales forecasts; $1,512,000, $1,250,000, and $1,325,000. To determine which sales forecast, which trend projection, has the highest probability of being achieved, the sales manager must now look at changes within the company and at changes outside the company that will affect 1992 sales. These trend projections, whether based on weighted or moving averages, have established some probable limits for the sales forecast that must now be refined. This same trend projection analysis should be prepared for each territory by the sales manager and appropriate sales person, representative, agent, or distributor.

Changes Within the Company

Sales for any future period are affected not only by past and present trends but by anticipated changes in your marketing plan. The ice cream company sales manager employs the following checklist for noting anticipated marketing plan changes that might affect his sales forecast: addition or loss of a salesperson, changes in sales force remuneration, introduction of new products, discontinuation of existing products, price changes, packaging changes, and changes in dollars spent on advertising.

In 1992 the sales manager anticipates hiring a new salesperson to specialize in vending services, replacing a weak salesperson, using a distributor to service "other" accounts, lowering draws but increasing commission rates, introducing several new dietary low cholesterol flavors and discontinuing several older nondietary ones, increasing prices 3 percent, adding a special dixie cup for vending services and a ten-gallon container for restaurants, and increasing cooperative advertising expenditures with drug and grocery stores from $25,000 to $30,000. Now the sales manager must evaluate the effect these anticipated changes can have on 1992 sales.

A new salesperson specializing in vending services should reinforce the past growth trend for that customer group and support the $110,000 forecast. Using a distributor to service "other" accounts should reduce selling expenses but have no effect on sales volume. With luck, replacing the weak salesperson will produce greater sales, and the higher commission rates should act as a stimulant for higher sales. The introduction of several new dietary low cholesterol flavors and the discontinuation of several older nondietary ones may increase sales in 1993 but should only offset each other in 1992. The effect of a 3 percent price increase should be nominal and not result in lower unit volume. The new dixie cup for vending companies should produce an immediate volume increase for that customer group. The new ten-gallon container for restaurants will immediately sell well but primarily replace smaller-container sales. The $5,000 increase in cooperative advertising expenditures should allow the company to maintain its grocery and drug store market share in 1992 and possibly to increase its market share in 1993. In evaluating the possible effects of these marketing plan changes, the sales manager feels most comfortable with a forecast between $1,325,000 and $1,512,000.

In looking at changes within the company that will affect next year's revenues, the sales manager for a garbage removal company considers the following:

1. Sales force remuneration is being changed from a primarily salary to a primarily commission basis.
2. The company's best salesperson is pregnant and will go on a four-month maternity leave.
3. In the first quarter, a new account contest will be announced; in the last quarter, a net revenue increase incentive program will be inaugurated.
4. Salespeople will receive car phones in June.
5. Recycling services will be introduced in February. Compaction equipment will be available in August. A fifteen-year-old rear-load truck will be retired in May.
6. The drivers' union contract expires in June.
7. After February corrugated materials will no longer be accepted at the landfill.
8. Because landfill disposal costs are rising, garbage pick-up prices must increase at least 10 percent by mid-year.
9. A customer service person will be hired in May and a sales administrator in July.
10. A direct mail piece will be sent in January to all construction firms.
11. The length of the service agreement contract is being increased from two to three years.
12. Payment terms will be changed in July from net 60 to net 30.

As sales manager you must share some of this kind of information with each salesperson, representative, agent, or distributor so that they can factor whatever is relevant into their territorial forecast. However, you might not want to share all such information, for instance, compensation and personnel changes.

Changes Outside the Company

Sales for any future period are affected not only by past and present sales trends and your anticipated marketing plan changes, but also by changes in the marketplace over which you have little control. The ice cream company sales manager, for example, uses a checklist for noting anticipated changes in the marketplace. The checklist contains four main headings: customers/prospects, competitors, demand trends, and business environment. Subheadings under customers include loss of existing customers, addition of new customers, changes in purchasing personnel, changes in customer needs, credit and policy changes, and customer expansion or retrenchment plans. Subheadings under competitors include market share, price changes, addition of new products, deletion of existing products, changes in sales personnel, and changes in policy. Essentially, sales managers need to know everything about the competition that they know about their own companies. Knowledge is power. The only subheading under demand trends is total national ice cream consumption. But if this is changing, the sales manager needs to know what forces, fads, or trends are at work that impinge both on the national appetite and on his particular share of the market. Subheadings under business environment include changes in the gross national product, local unemployment, total local employment, personal income, interest rates, retail sales, any special legislation affecting the product, and the weather.

In 1992 the sales manager anticipates that three restaurant customers will go out of business or become such poor credit risks that sales will have to cease. However, the addition of three new branches to an existing grocery store chain customer should more than offset this loss. The city purchasing agent for a major municipal customer will retire in 1992, and her replacement might ask for competitive bids on ice cream. Two of the vending service customers have just obtained major contracts for industrial lunchrooms that could generate more ice cream business.

In looking at customer/prospect changes that will affect next year's revenues, the sales manager for a garbage removal company considers:

1. Possible changes in the amount or type of garbage generated by major customers.

2. Customers who are considering recycling or compaction.
3. Targeting prospects with a probability of becoming customers. Prospects are ranked by each salesperson according to the probability of a contract being signed.
4. Current customers whose contracts are up for renewal.
5. Possible plant closings because of labor disputes.
6. Whether the local military base will be closed.
7. Election of city council members who favor contracting out municipal garbage collection.

In 1992 the ice cream sales manager anticipates that his two major competitors will raise prices 5 percent, making their products slightly more expensive than his. One competitor has licensed a celebrity name for a new higher-priced product line, which could have a negative impact on available shelf space and sales in grocery stores. The senior salesperson of another competitor plans to retire in 1992, which should open some doors for the sales manager's products. Another competitor has changed its terms from 2 percent-60 days to 2 percent-30 days, which might make some of its current customers receptive to a new vendor.

The sales manager for the local garbage company keeps a file on competitor changes that will affect next year's revenues. Information for the file comes from his salespeople, company truck drivers, landfill operators, equipment and supply salespeople who call on refuse companies, the local newspaper, and national trade magazines. The file indicates that one competitor will decrease the length of its service contract from two years to one, another will offer recycling and compaction, a third may go out of business because of financial and family problems, and another will no longer handle hazardous waste. Several competitors have bought software to automate their sales force and telemarketing. The major competitor is switching sales force compensation from salary to commission.

Your company sales forecast and each territorial forecast requires you to share information on customers and competition with each salesperson, representative, agent or distributor. Your field salespeople are a great source of information on customers and competitors.

In 1992 the ice cream sales manager anticipates no unit increase in the total market for ice cream. According to trade association sources, national annual unit consumption of ice cream has remained virtually unchanged for the past three years.

The garbage company sales manager anticipates a 10 percent volume yardage increase in the demand for refuse removal because of new EPA standards for hazardous and medical waste, because the city no longer picks up leaves, paper, or grass clippings, and because landfills are approaching capacity.

In 1992 the ice cream sales manager anticipates small increases in real gross national product, personal income, retail sales, and local employment, and a slight decrease in local unemployment. This would reverse current negative trends in these indicators. The sales manager bases his opinions on material published by the Boston Chamber of Commerce, the New England Business Association, Merchants National Bank, New England Electric, and articles in the *Wall Street Journal*. His boss, the company president, subscribes to an economic forecasting letter, avidly reads *Business Week*, and concurs with the sales manager's economic forecast.

A correlation exists between ice cream sales and summer temperatures. Generally, 50 percent of a year's sales occur in June, July, and August. During these months, hot weather can produce 10 percent greater sales than cool weather. The National Weather Service's long-range forecast calls for a hot summer in New England.

The garbage company sales manager feels that the lower interest rates predicted should boost construction activity and the demand for refuse removal. However, unemployment may rise because a defense electronics company has announced its closing. Energy costs and inflation remain under control, which generally increases consumption and waste generation. A major golf tournament this summer will generate a temporary demand for garbage removal.

Again, share this information on demand trends and the general business environment with your salespeople, representatives, agents, and distributors. You need it to prepare both next year's companywide and territorial forecasts.

Worst- and Best-Case Forecasts

After considering past and present trends, anticipated changes within the company, and possible changes in the marketplace, the ice cream company sales manager decides to prepare a "What if?" or worst- and best-case forecast. The forecast contains assumptions, critical risks, probabilities, and contingency plans. If 1992 summer weather proves to be unusually hot, and the major competitor's senior salesperson retires, and competition raises prices 5 percent, and a capable salesperson can be hired for vending services, and a strong salesperson can be hired to replace the current weak salesperson, then annual 1992 sales will be $1,512,000. If none of these things occur, the sales manager forecasts 1992 sales at $1,325,000. If some of them occur, sales will fall between these two figures. The sales manager decides to use the medium point of $1,420,000 as his preliminary sales forecast. He assigns a 90 percent probability to revenues reaching $1,420,000 and a 70 percent probability to their reaching $1,512,000. He also prepares contingency plans in case summer weather turns out to be cool, the major competitor's senior salesperson does not retire, competition does not raise prices 5 percent, and so on. For example, he is considering becoming a distributor for a line of low-fat yogurt, charging for delivery, and offering promotional programs to key accounts. Contingency plans take the emotion out of disappointment.

You also ask each salesperson, representative, agent, and distributor to prepare territorial forecasts containing best-and worst-case scenarios, the assumptions for each, the probabilities of each, critical risks, and contingency plans. This bracketing process takes the fear out of forecasting.

As the year progresses and more of the "What ifs?" become reality, you can make revisions to produce a more precise forecast. One small-company president humorously rated his sales manager high on producing accurate annual sales forecasts once the forecasted year's final quarter began.

Combing Sales Force and Management Forecasts Into a Final Forecast

You now compare your preliminary total company forecast with the sum of the territorial forecasts produced by your salespeople, representatives, agents, or distributors. Are the two forecasts close? If not, why not? What assumptions have you made that the salespeople did not? What information do they have available that you do not?

These questions are partially answered by comparing past and present sales trends in each territory and the company as a whole with each territorial forecast. If sales for a territory have remained unchanged for two years, why does the salesperson forecast a 28 percent increase next year?

You should also review how anticipated changes in your marketing plan and probable changes in the marketplace will affect each specific territory. Do territorial forecasts reflect your plans to raise prices next year? Has your Omaha agent adjusted her forecast to reflect credit problems in that territory and the possible loss of a major customer? Does the Minnesota forecast reflect the anticipated retirement of a competitive salesperson? Does the Washington forecast reflect the depressed condition of the lumber and aerospace industry? You should apply the same analytical techniques to each territory that you did to the total company forecast. Based on these techniques, you make adjustments and once again compare your total company forecast to the sum of individual territory forecasts. Are the two forecasts close, or do they require further adjustment?

You then continue discussing each territorial forecast and your suggested changes with the responsible salesperson, representative, agent, or distributor. You exchange information on how each of you arrived at the figures and then agree on a final forecast. These final individual territorial forecasts become the salesperson's, representative's, agent's, or distributor's objective or quota, which you use to measure, evaluate, and reward actual performance. To accept the sales forecast as a commitment, each salesperson must consider the forecast as a realistic, fair, and obtainable objective that reflects the territorial potential. The sum of these final individual territorial forecasts should equal or exceed your final total company forecast.

The bubble-up sales forecast, the result of this dialogue between you and the salesperson, has many benefits. Because you and the salesperson have used this process to arrive at the sales forecast, the salesperson has ownership and a commitment to its realization. The figures were arrived at through a rational process, not just plucked out of the air. The process gave you and your sales force an opportunity to evaluate factors inside and outside the company that drive sales as well as an opportunity to look at past and present sales trends. Sales management starts with a forecast and ends with an evaluation. The two are tied into the same circle. The bubble-up sales forecast does not force salespeople to accept unreasonable objectives. It gives management a realistic idea of future results based on many component pieces. And it is as applicable to outside sales representatives as it is to salespeople who are your employees. Try it and you will become a believer.

Management Review

Because of the final forecast's corporate importance, you should quickly share this information with other members of management. Arrange a meeting with the company president, controller, and operations manager to discuss the figures.

The operations manager may feel that he cannot hire enough skilled hourly people to provide the goods or services required by the sales forecast. He may suggest subcontracting certain work. On the other hand, the forecast might indicate an underutilization of equipment or skilled personnel, in which case he may wish to solicit subcontract work from another company.

Based on your forecast, the controller may immediately sense a need to decrease inventories or increase available bank credit. With your sales forecast, the controller can begin a cash flow projection and profit forecast for the next year.

The president may not accept the forecast as realistic, or as meeting long-range goals or short-term profit requirements, in which case further adjustments by you and the salespeople may be necessary. The president may also ask you to verify certain information by calling key customers.

Salespeople need to know that their input into the bubble-up sales forecasting process is essential but not the final word. They need to know that top management may ask for adjustments. In this situation, the sales manager goes back to the affected salespeople to discuss and get their commitment to such an adjustment. Likewise, top management needs to understand that adjustments must be realistic and realizable.

Evaluation of Sales Forecast

Obtaining the best estimate of future sales on the basis of current knowledge represents the ultimate objective of your sales forecast. Each year, you must compare actual results with forecast sales and evaluate how well you have met that objective. Was your forecast correct in units but wrong in dollars? Correct as to the direction of sales but wrong as to the magnitude of that direction? Accurate for one product line or customer group but inaccurate for another? Analyze the reasons for these variances and take appropriate corrective action on your next forecast. Possibly you should put less emphasis on general economic indicators and sales trends and give more emphasis to changes in industry demand, pricing, new accounts, and competitors' new products.

In addition, each month you compare cumulative actual sales for each territory with those projected, analyze the reasons for variances, and take corrective operational action. If your Ohio salesperson forecast $100,000 worth of sales in the first quarter but only booked $75,000, you would call to discuss the matter. Possibly you need to visit a major customer in Cleveland who has given more business to the competition, or the salesperson needs to travel more, or a major account is having credit problems. If your Minnesota salesperson forecast $225,000 of sales in the first nine months but only produced $150,000, possibly you should lower his draw or replace him.

Some small companies ask salespeople to forecast sales, but then never compare actual results with the forecast submitted. Under this scenario the bubble-up process becomes an exercise in frustration, a waste of time, and a demotivator.

Each quarter, you review the sales forecast for future periods and, based on any new information, make appropriate adjustments. For example, if a large customer unexpectedly goes out of business in the second quarter, the third- and fourth-quarter forecast will require adjustment.

There is no one best technique for forecasting sales, only what is most appropriate for your company's circumstances. Once you have arrived at an annual sales forecast figure, you use these same techniques to distribute sales by month or quarter.

The Sales Plan

The sales forecast is a number; the sales plan is the objective, action, and goal necessary for you and each salesperson, representative, agent, or distributor to achieve the forecast. The sales forecast says, "I want to get from point A to point B"; the sales plan says, "This is how I am going to do it." Sales plans and forecasts overlap and interrelate. Each year's sales plan is a simplified microcosm of this book.

Bite-Size Pieces

The sales plan starts by breaking down each salesperson's sales forecast into bite-size pieces. If a salesperson's annual sales forecast is $960,000, how does that break down by product line, new accounts, old account growth, customer group, gross margin contribution, and sales by month and week? A temporary help service divides $960,000 by forty-eight working weeks and 240 working days. The salesperson knows that to meet forecast, he or she must produce $20,000 of revenue a week, or $4,000 a day. The rule is no lunch until daily revenues reach $4,000. Each day the sales manager posts each sales person's dollar results and percent of forecast to a bulletin board in the hallway.

The $20,000 a week or $80,000 a month has product line, customer group, and pricing goals. Depending on the territory, these goals are different for each salesperson. For one salesperson the monthly goal is 50 percent office temps, 20 percent day laborers, and 30 percent medical technicians. Her monthly customer group goal is 40 percent state and federal facilities, 30 percent Fortune 1,000 customers, 15 percent nonprofit organizations, and 15 percent law and accounting firms. Other salespeople have different percentage goals.

In addition, each salesperson has pricing or gross margin goals, because a great deal of negotiation occurs in setting customer prices for each order. One salesperson has a pricing or gross margin goal of 30 percent, and another of 20 percent, because one territory has more competitors than the other.

Each salesperson has a dollar goal for generating new business versus maintaining or expanding existing accounts. For example, $100,000 of the $960,000 is forecast to come from new accounts. Ten new accounts are required to produce this $100,000 of business. Each salesperson's plan includes a list of target accounts ranked by the probability of opening them and their potential dollar volume.

The sum of all these bite-size pieces becomes your company goal.

Call Goals

Achieving each salesperson's territorial forecast requires call goals and so this becomes part of the sales plan. The more calls, the more dollars of sales. Based on the number of present and potential accounts, their density, the dollar forecast for new business versus retention or penetration, the temporary help company gives each salesperson daily call goals. The number of daily calls drives results. One person receives ten as her daily call goal, broken down into three new account calls, one service call, and six penetration calls. Another salesperson receives seven as his daily call goal, broken down into four new account calls and three penetration calls. It takes approximately twenty-five new account calls to open one account. The salesperson gets to ring a bell in the office whenever he or she opens a new account.

Staffing, Territories, Reporting, Training, Compensation

Achieving next year's sales forecast may require that you add or replace a salesperson or hire a customer service representative or a sales administrator. Your sales plan should state when each staffing change will occur.

Your sales plan should include any changes in territory boundaries as discussed in Chapter 4: Use a map to show the details.

Reporting requirements should be part of your sales plan and each of your people's sales plans: Do you require two sets of prospect profile cards? Do you require weekly route sheets or call reports? Do you require daily planners?

Include the training each salesperson will receive next year and where and when he or she will receive it. Training is an important part of the sales plan. Do your people need training in competitive advantage and time management? Will you provide this at sales meetings or in field training? When will this take place?

If you plan to alter sales force compensation next year or anticipate that you will have a sales contest, include these items in your sales plan.

Contingency Planning

Your own contingency planning might consist of preparing a list of the twenty most serious events that could have a negative impact on next year's sales. This list might include one of your best salespeople quitting, a competitor lowering its prices, a major account developing credit problems, or a shortage of raw material or skilled labor. As part of your sales plan, you should prepare a contingency plan for each such negative event. For example, if the competition lowered its prices, you would immediately have a salesperson contact each major account to resell your benefits, possibly offer enhancements such as faster turn-around times, and check for any dissatisfaction. If manufacturing was curtailed because of raw material shortages, you might part ship or allocate orders. Also you might want to notify all major accounts by phone and the rest by letter.

Wherever possible you involve the salesperson in his or her sales plan. As in sales forecasting, a major benefit of sales planning is the salesperson's involvement in the process. Again, you have a meaningful dialogue with the salesperson to agree on necessary action and that dialogue leads to ownership and a commitment for successful performance.

Sales Expense Budgets

At the same time you are forecasting sales and preparing a sales plan, you must budget the cost of obtaining those sales and executing the sales plan. For a company to be profitable, selling expenses must be maintained at a certain percentage of total sales.

Selling expenses can be grouped into fixed costs, which do not vary directly with sales volume and cannot easily be changed; variable costs, which do not vary directly with sales volume; and discretionary costs, which management has the ability to change on a short-term basis. Fixed expenses include such items as salaries, payroll taxes, group insurance, rent, and utilities. Variable expenses include such items as commissions, bonuses, and royalties. Discretionary expenses include such items as travel, entertainment, telephone use, and advertising. Although it is easier to budget

fixed costs than variable or discretionary ones, all expense budgeting requires assumptions, judgment, and planning.

Preparing a budget requires accumulating as much detail as possible
on anticipated monthly expenses from the sources of those expenses, whether
the sources be the sales manager, the sales force, or the sales forecast. This
bubble-up process results in greater accuracy, involvement, and commitment. Who knows better what expenses will be next year than the person
responsible for creating those expenses? Then each category in the expense
budget must be tested against the previous year's actual and figured as a
percentage of next year's forecasted sales.

The total sales expense budget requires review and approval by the
controller or accountant and the company president. The president decides
whether your expense budget realistically satisfies the requirements of the
company cash flow projection and profit forecast.

Preparing sales forecasts and expense budgets forces the sales manager
and the salespeople to plan the actions that influence sales and expenses.
As you can see, sales forecasts, sales plans, and expense budgets are closely
interrelated. These forecasts, plans, and budgets become objectives against
which actual performance can be measured and controlled. By involving
salespeople in the expense budgeting process, you get more accurate budgets and their commitment to keeping expenses within budget.

What happens when a company fails to maintain its selling expenses
at a certain percentage of total sales can be seen in the following example.
In the 1980s, a cellular phone manufacturer doubled its sales each year
until management declared voluntary bankruptcy. Each year the cost of
selling the product unexpectedly increased as a percentage of total sales.
Each year the company lost money, and to remedy this management
promised to lower selling expense as a percentage of sales. However, management never prepared an expense budget to use as a plan for lowering
those costs.

Had management prepared an expense budget it might have looked
like Figure 8-1 (see page 244).

Sales Force Discretionary Expenses

Sixty to ninety days before the start of your company's accounting year,
ask each salesperson, representative, agent, or distributor to prepare a
monthly budget for whatever discretionary reimbursable expenses he or
she will incur. If you use straight commission to compensate the sales
force and do not reimburse expenses, naturally you do not need this information. However, a company that does reimburse expenses should ask

the sales force for a monthly telephone, car, travel, and entertainment budget, including detailed information on lodging, food, transportation, and planned itineraries.

Once received, you compare each of these territorial budgets with the previous year's budget, with this year's actual territorial expenses/sales, and with next year's territorial sales forecast. Why does the Denver salesperson budget a 50 percent increase in expenses but no increase in forecasted sales? Why does the Minneapolis agent budget expenses at 3 percent of next year's forecasted sales, when the actual for last year's expenses totaled only 2 percent of sales? Why does the New York City distributor budget lower expenses but forecast higher sales for next year? You should discuss these questions with your salespeople, reaching agreement and making adjustments where necessary.

Each salesperson must accept his or her final expense budget as a realistic, fair, and obtainable objective. By asking salespeople to prepare their own budgets, by discussing these budgets with them, you obtain the salesperson's involvement and commitment to a realistic figure.

You use these territorial expense budgets to help plan, control, measure, evaluate, and reward actual performance. For instance, companies pay bonuses to salespeople whose expenses do not exceed budget. The sum of these adjusted territorial expense budgets becomes part of the total company budget.

Fixed and Variable Expenses

Next, start accumulating monthly figures for budgeted fixed costs, such as salaries, group insurance, payroll taxes, warehouse, showrooms, rent, and utilities. Prepare a worksheet listing yourself and all salaried personnel who report to you. By each name and under the appropriate month, place a figure equal to the budgeted monthly gross salary, taking into account any anticipated raises, retirements, replacements, or additions. Various sums of these figures then become the monthly totals for the company expense budget. Compare these totals with the previous year's actual expenses and next year's forecasted sales. Have they risen in dollars and as a percentage of sales? Are the increases justified?

Next, ask the controller or accountant to provide you with budget figures for group insurance and payroll taxes. He or she will ask for a schedule of your personnel and their anticipated compensation. Again, compare total budgeted group insurance and payroll tax figures with the previous year's actuals, and calculate what percentage of total compensa-

Figure 8-1. Cellular phone monthly selling expense budget (in thousands of dollars).

	Jan.	Feb.	Mar.	Apr.	May	June	July	Aug.	Sept.	Oct.	Nov.	Dec.	Total
Sales Management													
Salaries													
Office Salaries													
Salespeople:													
Salaries													
Commissions													
Bonuses													
Total Salespeople's Compensation													
Total Compensation (all sales personnel)													
Payroll Taxes													
Group Insurance													
Royalties and Licenses													
West Coast Warehouse													
New York Showroom													
Cooperative Advertising													
Trade Shows													
National Advertising													
Sales Aids													
Store Displays													
Models and Samples													
Telephone													
Travel													
Entertainment													
Rent and Utilities													
Postage													
Other													
Total													

tion and sales they represent. Be sure you understand the reasons for variances.

If you rent space for sales offices, warehouses, or showrooms, review the leases and add to the budget the appropriate monthly figures for next year's rental and utility expenses. If you share rented or owned space with other company functions, such as manufacturing or administration or research, ask the controller or accountant to allocate a portion of the anticipated monthly expenses to selling. Compare the total budgeted rental and utility expenses with the previous year's actuals and calculate what percentage they represent of total sales. Ask questions and, where appropriate, make changes.

Next, calculate monthly figures for the variable expenses that are a function of sales. Based on the final monthly sales forecast by territory, calculate each salesperson's commission and/or bonus due (if any). Then place the total figure in the company budget. Based on the final monthly company sales forecast, calculate your bonus and any royalty or license fees due, and place this figure in the company budget. Again, compare these figures with the previous year's actuals and calculate their percentage relationship to sales. Have budgeted commissions and bonuses risen as a percentage of forecasted sales? If so, is it because of a change in the compensation plan, because of an anticipated change in product mix, or because changes in territory boundaries have caused a redistribution of sales among salespeople?

Management Discretionary Expenses

Finally, you should accumulate monthly figures for remaining discretionary expenses such as your travel, entertainment, and telephone costs plus company advertising, trade shows, sales aids, models and samples. Prepare a monthly travel and entertainment expense budget for yourself using the same format previously suggested for the sales force. To arrive at a company total for this category, add your figures along with all other management sales-related travel and entertainment expense to the numbers submitted by the sales force.

Using last year's actual figures, and adjusting for rate changes and possible changes in anticipated activity, budget the sales office's and your business-related personal telephone expenses. Add this figure to the total of sales force reimbursed telephone expenses, if any, and arrive at a monthly total company budget for this category.

Prepare a monthly worksheet listing the various categories of sales-related advertising activity engaged in by your company. This might include trade, consumer, cooperative, classified, employment, institutional, newspaper, or magazine advertising, as well as displays, trade shows, sales aids, press releases, premiums, models and samples. Next to each category of advertising, budget the anticipated monthly expense. Then justify these figures with a more detailed plan. In what newspaper or magazine do you plan to run how many column inches of cooperative, consumer, trade, or classified advertising? What product, service, or employment will the ad feature? Which customers require how much cooperative advertising? What will each ad cost? In what months do you plan to purchase which displays, attend what trade shows, send out press releases, or give away samples; and how much will this cost?

The total of these figures becomes your monthly and annual advertising budget, which you then compare with the previous year's actual budget, and also calculate its percentage relationship to sales. Are you planning to spend more on advertising next year than last? Is it a higher percentage of sales? Do increased advertising expenditures result in increased sales? Would decreased advertising expenses result in decreased sales? The budget becomes your advertising plan, and raises questions that you must answer.

Finally, you total all the sales expense categories by month and for the year, then compare these totals to the previous year's actuals. You also calculate the percentage relationship of these budgeted expense totals to forecasted total company sales, and compare this percentage with actual past percentage figures. Negative variances require questions and answers.

Don't spend a great deal of time debating which company sales expenses are fixed, variable, or discretionary. It varies from one company to another. In a small company most selling expenses are fixed, and it is often hard to separate out the true variable costs. Do spend time accumulating data and discussing all sales-related costs, whether fixed, variable, or discretionary. Most sales managers don't know what their sales costs are.

Management Review

Because the selling expense budget represents a significant percentage of sales, you should share this information with the company president and accountant or controller. The controller/accountant needs these figures for next year's cash flow projection and profit forecast. The president may not accept your budget as realistic or as meeting profit requirements, in which case further adjustments by you and the salespeople could be necessary. The president may feel that continued growth requires more travel and advertising, or that the entertainment budget does not seem realistic, or that total budgeted selling expenses are too high a percentage of forecasted sales.

Both the sales forecast and the selling expense budget become part of a larger plan, the company cash flow projection and profit forecast. The president decides whether your figures realistically satisfy the requirements of that larger plan.

Evaluation and Use of the Sales Budget

Obtaining the most realistic estimate of future selling expenses necessary to profitably generate forecasted sales represents an important objective of the budget. At the end of each accounting year, you compare actual expenses with those budgeted and evaluate how well you have met that objective. Were actual selling expenses above budget because actual sales were above forecast? Did advertising expenses exceed budget because a new customer unexpectedly demanded a cooperative ad? Did higher than budgeted travel expense result from an unexpected trip to hire a new salesperson? Analyze the reasons for the variances and take appropriate corrective action in your next budget.

Each month, you should compare cumulative line item actual selling expenses to budget, analyze the reasons for variances, and, when necessary, take corrective action. If the Ohio salesperson budgeted $500 monthly for reimbursed travel expenses, but after five months has submitted receipts for $4,000, a telephone call is required to find out why. You may have him reduce traveling for two months unless his sales are ahead of forecast, thus justifying the budget overrun. After six months, telephone expenses may be several thousand dollars over budget either because of personal use or because of more business activity. You need to find out which.

Each quarter you should review the budget for future periods and, based on any new information, make the appropriate adjustments. For example, if a salesperson unexpectedly resigns in the second quarter and you decide not to seek a replacement immediately, the third- and fourth-quarter budgets will require downward adjustment.

Many small companies prepare sales expense budgets but don't use them. If you are not going to use them, don't waste time preparing them. But this chapter should show you the benefits of both preparation and use.

Territorial Profit-and-Loss Projection

Sales forecasts and selective expense budgets by territory produce information that allows you to prepare a territorial profit–and-loss projection.

You have already reached agreement with each salesperson on his or her sales forecast and, if appropriate, his or her reimbursed expense budget. By deducting from the territorial sales forecast all selling expenses directly applicable to that particular territory, the projected costs of manufacturing the goods, and an allocation for general, selling, interest, and administrative expenses, you arrive at various dollar margin figures that can be related to the territory's sales as a percentage; then you compare both the dollar and the percentage margins between territories.

Starting with the sales forecast, you deduct all selling expenses directly applicable to that particular territory, such as a salesperson's compensation, payroll taxes, fringe benefits, travel, auto, entertainment, phone, and rent costs, plus bad debts, freight, terms, discounts, and advertising expenses directly related to customers in that territory. This calculation produces a dollar margin figure that can be related to the territory's sales as a percentage, after which you compare both the dollar and percentage margins of various territories. For example, if the sales forecast for a territory is $400,000 and the direct selling expense budget totals $45,000, the resulting margin would be $355,000, or 88.75 percent.

You then deduct the projected cost of manufacturing the goods or producing the services being sold. Here you must rely on average costs or percentages for the entire company or product/service group, a figure available from the accountant/controller. You also deduct any royalties due.

For example, if the projected manufacturing costs average 65 percent of each sales dollar, you would multiply 65 percent by $400,000 of forecast sales to get a result of $260,000. Subtracting the $260,000 from the previous margin of $355,000 produces a contribution of $95,000 toward the remaining unallocated selling, administrative, general, and interest expenses. This contribution can be compared in dollars, or as a percentage of sales, with that produced by other territories. The $95,000 in the example, which represents 23.75 percent of sales, could be compared with another territory having $460,000 of sales and a $120,000, or 26 percent, contribution; or with one having $300,000 of sales and a $75,000, or 25 percent, contribution. You might set 18 percent as the minimum acceptable percentage contribution from a territory. Any territory making less than an 18 percent contribution would indicate a need for corrective action, such as a change in salesperson compensation, a change in territory boundaries, less advertising, or fewer discounts.

A further refinement of the territory profit-and-loss projection involves allocating the remaining selling, general, interest, and administrative expenses among territories on a percentage-of-sales basis. For example, if company sales total $2 million and the remaining unallocated selling, general, interest, and administrative expenses total $300,000, or 15 percent of sales, you would allocate 15 percent of each territory's sales to its remaining selling, general, interest, and administrative expenses. A territory with $400,000 in sales and a $95,000 contribution to selling, general, and administrative expenses would receive an allocation of 15 percent times $400,000, or $60,000, leaving a projected pretax profit margin of $35,000, or 8.75 percent of sales. You then compare projected pretax profit dollars and margins for various territories and take corrective action where goals are not met. At year end, actual territorial contributions to selling, general, and administrative expenses or actual territorial pretax profit margins should be compared with the projection and with other territories, and corrective action taken where necessary. On an actual basis you should be able to calculate the actual gross margin after cost of manufacturing for each territory reflecting product mix and off-price selling.

Territory Break-Even-Point Analysis

Using the territorial profit-and-loss projection may reveal unprofitable territories. By using these same techniques, you can forecast what level of sales and direct selling expenses will produce a break-even point or restore an acceptable level of pretax margin or an acceptable level of contribution to selling, general, and administrative expenses.

For example, a territory with $200,000 of sales, $45,000 of direct selling expenses, a 15 percent general, selling, and administrative allocation, and 65 percent cost of producing the product or service would show a $5,000 pretax loss. By using these territorial profit-and-loss projection techniques, you can calculate the performance necessary to break even: increase annual sales $15,000 to $30,000, or 7.5 percent to 15 percent depending on variable versus fixed expenses; or reduce annual direct selling expenses $5,000, or 11 percent. More specifically, you might calculate as necessary a monthly sales increase of $2,500, or a certain number of additional units; or a weekly increase of $577, or a certain number of additional units. You might decide to change the territory boundaries or product mix or to lower the salesperson's salary and travel expense by $1,500 each, and cooperative advertising by $2,000. You also might decide on a combination of lower expenses and higher sales to reach the break-even-point.

You perform this same type of exercise to arrive at the action necessary to earn a certain pretax territorial profit, for example, 10 percent of sales or $20,000. In this case, the salesperson must lower expenses by $25,000, increase sales by $75,000 to $150,000, depending on variable versus fixed expenses, or some combination of the two. Again, specific action can be planned to produce these dollar changes.

9

Performance Appraisals and Evaluations

Some sales managers would rather complain about a salesperson than analyze the underlying problems and attempt to solve them through a formal evaluation process. They dislike sitting in judgment and they especially dislike the disagreements caused by negative appraisals. When sales managers give a salesperson a poor appraisal, they are in effect evaluating their own performance as managers. The salesperson who started out well but has since gone downhill and now has to be dismissed might well have been rehabilitated along the way through regular performance evaluations. From a legal standpoint, regular performance appraisals can justify termination and avoid lawsuits by ex-employees. Evaluations let salespeople know in advance just where they stand.

As a sales manager, you have spent a great deal of time, energy, and money hiring, training, compensating, organizing, and motivating the sales force. It only makes sense to finish the process and ensure success with periodic performance evaluations. Performance appraisals actually make your job easier. As with sales forecasting, the process of evaluation—the meaningful dialogue, the goal setting, the attention, the accountability—may be even more important than the actual results. You can't afford to waste your most important resource, people.

Quarterly performance appraisals and evaluations represent an important means of communicating with and motivating the sales force. You should use them in varying degrees for everyone involved in sales: company salespeople, independent representatives, agents, distributors, customer service people, and sales administrators. Quarterly evaluations inform the salesperson what performance standards you expect; whether these standards are being met; and if not, what corrective action is necessary. Salespeople have a need and a right to know what you think of their work. They can't read your mind.

Performance appraisals establish a meaningful dialogue between the sales manager and salesperson and help develop an effective working relationship. You are in fact always evaluating salespeople whether in the form of hallway conferences or postcall field training critiques. Quarterly performance appraisals give you an opportunity to do this formally. The positive motivational message to each salesperson is that he or she is important to the company and that you care about his or her performance. That is why you are spending time together. Recognition of positive performance motivates a salesperson to do even better, and anticipation of such recognition stimulates self-motivation.

The evaluation process involves (1) deciding what you wish to appraise; (2) developing individual performance objectives and measurements for each salesperson; (3) observing, rating, and evaluating actual performance; and (4) discussing the evaluation with each salesperson. Most important, using the appraisal form, ratings, and discussion, you agree on future objectives and obtain a commitment from the salesperson to a plan and time frame for achieving these goals.

What to Appraise

The evaluation process starts by deciding what you wish to appraise. Prepare a list of activities, actions, characteristics, knowledge, skills, and results critical to the successful performance of a salesperson in your particular company. This will differ greatly from company to company and may even differ from salesperson to salesperson within the same organization. Performance appraisals are meant to be flexible. Start by reviewing the job description and candidate profile used to hire each salesperson. The job description lists a salesperson's anticipated duties, the candidate profile his or her personal characteristics. Next, review the format of your training program, which lists the skills and knowledge necessary for success. Then add any other items not mentioned in the job description, candidate profile, or training format that are important for effective performance.

Divide the appraisal list into twelve major categories: sales results, sales quality, sales activity, selling skills, job knowledge, self-organization and planning, participation, paperwork, expense control, customer relations, company relations, and personal characteristics. Whether your sales force sells soft goods or durables, products or services, to consumer, industrial, or government users, these twelve interrelated categories should prove helpful in deciding what to evaluate.

Sales results would include such items as total dollar and unit sales volume; sales volume as a percentage of quota or forecast; sales volume compared with previous year or month; number of new accounts opened; number of existing customers lost; and total number of active accounts. Did total sales, total revenues, total number of customers grow or decline, and how does the result compare with the forecast?

Sales quality would include such items as dollar and unit sales by product or service group, area coverage, pricing, credit losses, and territorial gross margin. Did the salesperson sell the entire range of products/ services or just a few? Did he or she concentrate on selling the least expensive and/or the least profitable? Did he or she maintain list prices or sell off price? Did the Ohio salesperson saturate the Cleveland market but neglect Dayton, Columbus, and Cincinnati? Did the Illinois salesperson call on appliance companies but not on printed circuit board manufacturers? Did the California salesperson call on chain and discount stores but not pharmacies and garden shops? How many new and existing accounts pay slowly?

Sales activities would include such items as number of calls per day or week on present accounts versus prospects, number of proposals, number of presentations, number of appointments. You know that certain activities lead to increased sales. You need to measure these against predetermined standards or objectives.

Selling skills would include such items as finding prospects, using referrals, calling on inactive accounts, upgrading accounts, conversions, creating empathy, identifying problems and needs, presenting benefits, answering objections, handling price increases and complaints, planning each call, closing, and using sales aids. You base your evaluations on observations made during field sales visits. Preferably, you spend at least several days a year with each salesperson, and part of that time is spent observing the salesperson relating to customers and prospects.

Job knowledge would include a knowledge of your company, its customers, the competition, competitive advantages, product/service features and applications, pricing, programs, market and industry information, and company policy. Information exchanged in call reports, phone calls, and meetings would feed into your evaluation along with actual observation in the field. During a customer visit, could the salesperson answer questions on product performance, competitive pricing, industry sales trends, or new applications? Did the salesperson know the buyer's name at all customer and major prospect companies?

Self-organization and planning would include the salesperson's efficient use of time in traveling the territory, allocating time correctly between different type accounts and different geographic areas, keeping accurate records on customers, setting up appointments, planning each day and week, planning each presentation, and keeping samples and sales literature neat. Does the salesperson call on clusters of customers, or spend many hours driving between accounts? On Monday morning does he or she call ahead for Friday appointments? Does the salesperson have an objective for each sales call, and know what happened on the last visit? Does the salesperson spend too much time at your office? Again, you base your evaluations on observations made during field visits as well as on information obtained from route sheets, call reports, phone calls, and meetings.

Participation would include prompt attendance at and involvement in sales meetings, trade shows, seminars, and setups, also promptly responding to company questionnaires. A salesperson who continually misses training sessions or fails to return memos on what new services are receiving the best customer response would receive a poor rating in this category.

Paperwork refers to the prompt submission of accurate route sheets, call reports, orders, service agreements, expense accounts, customer credit information, requests for advertising material, requests for return permission, and any other required written material. A salesperson who submits call reports once a month when you require them once a week or who submits requests for advertising material after the customer has run an unauthorized ad would not rate well in this category. Does the salesperson promptly update customer profile cards and account files? Are orders or service agreements filled out correctly in legible handwriting?

Expense control refers to the maintenance of reimbursable travel/entertainment costs, customer terms, discounts, promotions, and freight and advertising allowances at an agreed-upon budgeted level. If a salesperson's reimbursed annual travel expense is budgeted at $10,000 but actually amounts to $15,000, or if annual territorial cooperative advertising and freight allowances are budgeted at $7,000 but actually amount to $10,000, the salesperson probably would receive a negative evaluation in this category.

You may wish to carry the sales quality and expense control evaluation one step further by evaluating territorial profits. Using the territorial profit-and-loss analysis discussed in Chapter 8, you can rate each salesperson's profitability in total dollars and as a percentage of sales.

Customer relations include such items as solving customer problems, responding in a timely fashion to complaints and service calls, satisfying needs, providing technical knowledge, merchandising skills, stock counting, order expediting, and postdelivery follow-up services. Does the salesperson call on different type customers frequently enough, provide the necessary service and assistance, and develop positive relationships with customer personnel? A salesperson who visits customers only when he or she can write an order would rank poorly here.

Company relations involve abiding by company policies and procedures and cooperating with other company personnel. If it is company policy for salespeople not to call the sales manager collect more than once a week, yet one salesperson calls every other day, this would affect his or her rating. The salesperson who annoys fellow workers as a know-it-all or who yells at your secretary about late deliveries would not rate well in this category.

Personal characteristics would include such items as attitude, enthusiasm, self-confidence, assertiveness, aggressiveness, follow-up, drive, flexibility, persistence, judgment, stability, dependability, sense of urgency, imagination, initiative, responsibility, and appearance. The salesperson who fights any change in products, services, prices, procedures, or personnel would not be considered flexible. The salesperson you must remind for six months to call on a specific prospect would rank poorly in initiative. These qualitative soft issues, such as personal characteristics, are important to the success of your salespeople, but sensitive matters to discuss. Listing these qualities in your appraisal informs salespeople of their importance and forces a discussion of them.

Figure 9-1 lists the major categories you will want to appraise and the measurable features relevant to each.

Now you select specific objectives to fit the needs of each individual salesperson and territory. You have already reached an agreement with each salesperson on his or her forecasted total dollar, unit, and product line sales and on his or her budgeted expenses. The territorial forecast and budget become the salesperson's sales and expense objectives or quotas.

Bonuses and Quotas

Objectives can become quotas which then serve as a basis for both compensation and evaluation. Many companies include a bonus in their compensation plan as an incentive to attain objectives such a certain percentages of forecasted sales and budgeted expenses. For example, the bonus starts when actual sales reach 80 percent of forecast, but is greater if sales attain

(Text continued on page 257.)

Figure 9-1. The twelve categories on which appraisal is based.

Sales Results

Dollar sales volume
Unit sales volume
Percent of quota or forecast
Compared to previous year or month
New accounts opened
Existing customers lost
Total active accounts

Sales Quality

Dollar sales by product line
Unit sales by product line
Area coverage
Account type coverage
Credit losses
Gross margin
Pricing

Sales Activity

Number of calls per week on
    prospects vs. present accounts
Number of proposals
Number of presentations
Number of appointments

Selling Skills

Prospecting
Using referrals
Calling on inactive accounts
Upgrading accounts
Conversions
Using empathy
Planning each call
Presenting benefits
Handling objections, price increases, and complaints
Use of sales aids
Closing

(Continued)

Figure 9-1. *(Continued.)*

Knowledge of

> Product features
> Company strengths and policy
> Applications
> Pricing
> Customers
> Prospects
> Market
> Industry
> Competition
> Competitive advantages
> Programs

Self-Organization and Planning

> Traveling efficiently
> Customer records
> Allocation of time between accounts and geographic areas
> Planning each day, week, and presentation
> Condition of samples and sales literature

Participation

> Sales meetings
> Trade shows
> Seminars
> Setups
> Questionnaires

Paperwork

> Route sheets
> Call reports
> Expense reports
> Credit reports
> Return requests
> Advertising requests
> Orders

Expenses

> Travel and entertainment
> Freight and advertising allowances
> Terms and discounts
> Promotions

Customer Relations

Frequency of visits
Service and assistance
Personal relationships
Handling complaints

Company Relations
Policy and procedures
Personal relationships

Personal Characteristics

Attitude
Enthusiasm
Assertiveness
Self-confidence
Aggressiveness
Follow-up
Drive
Flexibility
Persistence
Judgment
Stability
Dependability
Sense of urgency
Imagination
Initiative
Dependability
Appearance

---

120 percent of forecast. The bonus may also be greater if the sales mix includes more high-profit items. Bonuses may also be paid for achieving objectives on the number of new accounts, credit collections, calls per week, territorial profits, gross margin or absenteeism.

A bonus can also be paid if actual expenses do not exceed budget, with the bonus increasing as actual expenses decrease. As previously stated, quotas must be mutually agreed upon by sales manager and salesperson and be obtainable through reasonable effort. Unobtainable quotas do not motivate the sales force to expend extra effort.

Counting, Measuring, Describing Individual Objectives

Once you have reviewed all the activities on your evaluation checklist, you can select those which represent the most critical areas for each individual salesperson. In order to set objectives, however, you need to develop valid methods for counting, measuring, or describing them. Territory by territory, salesperson by salesperson, you establish standards for measuring desired skills, activities, knowledge, personal characteristics, and results.

For example, one of your people spends too much time—more than 50 percent—with just a few customers. You want that reduced to 35 percent, with 65 percent allocated to other customers and prospects. Another salesperson opens many new accounts but then loses them the following year. You want that person to concentrate on maintaining accounts, and thus increase total active customers by 5 percent a year. Another salesperson averages only two calls a day and those are exclusively on existing accounts. You want that person to average three calls a day and to include at least one prospect. Yet another salesperson has only large accounts and needs to open a dozen smaller ones next year. Still another salesperson has only small accounts and needs to open two large ones next year.

One salesperson emphasizes product features rather than benefits; another does not carry catalogs. You want both deficiencies corrected. One salesperson does not write down buyers' names; another does not stay current with competition. Some salespeople do not submit call reports each week. Others phone orders to the factory rather than mailing the purchase order. These deficiencies also need correcting. Two salespeople show little concern for their personal appearance. You will ask them to wear suits when calling on customers.

Setting Up a Rating System

After you have decided what to appraise and developed some individual performance objectives and measurements, you must establish a meaningful rating system. Some companies use numbers 1 through 5 or 1 though 10; some use *poor, fair, expected, very good, excellent*; some use *poor, consis-*

tently below average, average, consistently above average, excellent; some use letter grades A,B,C,D,E with pluses and minuses; some use *strong, fair,* or *needs to improve;* some use arrows to show improvement or deterioration; some assign different activities different weights or importance; some use only *weak* and *strong* as ratings, or *exceeds standard* or *falls below standard.*

For example, one sales manager rates each salesperson's skills, knowledge, activities, characteristics, and results on the following basis:

Rating 1: Poor. Accomplishment
is significantly below
acceptable levels.

Rating 2: Fair. Performance is
close to but not yet at
an acceptable level.
Some improvement has
been made.

Rating 3: Expected. Performance
is at an acceptable
level, with accomplish-
ment very satisfactory.

Rating 4: Very good. Performance is above accept-
able level, and
accomplishment very
satisfactory.

Rating 5: Excellent. Performance
and accomplishments
are outstanding.

Each rating is accompanied by an arrow indicating whether there has been improvement or deterioration since the last evaluation. Each item on the evaluation sheet carries a weight indicating its importance: sales results carry a weight of 32, sales quality is weighted 16, selling skills, 9, knowledge 9, self-organization 5, paperwork 2, expenses 9, customer relations 7, company relations 2, and personal characteristics 9. These weightings total 100. Each item's weight is multiplied by the individual ratings, 1 to 5, to produce a number, which can then be added to the numbers for other items for a total evaluation. This evaluation form also contains room for written comments and plans for improving performance and objectives over the next ninety days.

In contrast, another sales manager rates each salesperson's performance for each activity only as strong or weak, with a note explaining next quarter's objectives and any necessary corrective action. Both sales managers consider their evaluation methods a successful and valuable tool.

Where possible, eliminate the middle ground from your ratings. For example, remove the word *average*. If you use numbers 1 through 5, remove 3. If you use numbers 1 through 10 remove 5 and 6. This eliminates the comfortable tendency to overuse middle ratings and forces you to make a judgment.

Select a rating system that is most appropriate for your particular sales organization—a rating system that accomplishes the desired results in the simplest, easiest, fairest way possible. Overly complicated rating systems prove hard to administer and understand.

Appraisal Interview

The ultimate effectiveness of the appraisal process depends on how you prepare for, organize, and conduct your appraisal interviews. Long before the interview, send each salesperson a copy of the appraisal form and fully explain the process. You may want to do this in a comprehensive memo, but you can also devote time at a sales meeting to this purpose. Include information on the goals, benefits, rating system, and interview, plus a copy of the evaluation form. Encourage questions so that your salespeople know what to expect and can express whatever concerns they may have. Remember, most salespeople have apprehensions concerning appraisals. Explain that your job involves helping the sales force to improve performance and that the appraisal form and interview assist in that task.

You should conduct performance reviews and evaluations four times a year. When you evaluate salespeople once a year, you are really evaluating only the last quarter. Quarterly evaluations allow you and the salesperson to set quarterly goals, which are more meaningful than annual goals. Quarterly evaluations take some of the emotion out of appraisals because the salesperson gets another chance in another three months; it thus becomes a helpful dialogue rather than a dreaded event, and salespeople don't feel you are using it as an excuse for reducing their compensation. Quarterly performance appraisals can significantly increase your sales force's productivity. If the sales force resides locally, conduct performance reviews at your office. If the sales force resides an airplane ride away, conduct the appraisal interview in your hotel room at the end of a field visit. Set appointments at least a week in advance. The meeting should last one to two hours.

Do not hold appraisal interviews at sales meetings or at compensation reviews. During a sales meeting you cannot devote the proper time to a performance review, and it detracts from the learning/social atmosphere necessary for a successful sales meeting. Combining them confuses and enervates participants.

Although appraisals certainly influence compensation decisions, the appraisal interview becomes too emotional if held as part of the compensation review. Salespeople may feel that the performance review is being used to justify lower compensation, and that attitude would make the appraisal much less effective.

Several weeks before the interview, send the salesperson a second copy of the appraisal form and ask him or her to use it as the basis for a self-evaluation. At the same time, you should start rating the salesperson for each item on the appraisal form, making written comments and noting any corrective action you feel is necessary and suggesting goals and objectives for the next ninety days. Do your homework. Don't wing it. Be prepared to discuss each topic. Review the past three quarterly appraisals for recurring problems, trends, and objectives.

Procedure

At the appraisal meeting, whether in your office or a hotel room, create a relaxed positive atmosphere. Don't accept phone calls, do offer coffee, and sit away from your desk in a comfortable chair. If you give your total attention to the salesperson and the evaluation, you add an element of importance and recognition to both.

After some small talk to set the salesperson at ease, review the reasons for the appraisal process and state what you hope to achieve. Restate the agenda. Pose broad opening questions. Stress the goal of mutually agreeing on guidelines, objectives, and action to improve future performance. Remind the salesperson that you are not here to complain about any substandard performance and that another appraisal will be held in ninety days.

Next and most important, review each section of the appraisal form, asking for his or her assessment and then giving yours. You will be surprised how often salespeople rate themselves lower than you do, admitting the need for improvement and help. This makes your job easier. The appraisal form thus becomes a basis or agenda for discussion; it provides a starting point for talking about the job (see Figure 9-2). Deal not only with results but with the knowledge, skills, activities, and personal characteristics that lead to results. Use "I" statements so that the salesperson knows you are expressing your opinion. Deal with issues, not personalities. When evaluating a friend, ask yourself: "Would the evaluation be similar if I did not like this person?"

Avoid the following pitfalls: Don't overemphasize one or two skills, activities, or results that could lead to an unbalanced evaluation of the person's overall contribution. Don't rely on impressions; rely on facts. Don't hold salespeople responsible for the impact of factors beyond their control. Don't compare one salesperson to another. Don't talk too much. Instead, listen to what salespeople need to work on. Restate what the person says to make sure you have understood it. Summarize points along the way to confirm agreement.

Explain your rating and justify it, using supportive feedback, but don't argue, complain, threaten, or lose your temper. Where appropriate, commend strong performance, good points, or improvement first before discussing weaknesses. Stressing the positive reduces defensiveness. However, never ignore unsatisfactory performance. Discuss the salesperson's ideas for improvement. Ask how you can be helpful. Develop trust. Be tactful, frank, and fair. Avoid negative words such as "fail," "neglect," "fault." Be specific, not general. Be flexible. Ask salespeople to discuss their reasons for poor performance. Encourage open-ended answers, not simply "yes" or "no."

If the techniques previously mentioned don't overcomes defensiveness, think about how the salesperson "feels" about the discussion. What is causing the defensiveness? Share your feelings, experiences, and personal information. Rephrase statements that become too emotional. Skip over sensitive areas of the evaluation and return to them later. Be empathetic to the salesperson's feelings and concerns. Usually appropriate doses of empathy, concern, recognition, praise, and understanding will correct defensiveness.

Most important, using the appraisal form, ratings, and discussion, agree on future objectives and obtain a commitment from the salesperson to a plan and a time frame for achieving these goals. The goals should correct weaknesses and build on strengths. Stress their benefits. The time frame should be long enough to achieve the desired goal, but short enough to maintain motivation. At the next quarterly appraisal you will discuss whether these objectives were met.

Close the interview with an upbeat, supportive summary of strengths, weaknesses, and goals. Ask, "Is there anything else you would like to discuss?" Then you and the employee sign the appraisal form, which makes it more of a mutual commitment.

For you the evaluation process is not only a means of communicating

(*Text continued on p. 269.*)

Figure 9-2. Sample quarterly performance evaluation form.

SALESPERSON: _____

DATE: _____

I. CUMULATIVE SALES RESULTS

PRODUCT LINE $GOAL $ACTUAL % OF GOAL $TO REACH GOAL $LAST YEAR

A _____

B _____

C _____

TOTALS

GOALS AND OBJECTIVES FOR THE NEXT 90 DAYS:

_____

_____

_____

II. MARKET PENETRATION

Number of active accounts at beginning of quarter ——

Number of new accounts added to account base ——

Number of accounts lost this quarter ——

Total number of accounts in territory ——

Total percentage increase of account base this quarter ——

GOALS AND OBJECTIVES FOR THE NEXT 90 DAYS:

_____

_____

_____

(Continued)

Figure 9-2. *(Continued.)*

III. PLANNING AND MONITORING SALES EFFORT

Requirements   Due   Received   % of Received

Itineraries

Call reports

GOALS AND OBJECTIVES FOR THE NEXT 90 DAYS:

IV. WORKING KNOWLEDGE

Product:	Exceeds standard Below standard	Programs:	Exceeds standard Below standard
Competition:	Exceeds standard Below standard	Prospects:	Exceeds standard Below standard
Market:	Exceeds standard Below standard	Pricing:	Exceeds standard Below standard
Competitive Advantage:	Exceeds standard Below standard	Company Policy:	Exceeds standard Below standard

GOALS AND OBJECTIVES FOR THE NEXT 90 DAYS:

V. PARTICIPATION

Sales Meetings:	Exceeds standard Below standard
Trade Shows:	Exceeds standard Below standard
Seminars/Setups:	Exceeds standard Below standard
Questionnaires:	Exceeds standard Below standard

GOALS AND OBJECTIVES FOR THE NEXT 90 DAYS:

_____

_____

_____

VI. PERSONAL CHARACTERISTICS

Appearance:	Exceeds standard Below standard
Attitude:	Exceeds standard Below standard
Flexibility	Exceeds standard Below standard
Self-organization:	Exceeds standard Below standard
Responsibility:	Exceeds standard Below standard
Follow-up:	Exceeds standard Below standard
Sense of urgency:	Exceeds standard Below standard
Enthusiasm:	Exceeds standard Below standard
Self-confidence:	Exceeds standard Below standard
Assertiveness:	Exceeds standard Below standard

(Continued)

Figure 9-2. *(Continued.)*

Drive to succeed:	Exceeds standard
	Below standard
Persistence:	Exceeds standard
	Below standard
Judgment:	Exceeds standard
	Below standard
Stability:	Exceeds standard
	Below standard
Dependability:	Exceeds standard
	Below standard
Imagination:	Exceeds standard
	Below standard
Initiative:	Exceeds standard
	Below standard

GOALS AND OBJECTIVES FOR THE NEXT 90 DAYS:

_____

_____

II. SALES ACTIVITIES   RATING

(1 = EXCELLENT, 2 = GOOD, 3 = FAIR, 4 = POOR)

Number of calls per day	1 2 3 4
Number of cold calls per week	1 2 3 4
Efficiency of geographical coverage	1 2 3 4
Coverage of all accounts	1 2 3 4

COVERAGE OF DIFFERENT TYPE CUSTOMERS   RATING

A. _____	1 2 3 4
B. _____	1 2 3 4
C. _____	1 2 3 4
D. _____	1 2 3 4
E. _____	1 2 3 4
F. _____	1 2 3 4
G. _____	1 2 3 4
H. _____	1 2 3 4

GOALS AND OBJECTIVES FOR THE NEXT 90 DAYS:

_____

_____

_____

VIII. SELLING SKILLS   RATING

Prospecting through inactive accounts   1 2 3 4
Knowledge of basics of selling   1 2 3 4
Overall usage of basics of selling   1 2 3 4

SPECIFICALLY:

  A. Introduction   1 2 3 4
  B. Presentation   1 2 3 4
  C. Closing   1 2 3 4

HANDLING OBJECTIONS: 1 2 3 4

SPECIFICALLY:

  A. Price increases   1 2 3 4
  B. Delivery problems   1 2 3 4
  C. Competition   1 2 3 4
  D. Soft retail sales   1 2 3 4

Usage of sales aids   1 2 3 4
Planning each day   1 2 3 4
Planning each sales call   1 2 3 4
Cold call closing percentages   1 2 3 4

GOALS AND OBJECTIVES FOR THE NEXT 90 DAYS:

_____

_____

_____

IX. CUSTOMER RELATIONS   RATING

Frequency of visits to A,B,C accounts   1 2 3 4
Service and assistance when answering complaints   1 2 3 4
Efficiency in handling complaints   1 2 3 4

GOALS AND OBJECTIVES FOR THE NEXT 90 DAYS:

_____

_____

_____

X. COMPANY RELATIONS   RATING

Understanding and usage of company policy   1 2 3 4
Pleasant relations with other company personnel 1 2 3 4

(Continued)

Figure 9-2.   *(Continued.)*

GOALS AND OBJECTIVES FOR THE NEXT 90 DAYS:

_____

_____

XI. SELF-ORGANIZATION   RATING

Time and territory management   1 2 3 4
Record/file keeping   1 2 3 4
Planning, setting goals and objectives   1 2 3 4
Keeping sales aids up to date and in good condition 1 2 3 4
Percent of time in office   1 2 3 4
Percent of time with customers   1 2 3 4

GOALS AND OBJECTIVES FOR THE NEXT 90 DAYS:

_____

_____

XII. PAPERWORK   RATING

TIMELY PREPARATION AND SUBMISSION OF THE FOLLOWING:

    A. Orders   1 2 3 4
    B. Daily activity sheets   1 2 3 4
    C. Weekly planners   1 2 3 4
    D. Credit applications   1 2 3 4

LEGIBLE HANDWRITING IN THE FOLLOWING:

    A. Order-writing   1 2 3 4
    B. Filling out dailies   1 2 3 4

UPDATING ACCOUNT FILES   1 2 3 4

GOALS AND OBJECTIVES FOR THE NEXT 90 DAYS:

_____

_____

I COMMIT TO THESE GOALS AND OBJECTIVES X_____
                                               Salesperson

                                        X_____
                                               Regional Manager

with salespeople but a way of controlling and motivating their behavior. In addition, you should use information gained from appraisals to improve training and update job descriptions. If you find most salespeople are not selling benefits, or are not calling on clusters of customers, or are not aware of competitive pricing, possibly your training program requires changing. If you find that most salespeople no longer service customers by counting stock or working with design engineers, possibly the job description requires a change.

Management by Objectives

Closely related to the evaluation process, but differing in emphasis, is management by objectives (MBO). The MBO concept calls on managers and their subordinates to jointly determine personal performance goals in terms of expected results. It requires that managers emphasize results rather than the activities, skills, knowledge, and personal characteristics that drive results. Although the evaluation process places heavy emphasis on results, such as annual sales, it places equally strong emphasis on the activities, characteristics, skills, and knowledge necessary to obtain those results.

Postappraisal Follow-up

Once the performance appraisal discussion has concluded, you should review any personal commitments you have made that require specific action. When and how will you do it? Also evaluate how effectively you conducted the session. Would you do it differently next time? What did you learn about the salesperson, the job, and yourself?

Be sure and follow up on whatever operational and developmental plans were agreed to. The entire appraisal process loses its impact without follow-up because the salesperson then assumes that no one really cares about his or her performance. Your follow-up in fact becomes the initial stage of your next appraisal.

A Successful Performance Appraisal

A Denver company employed three salespeople to sell oil and real-estate tax shelter investments. Once a quarter, the president, who also acted as sales manager, held appraisal interviews. Although he had daily contact with his salespeople, continually commented on their performance, and

suggested means of improving results, the quarterly appraisal process provided a more formal, comprehensive opportunity to review performance and set goals.

After offering coffee and once again explaining the evaluation process and its goals, he asked the salesperson how
she evaluated her dollar and unit sales volume. Susan replied, "I gave myself an excellent, a number five, because
last year my sales were 22 percent over quota, and for the
first quarter of this year 9 percent above quota." "I agree,"
replied Hal. "You have done a great job in surpassing your
total dollar quota, and I also rated you excellent, number five."
"Good," said Susan. "How about an increase in my bonus
and commission rate?" "We will discuss that at your compensation review in ninety days," replied Hal. "At this meeting I
want to discuss objectives for the next several quarters. What
sort of sales do you expect next quarter, Susan?" "At least a
10 percent increase," she replied. "Good" said Hal. "We will
discuss your sales plan and forecast in detail next month."

"How did you rate sales quality, Susan?" "I gave myself
another excellent, number five, for the same reasons we just
discussed," she replied. "How did you rate me?" "I rated you
number two, fair, because 80 percent of your sales are shallow gas projects and only 15 percent are real estate and 5
percent deep oil. Susan, do you present deep oil and real
estate ventures to prospects?" Susan answered, "I always
present shallow gas first because the cash return is faster.
Usually the prospect won't sit still long enough to listen to
another presentation on deep oil or real estate." Hal responded, "What if the prospect is more interested in a larger
tax write-off, which real estate makes possible, and less interested in a fast cash return from shallow gas? Assuming
you only have the prospect's attention for one presentation,
then presenting shallow oil first may lose a sale. Why not ask
prospects some questions to determine their tax shelter objectives, and then choose the appropriate program to present
first?" "I see your point," said Susan, "I'll try it." "Okay," replied Hal, "let's say that next quarter's objectives include a
30 percent increase in deep oil and real estate sales." "Fine,"
said Susan, "I'll start working on it today."

"How did you rate product knowledge, Susan?" "I gave
myself an average, number three." Hal responds, "You know

there is no number three, average, on the evaluation form." "I forgot, Hal. In that case, I rate myself number two, fair, because I am not confident in my knowledge of real estate and deep oil benefits. Maybe that's why I don't sell them." "Actually, Susan, I rated you four, very good, in product knowledge, but if you don't feel confident, I will give you more training literature today, and let's make some sales calls together this month." Susan replied, "That's fine, I will set up some appointments next week."

"How did you rate self-organization, Susan?" "I gave myself four, very good, because I keep great records." Hal responded, "In this area, I rated you fair, number two, because your call reports indicate a great deal of time spent traveling between prospects. Can you organize your week so that each day's appointments are closer together?" Susan angrily replied, "I see prospects when they can see me. If I travel a great deal between calls, that's not my fault. I deserve a very good, number four, on this rating." Hal calmly responds, "I will rate you a four on your next evaluation if you try to set appointments each day for one area of town. You suggest the appointment day to a prospect and then see if he or she will accept. Wouldn't that save you time and money?" Susan answers, "I guess it would. I'll try it this month and see if it works."

The evaluation interview lasted ninety minutes, and with the appraisal form setting the agenda all areas were discussed. As you can see, evaluation is a participatory process. Without the personal interchange of a meeting the process loses its usefulness.

10

Computers and the
Sales Effort

Whether your organization suffers from computer phobia or contains computer jocks, you must consider using computers to increase sales force productivity. Much of what we have discussed in previous chapters can be improved through computer-generated sales support systems. For example, computer-generated information gives salespeople immediate product, pricing, competitive and customer knowledge; faster hard copy communication to and from the home office; and the ability to do time and territory analysis and forecasting.

Most small-business managers avoid using computers in sales because of the expense, sales force resistance, training time required, small size of the sales force, fear of the unknown, or chronic inertia. But just as proper hiring, training, compensation, organization, time and territory management, motivation, communication and control, forecasts, budgets, and appraisals and evaluations of the sales force increase your probability of profitable growth, so does the use of computers. The use of computers in sales and sales management gives you a competitive advantage in the marketplace. Look at it as an opportunity, not as a problem. Computers are the most exciting advance in selling tools since the invention of the telephone. Used in combination with FAX machines and 800 numbers, results can be even more dramatic. In fact, recent surveys show that over a two-year payback period computers can increase sales force productivity 35 percent to 45 percent while also lowering selling costs.

Chapter 7 discussed the kind of information that flows to and from the sales force by way of route sheets, call reports, sales and expense reports, customer and product analysis, commission statements, orders, forecasts, budgets, phone calls, bulletins, and letters. Some of this information is computer-generated, some handwritten or typed and manually generated. Knowledge is power and time is a valuable resource. The use of computers by salespeople can reduce the time necessary to prepare, transmit, and receive these documents, and thus allow both management and its sales representatives to further refine the information and ensure its accuracy.

Salespeople complain that paperwork consumes 20 percent to 30 percent of their time, while management complains that salespeople spend less than 40 percent of their time with customers. Everything discussed in this book will help you to improve on those numbers, but sales force automation can create step-function improvements of a much greater magnitude.

Computers cannot sell products or services, they cannot smile, they cannot convert a salesperson's complacency into enthusiasm or convert a weak sales force into a strong one, but technology can give your sales force more quality time with customers. Information technology can give your small business a potent competitive advantage in the marketplace.

Sales management and selling are both processes. The selling process starts with creating demand, preselling, prospecting, and qualifying leads. It continues with an actual sales call that involves getting an appointment, using empathy to discover customer needs and problems, showing how the benefits and features of the product/service satisfy those needs and solve those problems, overcoming objections, and closing. Whether or not an order is written, each sales call requires follow-up work and preparation for the next visit. Computers help to integrate these elements so that they work together smoothly to ensure effective impact in the marketplace.

Successful small businesses focus on customers, quality, and human resources. The customer trend is toward placing smaller, more frequent orders so as to achieve greater inventory turnover; this requires successful vendors to provide a quick response. From apparel to bakery supplies and from giftware to pollution control equipment and aluminum ingots, users want products delivered closer to the time of use or, in the case of a retail customer, closer to the time of sale. To support this flow of products or services requires a flow of information. More customers require immediate, accurate, and detailed information from vendors concerning products/services, prices, orders, and delivery. Computers help provide that information, report on activities under way relating to the customer, give the customer comfort that obligations will be met, and ensure that order processing and production control are functioning properly. If each order requires a sales visit or a telephone call, then customer contact is more frequent, involves more information, and must be squeezed into less time to keep selling costs under control.

The use of computers in selling and sales management is being driven by these customer needs, but also by the availability of powerful low-cost microcomputers, desktop portables, laptops, and low-cost proven software programs. The use of telecommunication networks that transmit computer data at higher speeds and lower costs than voice messages further fuels sales force automation. The need for teleprospecting, telesales, and telemarketing also requires computer assistance.

Major Systems Applications

Now that you are committed to some action in developing an automated, computer-driven sales support system, let's discuss the tasks it can perform. It is wise to start with those applications that deliver the greatest customer benefits. Possibly you are already using computers for some of these functions. Now consider using them for additional functions. After all, in the 1990s you are no longer a pioneer in the use of computers for sales and sales management. You are just catching up. The objective of this chapter is to convince you of the benefits and many applications of computers in selling and sales management. Once you are automated, you will have to rely on in-house management information systems people, if available, and on software and hardware vendors for additional guidance and direction. A list of uses for computers in the sales function includes:

Order entry and processing	Account management
Checking order status	Analyzing customer requirements
Checking inventory	Telesales
Checking shipping status	Maintaining customer and pros-
Pricing and proposal preparation	pect files
Customer service	Sales analysis
Lead tracking and qualifying	Sales presentations
Telemarketing and teleprospecting	Direct customer support
Direct mail	Evaluating salespeople
Database management	Market research
Target marketing	Preparing forecasts
Time and territory management	Training
Planning and scheduling	Word processing
Expense reporting	Spreadsheet analysis
Call reports and route sheets	Electronic mail

Order Entry and Order Processing

Of the twenty-nine applications listed, most small companies average eight, with automated order entry the most common. Order entry is generally the first priority for computerization of sales functions because it drives customer billing, accounts receivable, inventory, and other general ledger accounting-related functions already on the computer.

A giftware importer with twenty commissioned field salespeople, five showrooms, 5,000 SKUs (stock keeping units), and 20,000 active accounts found that errors in order entry and lost orders were becoming a nightmare. As annual sales had risen from $2 million to $20 million, the company had expanded the number of people in its manual order entry department. The Christmas-oriented seasonality of the business and long lead time for importing compounded problems. For many years, billing, accounts receivable, inventory, and most other accounting functions had been prepared on the company computer.

Once order entry was added to the computerized functions, errors in addresses, product codes, shipping dates, terms, and arithmetic were virtually eliminated and orders no longer mysteriously disappeared in the warehouse. This initial program was so successful that each salesperson now enters orders directly from the field by using a laptop computer that is linked to the mainframe. The system not only improves speed and accuracy of order processing but provides information to sales personnel on availability of items, price changes, and shipping dates. Management, salespeople, and customers are all happier because the system has shortened lead time for importing, increased inventory turnover by reducing the order shipment cycle, and provided faster customer service.

Previously customers and salespeople had often called customer service to confirm shipping dates on seasonal merchandise. Accurate information was seldom available. Now each customer order and each item on the order can be tracked as to availability. If an item is not in stock, the quantity on order from overseas and the expected arrival date are shown. Soon this information will be available to field salespeople on their computers.

A local bakery supplies distributor with 2,000 SKUs, ranging from flour and butter to mixes, toppings, and fillings, employs five salespeople to service 1,000 bakery, grocery store, hotel, and restaurant customers. This distributor promises shipment within twenty-four hours of order receipt. If the order is received by 2:00 P.M., it will be shipped the next morning. The route sales/service person enters the customer's inventory of cookie batter, frozen brownie mix, and lemon meringue pie filling on a laptop computer that creates a complete reorder for all products and suggests related ones not currently carried. The salesperson can now make twenty calls in a ten-hour day, almost double her previous number of twelve. Bakery supplies is a very competitive industry, but this computer-generated twenty-four-hour delivery program allows this distributor to obtain a premium price.

A local commercial yarn and thread distributor who must ship within twenty-four hours of order receipt used to have his salespeople phone in orders each afternoon. From 2:00 P.M. to 5:00 P.M., five customer service people were needed to process orders. From 8:00 A.M. until 2:00 P.M. only two were needed. Recruiting three extra people for three hours was difficult and expensive. Now orders are entered from the field by means of a touchtone telephone that is connected to an order-processing system in the office. Using the touchtone, the salesperson calls the office, enters a password and ID number, and gives the order information. A synthesized voice then responds with the customer's credit status and the availability of the product. By computerizing, the company was able to eliminate the three part-time customer service representatives.

Telemarketing and Telesales

Both the giftware company and the bakery supply concern rely on tele-marketing to service small accounts. The giftware salespeople make four to five calls a day, and the bakery supply route salespeople fifteen to twenty. These numbers include reorders and prospecting for new accounts. Based on the amount of time devoted to the customer and the salesperson's com-mission and/or salary, the giftware company and its salespeople lose money on an order under $1,000. The bakery supply company and its route salespeople lose money on orders under $1,300. But if the sales/service expenses are reduced, these small customers and small orders then become important profit generators for both concerns. Telemarketing/telesales solves this problem and satisfies the need, and the smaller customer finds it an efficient way to order.

Both the giftware and bakery supply company also rely on telemar-keting to follow up on inactive accounts. For both, 25 percent of the cus-tomer base turns over annually. Any customer that has not purchased in eighteen months pops up on a monthly report along with the account history, telephone number, address, contact person, and salesperson. The telemarketer then calls the account with a list of questions as to why it has not purchased in eighteen months. Accounts that have gone out of busi-ness or have moved are purged from the database. Accounts that require follow-up are sent to the appropriate salesperson and tracked like any other prospect.

The use of telesales for taking orders, answering inquiries, and tracking inactive accounts requires a computerized sales support system to provide information quickly on pricing, inventory, and customer history.

A local waste disposal company with ten trucks and five salespeople uses telesales to contact customers once a month concerning service increases, size of containers, frequency of pick-up, and service problems. The assigned field salesperson contacts the account quarterly concerning contract updates, landfill regulations, and new services. Using telesales to make retention calls allows the salesperson more time for prospecting. To accomplish his job the telemarketer requires ready access at his work station to the customer's needs, credit standing, and history with the waste disposal company. The telemarketer also has information available on customer personnel, disposal pricing, container availability, and route scheduling.

Similarly, telemarketers/teleprospecters are used to qualify prospects and generate leads that field salespeople follow up on. The telemarketer calls restaurants, apartment complexes, retailers, and construction companies to find out their current needs for garbage disposal, their current hauler, if possible the price they are paying for the service, and when their contract expires. This informataion is fed to field salespeople via a computer-generated report and then followed up on by the salesperson and the computer.

Pricing

Salespeople offering a large variety of products or services with price discounts based on volume benefit from computer access when writing and pricing orders. An importer of Christmas trees and lights offered volume discounts based on the total number of units ordered and the date of order. The more a customer ordered and the earlier the order was placed, the greater the discount was. However, the discount varied by style of light and by style of tree. What at one time took salespeople an hour to calculate can now be accomplished in minutes with a computer program. Salespeople now leave the customer with a correctly priced order copy and with additional time free to make several more calls a day. Price changes used to be a nightmare. Now they are rolled out effortlessly by the computer program.

Portable computers are even used by universal life insurance salespeople to illustrate options and variables and to close a sale. Using a laptop, a tree-care company salesperson can quote prices for different packages of services on various numbers of trees. This image of professionalism in an unsophisticated industry helps to close sales.

As the clean air/acid rain legislation made its way through the maze of congressional committees and votes, coal-burning public utilities realized the need to significantly reduce sulphur and particulate emission in the 1990s. Deadlines and fines for violating emission standards greatly concerned top utility management. Suddenly the handful of companies that design and erect wet and dry scrubbers and electrostatic precipitators, which reduce sulphur emissions, were deluged with requests to bid on multimillion dollar projects. Previously, these companies had prepared a dozen bids and proposals each year by manually building component costs up to system costs. Now they had fifty bid requests that would have taken years to prepare. Fortunately, several systems suppliers had computerized initial pricing and bidding through the use of databases and models. Within weeks these companies were able to quote prices that became the first step in contract negotiations. Several tier bids were submitted showing alternative prices for systems with various features.

Lead Tracking and Qualifying

Marketing and sales productivity can be increased by establishing databases to qualify and track leads. A local pesticide service received hundreds of leads each month from sending out direct mail ads and running press releases, newspaper advertising, and radio spots. The company's growth depended on new business, and so 10 percent of each sales dollar was invested in generating leads from these sources.

These leads were then sent to the salesperson who covered the appropriate territory. Salespeople at first disregarded the leads, claiming that they were a waste of time and that cold calling produced better results.

To better utilize these expensive leads, the company took the following action. All leads were entered into a database according to established criteria. Leads were rejected from the database if they had been entered previously or were outside the service area. Each lead was coded according to zip code; industrial, commercial, or consumer type use; date of receipt; and the medium by which it was generated.

This is how the system works. A teleprospector next calls the lead to ask key questions concerning problems, needs, time frame, history, and decision maker. All this information is entered into the database. At this point, some leads are purged and some are sent to the sales manager, but most go to the appropriate field salesperson. At the same time, the computer produces a direct mail label and one of several letters following up on the phone call, which is sent along with appropriate sales literature to the prospect.

The computer ranks the leads using target account and ideal candidate criteria. Commercial accounts with more than a hundred employees are ranked above household prospects, and food-service companies are ranked above machine-tool companies.

The salesperson must call on the lead within two weeks and report on what transpired. This information is entered into the database along with the next required call date. Five days before that call date the computer automatically generates a contact reminder so that viable prospects are not ignored. Each salesperson receives a comprehensive list of all customers and prospects to be seen in the coming week along with vital background information for the call, the prospect/customer profile data. After the visit, the salesperson returns the call report to the home office, detailing the status of the account and any new information on needs, problems, competitors, time frame, and decision makers. The salesperson indicates why and when to follow up on the prospect. All this is entered into the database, and the computer automatically follows up on the account, reminding the salesperson a week before the next contact date.

The pesticide service company's sales are growing and its commission sales force is happy. Salespeople claim that this automated sales system allows them to manage 40 percent more prospects in the development stage. Management claims that it now knows what trade shows, advertising, and public relations sources produce both leads and sales.

Direct Mail

As the pesticide service firm grew so did its mailing list. It reached 25,000 names collected from customers, advertisements, purchased lists, public relations, trade shows, and direct mail. The mailing list was a valuable but costly asset to use. As the firm offered new expanded services, reaching customers and qualified prospects by mail became more important. By using selection criteria and coding names (by various industries, commercial type, uses, consumer demographics, purchasing potential, title, and location) the firm could use the computer to target mailings, which improved results, eliminated inappropriate names, and lowered costs. The computer was occasionally used to produce personalized direct mail cover letters. The data base required continual updating of addresses, titles, credit, and industry. Salespeople were asked to assist with this. Again all direct mail campaigns were tracked from response to order entry and results were organized by type of customer.

Time and Territory Management, Route Sheets, Call Reports

Salespeople spending more time in front of the customers and less time in front of the windshield maximizes company revenues in a territory and minimizes sales travel expenses. Many events are required to generate a sale. Each event, whether planning for an appointment or demonstrating the product or service's features, requires time and planning. Time and knowledge are a salesperson's most important resources. Computers can help salespeople efficiently plan their day and reduce the time necessary for record keeping. These functions are distinct from order entry and processing, telemarketing, and pricing, which are transaction-oriented.

A garbage disposal company asked each of its five salespeople to make fifteen calls a day, five on customers whose contracts were up for renewal, five retention calls to upgrade service on current customers, and five on prospects. It averaged five calls to close a prospect. Each salesperson handled 500 to 600 active accounts, and each territory contained thousands of prospects. Territories needed to be gridded and accounts worked in clusters to accomplish these call objectives. Salespeople submitted weekly route sheets and daily call reports to help organize themselves. The volume of material, however, became impossible to cope with.

Management automated call reports and route sheets by key punching certain information into a computer. Salespeople submitted lists of all their customers and prospects complete with addresses, account history, type and frequency of service, key competitors, key decision makers, monthly billing, call frequency, pricing, and contract expiration dates. Using this information and a software program, the computer generated daily route sheets for the salespeople with five contract renewal calls, five retention calls, and five prospect calls. All fifteen calls were clustered geographically and presented in route sequence.

These daily route sheets contained all the available information previously submitted on each customer and prospect, including the date of last visit and what had transpired. Attached to the route sheets were the appropriate computer-generated customer/prospect profile cards.

Each Friday the sales manager reviewed this information and gave salespeople the next week's itinerary. Often salespeople were unable to complete the calls because the customer/prospect was unavailable or because the salesperson was required to put out a fire in another area of the territory. These missed calls were made up later on swing days or when the salesperson was nearby on another call. The system was not perfect and always required personal judgment, but it did help salespeople to better organize their time and contained a great deal of useful information.

After each call salespeople recorded on the computer-generated route sheets when they had seen the account, what had happened, and any information relevant to further calls. This became their call report. For example, they might write, "suggested more frequent service or a larger container," "signed new contract," "owner on vacation until February," "competitor has offered prices 20 percent below ours," "restaurant about to be sold." This new information was reviewed by the sales manager and then key punched into the database, so that it would appear on the next route sheet. Salespeople received two copies of the daily route sheets, one of which they kept and one of which they returned to the office with comments.

Turnover of salespeople and customers in the garbage game is high. Customers and prospects are often shifted from one salesperson to another. With this automated system a new salesperson hits the deck running with a good customer database and an organized territory. This benefit alone has paid for the system. When account representation changes, letters introducing the new salesperson and appropriate mailing labels are generated by the computer. Management is now considering having salespeople input customer/prospect data with handheld computers or tape recorders. Management has already added car phones to save time and allow salespeople to quickly respond to unplanned events. Salespeople have stopped complaining about too much paperwork because these highly repetitive nonselling support tasks are now automated.

The sales manager has more accurate and timely information on which to evaluate and help salespeople. A sales manager can quickly obtain information on how many calls each salesperson makes, what type of establishments are being called on, what type of service is being offered, and how many calls it takes to close a sale.

A database and system similar to the one just described convinced a packaged meat processor, which sold corn beef, pastrami, and ham to delicatessens and grocery chains, to eliminate its broker/distributor network and sell directly to the retailer. The company's expenses and break-even point declined, and sales and profits increased.

Direct Customer Support

Most small businesses sell to and buy from large businesses. Many large retailers, manufacturers, and service customers require and benefit from direct access to vendor computer databases. Selling to large accounts involves establishing partnerships. Part of the partnership is the customer's ability to order and obtain pricing, product, and availability information without a salesperson. This is done by the customer's computer talking over telephone lines to your computer.

One small software company demonstrates its new programs with a diskette located at its main office but transmitted by phone lines to the prospect's computer terminal. The demonstration can take place in person or over the phone. This saves both the customer and the software company time and money.

Forecasting and Market Research

The information collected in the various databases described here can help you in forecasting sales and evaluating market potential. To forecast next year's sales you start by projecting into the future past and current trends by territory, product/service, and customer. You also prepare a list of target accounts with the probability of closing each. You look at changes in your customer bases. At major customers, what changes in purchasing personnel, decision makers, needs, problems, and economic factors might affect your business? What changes that your competitors might make in terms of pricing, promotion, products or services offered, and personnel might affect your future revenues? With automation, this information is in the database and can be coded by, and retrieved by, territory, customer, product, or competitor.

Similarly, this same data should help you estimate your total market size in terms of annual revenues and number of accounts, what percent each major segment represents, which are growing, and each competitor's share. For example, from the database described in this chapter, a neckwear manufacturer determined that annual sales of men's neckwear in Illinois, Wisconsin, and Indiana was approximately $40 million and growing annually at 7 percent. Forty percent of the market was sold through chain stores and mass merchants, 40 percent through department stores, and 20 percent through specialty stores. In total, there were 8,000 potential accounts. Rep ties accounted for 10 percent of the market, prints for 60 percent, and wovens for 20 percent. The neckwear manufacturer sold $1 million in these three states, its largest domestic competitor $4 million; another $4 million went to direct imports, and the remainder was divided among a hundred other neckwear firms. This information helped the neckwear sales manager prepare a sales plan.

Personal Applications

Field salespeople can use computers for word processing, spreadsheet analysis, database management, and electronic mail. With a computer, they can toss off follow-up letters to customers/prospects; analyze travel expenses or gross margin by customer; record buyers' birthdays by month; and instantly transmit hard copy from the field to the home office. Salespeople very much appreciate these features.

Implementing an Automated Sales Support System

As the sales manager of a small company contemplating a computer support system for the sales force, you should be thinking in terms of stages and the assistance of outside experts. To go about this you need to:

1. First establish service goals and objectives, deciding what problems the system can solve and what opportunities it offers. Then prioritize these and break them down into bite-size pieces.
2. Prepare a formal proposal with a detailed budget and time frame. Include initial investment and operating costs.
3. Decide what portion of the work will be done internally and what portion will be contracted out.
4. Test the proposed system with a pilot program, evaluate results, and make modifications.
5. Install the system for the entire sales force.

A committee should be established with responsibility for steps 1 through 5. The committee should include your company's chief operating officer, chief financial officer, the management information systems manager, the sales manager, and a representative from marketing, customer service, sales administration, and the sales force. In a very small company, this could be two people, the president and the sales manager. In larger companies it could be eight. Each member represents the people, needs, problems, and opportunities of a department. Each committee member should be assigned specific tasks. Be sure to survey the field salespeople to find out their priorities.

Goals and Objectives

Decide on the specific problems you wish to solve. These might be orders getting lost or containing incorrect information; the unprofitability of calling on smaller customers; salespeople refusing to follow up on leads generated by advertising; many sales mailings being returned; salespeople spending only 25 percent of their time with customers; or salespeople and customers ordering products that are out of stock or discontinued.

Decide on the specific opportunities available to increase sales force productivity and better serve customers. These might include increasing the number of quality calls per day from five to six; reducing the time between order receipt and shipping from seven days to five; reducing the customer service staff from five to four; allowing customers to get information immediately on availability and pricing directly from customer service, your computer, or your field salesperson; knowing how many leads and sales are generated by each ad; improving lead quality and closing ratios through telemarketing; and increasing direct mail responses.

Prioritize and rank the problems and opportunities. Which are the musts, which are the wants? Which are the easiest to accomplish, which the most difficult? Which will increase sales the most? Which will decrease costs the most? Which require the greatest investment and highest operating costs? Which can be done the quickest? What are the risks and rewards of each? In what order would you like to solve the problems and realize the opportunities?

Formal Proposal With Detailed Budget

Once you have established specific goals and objectives, find out what hardware, software, and human and financial resources are required to meet them. A formal proposal reflecting this must be approved by the committee. The formal proposal requires agreement on objectives, applications, estimated investment, operating costs, performance standards, a timetable of events, checkpoints, a pilot program, and how to evaluate benefits and results. The approved proposal provides the plan for implementing and developing the system. It should take advantage of information sharing and task coordination. Different salespeople have different problems and opportunities. Customer service looks through a different frame than order processing. You don't want four incompatible minisystems.

The detailed budget should include estimated costs for the initial investment in software, hardware, consultants, programming, installation, and training, as well as estimates for the annual operating/maintenance costs, which might include additional personnel. The budget process will force you to look for hidden costs and hard-to-quantify benefits. For instance, during the first two months after rollout, sales force productivity falls off as salespeople learn to use the system. You must consider the cost of a backup system or contingency plan or lost time when the system malfunctions. The budget process forces you to seek the advice of hardware and software vendors, consultants, and independent programmers.

Costs are so dependent on applications and on your current hardware—and are also decreasing so rapidly—that it is difficult to give guidelines. Every year personal computers and software can do much more for much less. However, a typical outlay per salesperson runs $6,000, sales management programs might total $20,000, and telemarketing another $20,000. Hardware costs for sales support systems vary widely depending on whether your company uses terminals, desktop computers, portable computers, or laptops. If you decide on portable units, not every salesperson needs one, but certainly the sales manager does. The current trend, especially for sales forces with under ten people, is toward the use of laptops and away from desktops.

The cost of laptops ranges from under $1,000 to over $7,000, with the median figure hovering around $3,000. After the first-year warranty, maintenance costs run about $350 per annum. Always buy a few more laptops than you need to replace machines out for repair. Also in the first year add $500 for supplies.

Software depends on applications and the number of terminals or salespeople, but will probably range from $12,000 to $50,000. You might figure on $1,000 per salesperson in year one and another $1,000 in year two.

Implementation costs will include both training costs for users and the cost of a consultant to advise you on the choice of software and hardware. Training will be $500 per user, and sales force automation consultants charge between $5,000 and $15,000 for the project.

After year one, software upgrades should cost $100 per user, insurance on the laptops also $100 per user, and maintenance, as mentioned previously, $350 per user. If you want your salespeople to communicate by electronic mail over telephone lines, that will cost $150 per user per year.

Estimating, quantifying the financial benefits of your automated sales system is extremely difficult. How much will improved sales force productivity or improved customer service increase sales? The more you use the system the more valuable it becomes. Three out of four companies employing under ten salespeople reported that sales force automation significantly improved productivity and increased sales.

Internal Development vs. Contracting Out

Your next major task is to decide what portion of the work will be done internally and what portion will be contracted out. In deciding whether to develop a system internally you must consider:

1. *The human resources.* Do you have capable systems designers and programmers available to write the software?
2. *The cost of time.* How much longer will it take to develop a system internally than to buy one on the outside? Multiply that estimate times 2 or 3. How important is time to this project?
3. *The cost and cash flow difference.* It may cost more to develop a system internally, but you are already employing the necessary system designers and programmers.
4. *Whether your people or an outside vendor would better understand the problems, needs, and opportunities of automating the sales function.* Sales/marketing and management information systems (MIS) people seldom speak the same language. Sales and marketing managers think about sales force productivity, while MIS people focus on technical considerations. You must decide who can work better with the sales force and then facilitate communication.
5. *Who will be responsible for monitoring and repairing the system when it malfunctions?*
6. *How to protect yourself should the vendor company fail.* Will the vendor make the source code in which the computer program is written available to you or place it in escrow?

Three-fourths of companies with operational sales support systems developed their systems in-house; the remainder bought turnkey systems. As outside vendors develop more experience in computerizing various selling functions, and as the cost of programs decreases, more firms will contract out the work. For a small company with limited human and financial resources, especially in MIS, using outside experts makes sense.

In the end you might split the responsibility. For example, you could use inside people to automate functions such as order entry, pricing, direct mail, and order processing, but use outside contractors for automating telemarketing, lead tracking, and time and territory management.

An acceptable turnkey system can save development time, create an operational system sooner, take advantage of the vendor's prior experience with similar installations, provide more reliable cost estimates, and avoid costly surprises. As more off-the-shelf systems become available, the likelihood increases of one meeting your needs with minimum modifications. Early in the software selection process obtain an evaluation copy of the program rather than a demonstration copy. Although free, demos are basically selling pieces. Evaluation copies, which you pay for, are full-blown versions of the product that allow you to gain hands-on experience.

Before contracting with an outside vendor for programming, systems modifications, hardware, or a turnkey system, check with previous users concerning:

1. *The experience and track record of the system and vendor.* What sort of expertise do they have in computers, data communications, and software technology? What expertise do they have in marketing and sales problems and opportunities? What specific experience do they have in your industry and your applications? How good were they in training the sales force on usage? How well did they overcome sales force resistance to implementation?

2. *The modifications of existing software that were necessary.* Does the database program have a full import/export capability that allows files to be converted to the necessary format?

3. *The package's final cost,* including hardware, software, communications, maintenance, and training.

Twice a year *Sales and Marketing Management* magazine publishes a list of software vendors by application. The index includes addresses, prices, and services. The purchase of software for sales automation applications is growing at 40 percent a year and now has an installation base of several billion dollars.

Your choice of software will determine your choice of hardware. Therefore, make the software decision first. Choosing hardware before software is like buying tires before you purchase a car.

Establishing a Pilot Program and Evaluating Results

Because launching a full-scale system is complex, expensive, and risky, most companies use pilot programs and test the results. Establishing a realistic pilot program requires many decisions. You must choose what functions to test, how long to test them (usually two to six months), what people to use in the test, and how to measure results. For a small company a ramp up or rollout strategy makes sense.

First choose representative salespeople, customer service people, and telemarketers to participate in the pilot program. Include people with computer phobia as well as people with computer proficiency. Start by automating one function at a time, but make sure that the test includes automating all proposed functions for a territory, region, product, person, or department so that you can evaluate the total system's complexities, problems, and effectiveness. Critical performance results and limitations may remain hidden unless the complexity and scale of the tests parallel the system's actual use.

You might choose to test lead tracking first just because it can show the greatest results and contains the least risk. You might then add time and territory management, telemarketing, direct mail, pricing, order entry, order processing, direct customer support, market research, and forecasting in that order. You must choose a territory, region, salesperson, product, customer service representative, telemarketer, or some combination to test the functions on. Make it user-friendly. Pilot programs should start with projects that produce the most benefits for salespeople, like lead tracking or pricing modules. You will have an easier time selling and training the entire marketing/sales organization on automation if these tests go well. The salespeople involved in testing the various automated functions at the bakery supply, giftware, apparel, and waste disposal companies enthusiastically sold it to their colleagues. Once the salespeople realized the system's benefits—less paperwork, fewer mistakes, more time with customers, better leads, and higher commission income—they endorsed it.

Test programs should bring problems to the surface, identify the modifications required, and conserve cash outlays. Possibly the database on direct mail needs to be sorted differently, or telemarketers require more information more quickly. The weekly route sheets don't take into account traffic patterns, or new accounts require a code for order entry. Possibly pricing must be done by total order size rather than by item quantity. Automating your sales force over two years rather than over two months also conserves cash by spreading out the capital outlays.

The exact results of pilot programs are often hard to measure. When establishing the test program, decide how you plan to measure results. Is proof of success faster order turn-around time, a better closing ratio, more time with customers, more new accounts, fewer pricing mistakes, lower cost per call, greater dollar sales per call, more calls per week, or some other criterion?

Installing the System for the Entire Work Force

As each application becomes debugged in the testing phase, roll it out to the entire sales force, or customer service representatives, or telemarketers. The rollout by function should also be in increments by person, territory, region, or product. That is, implement the successfully tested programs in stages. Make sure that one region or one salesperson is up and running before going to the next.

Develop a formal training program to assist salespeople, telemarketers, customer service representatives, and order processors in the proper use of the system. Make this computer program part of a new hire's initial training, add it to the job description, and include it as a topic at sales meetings. The training program requires classroom presentations, videos, exercises, a telephone hot line, users' guide, field training, and follow-up evaluation. Many worthwhile sales automation programs fail because of poor training.

During the long, complex process of designing, testing, and implementing an automated sales system, responsibilities and project accountability may become blurred. Every few months define or redefine who is responsible for what in the startup and continuing operation of this system.

As noted earlier, salespeople will resist this system because it invades their privacy, challenges their abilities and authority, quantifies an amorphous skill, causes concern about more administrative work, requires change, makes them feel insecure, and raises the fear of replacement. You overcome their resistance by selling the system's personal benefits. Successful systems boost salespeople's self-image, morale, and motivation. They are proud to be part of a forward-thinking organization. The sales force's use of computers enhances its credibility with customers.

To successfully implement an automated sales system, you must be willing not only to alter technology to accommodate the sales/marketing environment but also to alter your organization to fit the technology. If your salespeople work out of their homes far from any company office, you may have to use portable laptops rather than a shared terminal or micro at your sales office. If salespeople have never used call reports or route sheets, the time and territory program may ask for less participation on their part.

Don't delay. Postponing the automation of your sales and marketing functions is counterproductive. Your customers are demanding it, and these systems provide your firm and its sales force with a competitive advantage. Could you run your small business without a computer? Have you found the FAX machine, telemarketing, and car phones helpful? By automating more aspects of the sales function, your firm derives more benefits from the computer, FAX machine, telemarketing, and car phones.

If you look at automating certain sales force functions as a process with steps along the way, the task is much more manageable. The benefits are tremendous and by following the procedures suggested here risks are reduced. Marketing and sales costs generally represent from 18 percent to 25 percent of your sales dollars, which is probably more than your firm's direct labor costs. Over 75 percent of companies using computers for applications described in this chapter reported significant increases in sales force productivity.

11

Exporting

Two small software companies, a men's belt company, and a small specialty chemical company have one thing in common. In 1989 they all lost money and none of them sold overseas; in 1991, 40 percent of their revenue was generated by exports and all four companies showed a profit. One software company specializes in sales management functions, the other in databases for museum collections. The specialty chemical company followed its customers, who relocated in Europe. The belt company sold Western looks to Italian consumers. One software company does just under $1 million in business annually, the other just over $1 million. The specialty chemical company and the belt company each have annual shipments of $8 million.

Until several years ago, I suffered from export phobia. Now I have become an export enthusiast. Your potential export market is probably at least four times larger than your domestic market and growing. If you sell in New York, California, Florida, and Texas, why not sell in Canada, South America, Europe, and the Pacific Rim?

Recent studies by the U.S. Department of Commerce indicate that the growth in exports has been fueled by small to medium-size companies and that there are at least 25,000 U.S. companies not selling overseas but with export-worthy products/services. Only about 10 percent of eligible American companies export; yet one out of four exporters are companies employing under a hundred people, and 80 percent of U.S. exporters employ under five hundred people. The Census Bureau reports that 86,500 companies are infrequent exporters, averaging nine overseas shipments annually; 9,900 are growing exporters, averaging 116 overseas shipments annually; and 3,600 are frequent exporters, averaging 4,410 shipments annually. Among small companies contacted in a recent Small Business Administration survey, 56 percent of those involved in exporting said that their overseas sales had increased over the previous year, and 41 percent that export sales had grown faster than domestic sales.

If your small company is successfully selling a product or service in the U.S. market, and if similar needs exist overseas, you should investigate exporting. Needs also exist in Third World countries for older, less expensive, less sophisticated products/services that might be considered obsolete or inefficient by American standards. Here exporting can extend a product's life cycle and, with little additional cost, increase your company's profits.

Although the dollar's weakness makes exports more appealing, most American goods sold overseas, like goods sold domestically, are not bought strictly according to price. They are bought because the product's benefits solve a problem, satisfy a need. Value that includes many areas is more important than price.

However, exporting requires the same skills, analysis, planning, and commitment as selling domestically. Don't export just because you enjoy traveling. Do consider the following points:

• *Experience*. Have you received inquiries from overseas about exporting? Are you currently selling some products/services overseas? What products/services and which countries appear to generate the most interest? Are your actual export sales growing?

• *Competition*. Who is the competition overseas? How do they compare with your domestic competitors? What are the competitive advantages of your products/services' features/benefits in the various overseas markets?

• *Market/Product*. How can overseas customers be identified? Does your product/service need to be modified for export? What minimum quantities are required? Is overseas licensing or manufacturing a possibility? How does your quality compare with the quality available in the export markets? After you factor in transportation, duties, and export selling expenses, how does your final overseas selling price compare with that of the competition? Must your catalogs and brochures be translated into a foreign language?

• *Management, Personnel, Human Resources*. Who will be responsible for export sales? Does your company's management and support staff have the time or must additional people be hired? What effect will diverting human resources to exports have on domestic sales?

• *Financial Considerations.* How much capital is required? What is the expected annual profit for the next five years on best- and worst-case sales? How does this translate into return on investment? How does this compare with domestic opportunities? Is the potential reward worth the risk? What is or will be the annual operating expense budget for the export department? What credit terms will the market require and how will claims be dealt with? Does your company have the necessary financial resources to handle these additional demands?

• *Production/Service Capacity.* Does your company have the capacity and flexibility to satisfy overseas markets? What opportunities exist domestically for expanding sales? Do you have excess goods or seasonal lulls where exports could prove helpful? What would it cost to increase capacity? Will added sales volume from exports significantly lower production or overhead costs per unit?

It is also worth considering that through exporting your company might discover new product variations or a technology appropriate for the domestic market. Also by diversifying into other export markets you reduce the risks of U.S. business cycles.

Today we live in a global community with global markets. Rather than complain about imports why not investigate exporting? Markets in Asia, Europe, and Canada are all growing faster than those at home. Advances in FAX communications and the proliferation of international air freight services will help make your job easier. Importing requires time and patience, but it is an opportunity to greatly expand your markets for only a small increase in costs.

Market Research to Target Overseas Markets

You have decided that exporting is worthy of serious consideration. As with any domestic market, you must consider where the greatest need for your product/service is and where or if a competitive weakness exists. Which foreign markets have the best potential? You need to know market size, growth, trends, conditions, and practices along with your competitors' strengths and weaknesses. How can you determine this quickly and inexpensively? After all, you have a domestic sales organization to manage.

Contact the Department of Commerce (DOC) or your local library to obtain copies of the *Export Statistics Profiles (ESP)*. The *ESP* analyzes U.S. exports by industry for thirty-five countries on a product-by-product, country-by-country basis for the last five years. It also includes information on competition, growth, future trends, prospects, performance, and leading products.

If *ESP* does not cover your industry or the countries that represent your potential markets, consider using the Department of Commerce Custom Statistical Service. DOC will search its database to prepare a custom report on countries, products, and industries of interest to you. Data are available not only in dollars but in percentages, quantities, and unit values.

The U.S. Government Printing Office publishes a monthly *Foreign Trade Report,* FT410. The FT410 provides monthly statistics on shipments of all merchandise from the United States to foreign countries, including units (quantity) and dollar value by country.

The DOC publishes *International Market Research* (IMR) reports, which provide in-depth analyses for a particular industry in a particular country. *Country Market Surveys* (CMS) summarizes several *IMR*s by industry, highlighting market size, trends, and prospects. The DOC also publishes competitive assessments of certain industries in overseas markets.

Use this data to narrow your focus. What are the top ten export markets (countries) for your product/service? If Canada and Mexico are two of them, consider test marketing there through your own sales force. Can you cluster target markets to make distribution and travel more efficient? England and northern Europe might be one cluster, New Zealand and Australia another.

In ranking the top ten export markets, also consider currency fluctuations, possible product/service modifications, political and economic stability, language barriers, government barriers or regulations, present and future market growth, and competition. Once you have targeted and ranked the top ten markets (countries), obtain more detailed information on each. Visit an appropriate trade fair, talk to noncompetitive companies that export related products/services to the target markets. Analyze factors affecting the end use of your product/service. Identify any U.S. or foreign government incentives to promote exporting in your industry. If possible visit but certainly call the appropriate DOC country desk officer in Washington.

When you arrive at a short list, maybe five countries, do additional analyses of possible product modifications necessary because of the climate, electrical standards, shelf life, spoilage, packaging, sizing, or relabeling. Look more carefully at channels of distribution. Can you sell direct or do you need a middle person? Will your landed price be competitive? Are the legal systems and commercial practices compatible with ours? Is foreign exchange readily available? How are competitive products distributed, promoted, and sold?

Export and foreign market information and assistance are available not only from your local Department of Commerce but also from the U.S. and Foreign Commercial Service (US&FCS) offices abroad, its export counseling centers, market research divisions, and industry and country specialists. The Small Business Administration, trade associations, trade publications, the Department of Agriculture, and the Foreign Agricultural Service (FAS) can also provide assistance and information. Recently a dozen states have established export finance funds for small and midsize businesses. Many regional banks now offer private export financing. State governments that promote exports and banks that finance them can provide even more assistance and information.

The Export Trading Company (ETC) Act of 1982 has allowed banks and groups of U.S. companies to cooperate in their export efforts. Major corporations such as Sears, Roebuck and General Electric have ETCs. Many groups of smaller companies have also formed ETCs so as to share their export staffs, financing, and costs. The appropriate ETC can provide you with market data. Closely related to ETCs are Export Management Companies (EMCs), which also can provide useful information.

For an even more complete guide to assistance and information, buy the Department of Commerce's *A Basic Guide to Exporting*. Don't leave home without it. Other sources of market research (and their publishers) listed in this guide are: *Annual Worldwide Industry Reviews* (US&FCS), *Product Market Profiles* (US&FCS), *Comparison Shopping Service* (US&FCS), *Market Share Reports* (DOC), *Export Information System Data Reports* (SBA), *Directory of Market Research Reports, Studies, Surveys* (Information Clearinghouse), *Country Market Profiles* (US&FCS), *Country Trade Statistics* (US&FCS), *Foreign Economic Trends* (US&FCS), *Overseas Business Reports* (U.S. Government Printing Office), *Background Notes* (GPO), *Exporters Encyclopedia* (Dun's Marketing Services), *Statistical Yearbook* (United Nations), *World Population* (U.S. Bureau of the Census), *International Economic Indicators* (DOC), *International Financial Statistics* (International Monetary Fund), and the *World Bank Atlas* (World Bank Publications).

There is in fact as much market data available for overseas countries as for the United States. It takes time to locate and analyze the data. The time to do your market research is before you commit to an export program, not afterwards. Many small businesses complain that the information available through various U.S. government agencies is difficult to obtain, incomplete, outdated, and sometimes inaccurate. Dealing with the bureaucracy is frustrating, but generally valuable information is available if you know where to look.

Exporting Services

Domestically, services account for two-thirds of the gross national product and for over 70 percent of all small businesses. Today services constitute 25 percent of overall world trade. In 1987 the United States exported $185 billion worth of services, including $15 billion of professional and consulting services. So consider the possibility of exporting even if you are in a service business.

Our greatest service exports relate to knowledge and education, including construction, design, and engineering; teaching services; banking and financial services; insurance services; legal, accounting, and management consulting services; computer data processing and software services; franchising; and tourism. Because services are intangible they often require face-to-face selling by the principals. Generally, smaller U.S. service firms go overseas to provide services to an American client with foreign operations. Once there, however, they see similar needs and problems in local markets, make contacts, and expand their presence.

Because services sold overseas are difficult to finance through banks, the client and provider must negotiate down payments, progress payments, benchmarks, performance expectations, and time frames. You can obtain advice on payment techniques and leads for clients from the Office of Service Industries within the DOC. Other sources of client leads and assistance include the U.S. Agency for International Development (AID), the U.S. Trade and Development Program (TDP), the Export-Import Bank, Commercial News USA, New Product Information Search (NPIS), and International Market Search.

Finding and Establishing Channels of Distribution

You have decided the export market is worth exploring and through market research targeted the ten countries with the greatest potential. Now, as with any domestic market, you must choose the most appropriate form of distribution. You can sell direct from the United States, you can hire full-time salespeople in target markets, or you can use overseas sales representatives, agents, or distributors. You may wish to consider indirect distribution through one of the following channels: commission agents, export management companies (EMCs), export trading companies (ETCs), export agents, merchants, remarketers, piggyback arrangements, or state-controlled trading companies.

Your choice of a distribution channel depends on the nature of your product, the type of customer, your company's size and experience in exporting, and your available human and financial resources. But your choice of a distribution channel and your choice of a foreign representative can make or break your export program. Just as you do for domestic markets, you need to prepare a job description and candidate profile. What are you looking for, and what do you want that person or company to do? What are the anticipated duties, and what experience, knowledge, activities, and skills are needed for success?

Indirect Exporting

Indirect exporting involves using a second U.S. company as your sales organization. This company assumes responsibility for finding overseas buyers and for shipping the product or providing the service. Indirect marketing provides a way of penetrating foreign markets without becoming involved in the complexities and risks of exporting. Your choice among several kinds of intermediary companies depends on the services they offer and your company's and the customer's needs.

Export management companies (EMCs) and export trading companies (ETCs) act as the export department for several manufacturers of noncompetitive products. They may sell overseas under your company's name or under their own. They can be paid by commission (usually 10 percent or 15 percent), salary, retainer, draw, or some combination. Some larger EMCs and ETCs provide immediate payment by arranging financing or taking possession of the goods and reselling them. EMC/ETCs that take possession and resell to the final user want a price that's 15 percent below your domestic distributor price.

There are 4,000 EMCs and ETCs in the United States. Most are small and specialize in a particular industry or country. Using an EMC/ETC gives your company fast access to foreign markets because the distribution system is already in place. It also lowers your initial export expenses, gives you an opportunity to learn exporting, and provides you with immediate access to export expertise. Often your export needs can be serviced more effectively at less expense and risk by utilizing the international marketing and financial expertise of a specialized EMC/ETC. You gain the services of a bank, export sales representative, freight forwarder, shipping underwriter, and international business consultant from one resource.

EMCs and ETCs set your overseas prices, choose distribution and trade shows, formulate advertising and marketing strategy. The disadvantages of using EMCs and ETCs include loss of control, competition for their time from their other principals, forgoing customers who require to deal directly with you, and added costs, which may increase your prices. Essentially it is like using a domestic distributor. You may not even know who your overseas customers are.

You can find an interested and qualified EMC/ETC by asking the international department of your bank or Chamber of Commerce or the local DOC office. You could also advertise in the *Wall Street Journal, Journal of Commerce,* or your industry trade publication. The National Federation of Export Associations (NFEA), 1511 K Street, N.W., Washington, D.C. 20005 lists most EMCs/ETCs. DOC also publishes the *Partners in Export Trade Directory* (PET), which lists 4,500 banks, EMCs/ETCs, and other organizations involved in exports; a *Directory of Export Management Companies;* and a *Contact Facilitations Directory.*

In selecting an EMC/ETC, don't give too much weight to its geographic proximity to you in the United States. Pay more attention to its management, overseas customer list, distributor system, success with other companies like yours, other noncompetitive product lines handled, and available services offered. Ask for a list of its overseas customers, banks, and domestic clients that you may contact as references. Because EMCs/ETCs are generally highly leveraged, check their credit.

Send possible EMCs/ETCs a list of your major domestic customers and markets, catalogs of your products/services, and your results to date, if any, in export markets. Visit the office and meet the staff of two or three of them. Do they farm out freight-forwarding functions or do them in-house? What languages does the staff speak? How many agents do they have and where? What are their strengths and weaknesses?

One of the keys to working with EMCs/ETCs or any overseas representatives is a proper contract. A contract must express the spirit of clear and mutual interest. Have a lawyer with export experience draw up the document. Don't accept the EMC's/ETC's or overseas representative's boilerplate.

The agreement should cover term, causes for termination, territories, products/services, and if certain types of customers, such as post exchanges, are excluded. Include performance standards for you and the exporter, the domestic and export pricing system, payment terms, transfer of title, delivery commitments, marketing expenses, compensation, insurance, product liability, and arbitration. Terms generally run one to three years, with renewals based on performance.

Whatever form of overseas representation you choose requires your commitment to provide assistance. Overseas representatives require the same levels of training and management selling as domestic distributors.

Other indirect methods of exporting include commission agents, export agents, merchants, remarketers, piggyback arrangements, and state-controlled trading companies. Like the EMCs/ETCs, each of these types of distribution must be evaluated in terms of your companys capabilities, products/services, markets, and customers. These types of distribution are not mutually exclusive. Where appropriate, it makes sense to use several.

Commission agents/buying agents represent foreign companies wishing to purchase certain U.S. products/services. Just as U.S. companies use overseas agents to find the best suppliers (exporters), so do foreign firms wishing to import. These agents are paid by their foreign clients to find the best source of supply, the best, most reliable value. This category includes foreign government agencies or missions and state-controlled trading companies. Use the references mentioned earlier to locate these agents.

Export agents, merchants, or remarketers purchase products/services directly from you, packing and marking the products according to their own specifications. They then sell overseas through their distribution network, under their name, and assume all risks. You relinquish all control over pricing, customers, markets, advertising, and strategy.

In piggyback marketing, an appropriate overseas company sells your product/service along with its own. Many small U.S. software, publishing, apparel, and drug companies have overseas software, publishing, apparel, and drug companies carry their line. Here you have to find a foreign company that reaches your target market with complimentary products/services. Your products/services must fill a void in their line and be needed by their customers.

Some piggyback arrangements involve commission, others possession and stocking of the line. When doing your initial market research on each country, look for potential piggyback companies. Send them product/service literature to see if they are interested. You will need a contract similar to the one described for EMCs/ETCs.

Direct Exporting

As a direct exporter you select markets you wish to enter, choose the best channels of overseas distribution, bypass U.S. intermediaries such as EMCs, and deal directly with foreign sales representatives, agents, distributors, retailers, and end users. Direct exporting more closely parallels your domestic distribution.

The advantages of direct exporting for your company include more control over such areas as pricing, labeling, and distribution, greater profit margins, and closer ties to customers and markets. The disadvantages include a greater commitment of human and financial resources. Direct exporting costs more, but you can make more. You must decide whether the reward is worth the risk. Direct sales can accelerate your export sales volume in the long run, even though a well matched EMC/ETC may get faster initial results.

Exporting directly to foreign markets requires you to separate the management of exports from domestic sales. You must hire or train someone to manage the export business. Look for someone inside or outside the organization with strong marketing skills. Correct decisions on overseas target markets and distribution prove as important to export success as the product features. This person's responsibilities will include choosing and managing sales representatives, agents, and distributors and handling accounts you sell directly. Different distribution channels may be used for different markets or countries. You still have the option of using an overseas resident export manager for certain areas, for example, the Pacific Rim, and a New York consultant to assist with contacts in Europe.

Sales Representatives and Distributors

Overseas sales representatives receive a 3 percent to 15 percent commission for selling your product/service to customers in their market area. You ship direct to the customer, assume credit risks, and carry the inventory. You must hire, train, motivate, and evaluate foreign representatives using the same techniques described in this book for domestic reps. The rep handles complimentary local and imported products/services from other principals selling to the same target markets. Representatives have greater rights under foreign law concerning termination, so to avoid costly problems you should consult a local attorney.

Overseas distributors buy your product/service, clear the goods for import, and resell them. They assume credit responsibility and inventory risk. You sell to them at a discount from the suggested list price. Distributors handle many noncompetitive products/services and seldom pursue any of them aggressively.

Distributors are more appropriate for products/services with pull-through, such as brand names, proprietory designs, or those with established customer recognition. Distributors are more appropriate for products that require spare parts, follow-up services, or support and for low-ticket items with high inventory turnover.

Sales representatives will do missionary work and are more appropriate for breaking into a market where your offering needs pushing. Although it is expensive, some exporters find it necessary to use both sales representatives and distributors in the same market.

You locate foreign representatives by first researching secondary sources of information. Check with your American trade association, which may have requests from foreign representatives. *Trade Directory of the World* (Croner Publications) contains information on foreign sales organizations. The American Chamber of Commerce in the countries where you are seeking distribution can contact foreign industry associations for salespeople. Consider advertising for representation in overseas trade journals. There are DOC, FAS, and other government programs such as Agent/Distributor Service (ADS), matchmaker events, *World Traders Data Reports* (WTDR), *Foreign Trades Index* (FTI), and *Trade Opportunities Program* (TOP), which can help you locate and gather information on overseas representatives and distributors. The Agent/Distributor Service uses DOC offices overseas to conduct a search and identify up to six foreign companies interested in representing your product or service. FTI is a databank of 140,000 companies in 130 countries and includes sales representatives, distributors, retailers, and end users. The FTI is designed to produce lists of companies interested in representing or buying from American exporters. TOP is also a computerized information service that provides data on overseas agents and distributors.

Once you have a list of possible representatives/distributors, send out letters expressing your interest and describing your products/services and markets. Ask them to provide the following information in their replies:

1. A list of the industries/markets they call on
2. A list of their primary customers
3. Other products they sell and companies they represent
4. The number of salespeople employed and geographical areas covered
5. Facilities such as warehouses, offices, FAX and Telex machines
6. Banking and trade references, years in business, and names of principals

World Traders Data Reports can also provide you with much of this information.

Prepare a list of criteria for identifying the type of company that fits your company's export needs. This would be similar to the candidate profile you use in hiring domestic salespeople. Also prepare a job description for your foreign representative, listing anticipated duties.

When you get to the short candidate list, call the other companies the finalists represent and ask if they are satisfied. Specifically ask what the sales representative or distributor did to pioneer their product/service. Also seek background information on the principals. Check with the bank references provided and run credit reports from several sources. Your bank may be able to obtain credit information for you.

Provide overseas companies on the short list with full information about your company's history, facilities, resources, people, products/services, and previous export activity. Send them pertinent product literature.

The next step in deciding on an overseas representative is a personal meeting. If convenient and economical, visit the facility and meet the staff. If this is not practical, meet at a trade show or at your facility. You would not hire a domestic sales representative or distributor without a personal meeting. The same applies to overseas representation.

Be sure and sign a foreign sales agreement with your overseas representative or distributor even if you are starting on a trial basis. Use an attorney with a working knowledge of agency and commercial law in the countries involved. Consult the appropriate country desk in the International Economic Policy Section of the DOC and inquire about problems arising out of similar agreements in the specific country. Refer to the DOC publication *Foreign Business Practices,* which discusses agency/distributor termination laws in different countries.

Your foreign sales agreement should include:

1. An exact description of the product, service or product/service lines that are included and of those related lines that are excluded.
2. The exact boundaries of the territory.
3. A statement as to whether the arrangement is exclusive.
4. Conditions for termination, including representing competitive lines, not meeting specific performance standards, and nonpayment of invoices. Because they have more rights, it is much more difficult to terminate foreign representatives than domestic ones. Penalties are often imposed. Also, using conflicting lines as a basis for termination may violate antitrust laws.
5. The term of and conditions for renewal of the agreement, including minimum annual sales volume.

6. Commission rates, price or cost basis for commission, current dated price list for each item, and payment terms.
7. Confidentiality clauses.
8. A statement on the duty of overseas representatives or distributors to refer pertinent inquiries from outside their territory to you.
9. A list of duties and responsibilities for both parties.

Foreign Retailers and End Users

Some consumer goods companies sell directly to major retailers overseas, bypassing domestic and foreign intermediaries. Some business-to-business products are also sold directly to end users. This approach is appropriate if your product/service has a limited base of major easy-to-identify customers, if the product/service does not require a great deal of follow-up service or missionary selling, and if you offer a narrowly focused line. This direct approach creates more work for you, but builds direct relationships and saves the cost of commission or the distributor's discount. Many companies start out selling direct in response to overseas customer inquiries and then go to intermediaries when they want to expand distribution. Selling direct makes you responsible for shipping, customs, credit, collections, and service.

The direct approach requires you to contact prospects by mail, qualify them by phone, and then personally visit them. You might also encourage them to visit your U.S. facility. Exhibiting at international trade shows and participating in matchmaker programs are excellent ways of meeting prospects. Advertising in foreign trade journals with a return coupon or number to call is an excellent way to produce leads.

Names of potential customers and retailers for your mailing list can be found in the *Foreign Traders Index* (FTI), *Stores of the World Directory* (Newman Books Ltd., London), and the DOC publication *Great Stores of the World*. These reference books contain information on size, locations, management, merchandise offered, and type of business.

In selling direct, don't overlook the industry group trading offices of socialist countries. Also contact the Japan External Trade Organization (JETRO), whose job involves assisting American exporters in finding Japanese customers. It has offices in most major American cities, as do Sogo Shosba which are Japanese trading companies. There are nine major trading companies, including Mitsubishi, Marubeni, and Mitsui. Korea, Taiwan, Singapore, and Hong Kong also have major trading companies with offices in the United States.

Foreign Partners

You can profit from overseas markets with limited risks through licensing, franchising, contract manufacturing, or joint ventures. Don't overlook these possibilities. It allows you to eliminate the cost of duties and freight and possibly take advantage of a more efficient or less expensive labor pool.

To license or franchise you need a proprietary process, product, service, technology, or trademark. Many American apparel companies, for example, Jockey, license their names in Europe, and many European designs, for example, Yves Saint Laurent, license their names in the United States. American chemical and software companies license their proprietary technology around the world. Fast-food restaurants and retailers franchise their proven formula for success in many foreign countries.

Using the many sources already discussed, you can find licensees and franchisees. You should evaluate them in the same way you do other foreign representatives. Have a lawyer with overseas offices and an intimate knowledge of local laws draw up the necessary contracts. The agreements must give you control over quality, guarantee payments, protect you against pirating, and establish high enough minimums to reflect market potential.

You can also contract the manufacturing of products overseas for foreign markets, and then sell through local distributors or sales representatives. Your product must be capable of generating considerable volume to justify the economies of scale necessary for local manufacturing. Generally, you consider contract manufacturing after first establishing distribution and experiencing a successful sales history in a region.

Joint ventures are worth considering as an initial means of entering a region or market. Each partner contributes varying degrees of money, expertise, and knowledge, which reduces risks and increases the critical resources. Each draws from the other's strengths, which may include efficient manufacturing, technical expertise, brand recognition, marketing savvy, or effective distribution. If both partners are compatible, you may have the best of both worlds. Be sure and consult your accountant concerning tax advantages.

Product Modification and Selection

To successfully sell your product or service you may have to make modifications to conform with government regulations, geographic and climatic conditions, buyers' preference, or shipping, branding, labeling, and packaging requirements. In addition, you must select that portion of your line most appropriate for each overseas market. You would not offer wool over-the-calf hose in Saudi Arabia but would offer them in northern Europe. For Pacific Rim countries you must knit smaller socks than for Europe. In Eastern Canada all labels must be in French and English. Whatever the destination all socks would be shipped in bulk cartons to lower the freight cost. A men's belt company found that European men required larger wallets for larger bills.

Through potential customers and your channels of distribution, research the unique chacteristics of each target market or country. Choose those models and items that are best suited to satisfy the customer's needs. Seek out opportunities that create competitive advantages and isolate problems requiring modification. You might add several features to your software package that are not available overseas. You might modify the software to run on a popular European platform not used in the United States.

Enhance the product with service and quality. You seldom win on price in the export market. Is installation, training, maintenance, and quick response on spare parts critical for success? How will you provide this? Imported products raise concerns about service, defects, and return policies. Guarantees and service contracts can overcome these concerns.

What foreign government product specifications and regulations apply in each country? Are there health, environmental, electrical, energy, or measurement standards (metric) that must be met? Is space a problem, or high energy costs, or power outages? Do instructions or documentation need to be translated into another language? In Japan, tasteful packaging communicates a positive image; in Mexico, anything but utilitarian packaging is considered wasteful. Where illiteracy is high, use pictures. Third World countries might be most interested in the lower-priced portion of your product line, while highly industrialized nations might want the top models. Ask yourself whether the potential volume from a region is great enough to justify the costs of any product modifications?

Does your brand name have a meaning in another language that might be negative? Are you infringing on an existing trademark? Can you protect yours? You need to consult a local attorney for answers to these questions.

Creating a Demand, Reaching the Customer

Whatever channels of distribution you choose—EMC, ETC, export agents, remarketers, piggyback, sales representatives, distributors, or retailer/end user direct—you must create a demand for your unknown products or services. In joint ventures, licensing, and franchising, this is done for you.

Direct Mail

Direct mail to the target customers is the least expensive and most effective means of initially reaching your overseas market. Translate your product literature into the local language and include a covering letter introducing your company and local distributor. Be sure to include a return-address post card and local phone number. Consider buying a mailing list from a trade magazine or trade association, or possibly use your distributor's list. It is less expensive to have your distributor do the mailing locally and sometimes even the printing. For additional qualified names, consult importer directories, foreign visitor lists at appropriate domestic trade shows, visitor lists from overseas American pavilions, classified telephone directories in the foreign country, and associate foreign members of your U.S. trade association. Blytman International, Healdsburg, California, sells lists of overseas end users, retailers, wholesalers, representatives, and distributors by product/service category.

Also consult government publications such as *FTI* and *TOPS* for names of qualified leads. The DOC has an Export Mailing List Service (EMLS) that contains a database of manufacturers, agents, retailers, service firms, government agencies, and other end users. You can request on-line custom retrievals based on specified market criteria. Output is available on mailing labels, printouts, or computer tape. You can request trade lists of companies in a single country across all product categories or companies in a single industry across all countries. Information available includes names, addresses, cable and telephone numbers, name and title of a key official, products/services, and year established. The source is the DOC's world-wide database of foreign companies.

Media Advertising and Press Releases

Consider advertising in and sending press releases with pictures to appropriate foreign trade journals or domestic journals read overseas. You might consult *Trade Directories of the World*, published by Croner in Queens Village, N.Y. Share the ad cost with your overseas distributor or representative or domestic EMC/ETC. If you sell to a major retailer, discuss cooperative newspaper ads, catalogs, and statement stuffers.

Consider using an overseas advertising agency to assist in creating and placing ads. For names of agencies, consult the annual international issue of *Advertising Age* and the International Advertising Association in New York.

The DOC monthly publication *Commercial News USA* offers inexpensive ($150) display and editorial advertising. New U.S. products and services available for export are described and pictured in each issue along with the manufacturer's or provider's address. Then several times a year an entire issue is devoted to a single industry, its technology, products, services, and exporters. *Commercial News USA* is disseminated through 240 U.S. embassies around the world to 200,000 overseas business readers and through 96 consular posts to another 80,000 businesses.

Trade Fairs, Catalog Exhibitions, Trade Missions, and Matchmaker Events

Trade fairs include the domestic shows at which you exhibit and overseas events. Alert your salespeople at domestic trade shows to be on the lookout for foreign customers. Overseas customers attend, but we often neglect them. Contact the DOC to find out which domestic trade shows attract the greatest number of foreign buyers. The DOC promotes certain domestic trade shows for export through its newsletters *Commercial News USA* and *Business America*. Also the DOC foreign buyer program will provide you with translators for domestic trade shows and on-the-spot export counseling. A men's Western belt company met its major Italian export customer at an industry trade show in New York City.

Once you have decided on the target countries for exporting, find out where and when your industry holds its foreign trade fairs. Start out with regional fairs that address your target customers. Regional fairs are less expensive. Eventually you can move on to bigger events. Your local representative or distributor should share the cost, recommend the best fairs, and help man the booth. The local overseas trade publications and associations can also recommend appropriate fairs. If you do not have local representation, if you are selling direct, and you do not speak the language, hire a translator.

Contact the DOC to see what fairs will contain a US&FCS-managed American pavilion. These pavilions represent a low-cost opportunity to participate in overseas trade fairs.

Create an attractive booth that quickly tells your story. Signs and printed matter should be in the local language. Consider a continuous videotape in the local language explaining the benefits, features, and competitive advantages of your product/service. Try to set up dates with qualified prospects for immediately after the fair.

Foreign trade fairs are not only an efficient way to prospect for new customers but also a good way to find or test local sales representatives and distributors. In several days you can meet a lot of industry people and obtain a better understanding of the market. Potential buyers have an opportunity to see your product or service and to meet company representatives. Overseas trade fairs are "shop windows" where thousands of buyers and sellers can meet at their mutual convenience.

Several weeks before the show, mail out product literature with your booth number to attendees. Also send out press releases and pictures to the trade journals covering the fair. Volunteer to participate in workshops or seminars given at the fair. You will learn a great deal and receive free publicity.

Spend time touring the fair to obtain competitive knowledge. Who are your competitors? What are their competitive advantages?

Have business cards printed in English on one side and in the local language on the other. Include your FAX and telex numbers.

Plan on staying in the area after the show to follow up on prospects. Strike while the iron is hot and take advantage of your presence.

Catalog shows are a bargain-priced ($150–$300) international marketing tool. You may test product interest in foreign markets, develop sales leads, and locate agents or distributiors through catalog exhibitions sponsored by the DOC. These exhibitions are held at U.S. embassies or trade shows and contain a large number of U.S. product/service catalogs and videotapes. Catalog shows prove most appropriate for overseas markets in developing nations and hard-to-reach countries, that is, in places where the opportunity to see your product is rare. The DOC organizes a limited number each year for specific products in key foreign cities in a region. An industry spokesperson is chosen to attend and answer questions.

Trade missions and matchmaker events are planned visits by groups of industry participants to potential overseas customers. The DOC, state export development agencies, trade associations, and chambers of commerce sponsor and organize these trips. Each group generally contains five to twelve executives. Depending on your needs, appointments are made for you in the target countries with appropriate prospects, distributors, sales representatives, joint venture or licensing partners. You pay your own expenses in addition to a portion of the cost of organizing the visit ($4,000 to $7,000 total).

There are also U.S. seminar missions that promote an entire industry, such as medical waste management or museum collection management software. These missions concentrate on concepts and systems rather than an individual companies' competitive advantages. They address the particular needs of the host country and of the target industries.

Other Means of Reaching Customers

The Foreign Agricultural Service (FAS) administers export programs for the U.S. Department of Agriculture (USDA) through its marketing arm, Agricultural Information and Marketing Services (AIMS). AIMS helps American companies find foreign buyers of food and agricultural products. Their many programs parallel those described for the Department of Commerce.

U.S. banks with international departments and overseas correspondents can prove helpful in developing business. Many states, counties, chambers of commerce, and ports have export programs that parallel those described for DOC. These local programs avoid the immense bureaucracy of the federal government and often produce better results.

Pricing

You should price your product/service on a country-by-country, market-by-market basis to maximize dollars of profit. You charge what the market will bear based on competitive advantage, value to the customer, image, benefits, type of product (staple, homogeneous versus specialty, heterogeneous), and type of customer (leader versus follower). The last area you must check to verify the soundness of the price is the cost and contribution margin for each product or model. Depending on your objectives, you may be willing to accept different contribution margins. If your export objective is closing out last year's models, you would accept a lower contribution margin than if you were offering the newest style or product. Generally the contribution margin is a product's net price less its direct variable costs such as factory labor, materials, commission, and shipping, that is, the dollar and percentage contribution to fixed expenses. You should establish a minimum acceptable contribution margin.

Proper pricing requires market research, which you should begin when making your initial decision on whether to export. The time to decide that your prices are not competitive is not after you have spent thousands of dollars developing distribution. You continue acquiring and refining market research information on pricing on a market-by-market, product-by-product basis as you select distributors, target customers, and attend trade shows.

Many export transactions, particularly first-time ones, begin with an inquiry from abroad followed by a request for a quotation or "pro forma" invoice. Once you choose an EMC/ETC, overseas distributor, sales representative, or other form of distribution, you must start quoting prices. Be precise in all elements of your quotation by including model, price, quantity, method of payment, and shipping terms.

Costs

Export costs include certain expenses not present in domestic sales such as export documentation and packaging, long-distance multicarrier shipping, ocean freight, exchange rate contracts, insurance, discounts, allowances, financing, and import duties. To arrive at a final cost to the retailer, consumer, or end user, you might have to add the distributor markup and/or retailer markup. To arrive at your final costs, you might also want to allocate certain export-related overhead expenses such as market research, credit checks, travel, telephone use, consultants, freight forwarders, product modifications, and special packaging.

As an exporter, you must understand packaging costs and the costs of alternative transportation. Proper packaging is critical to ease of handling, controlling transportation costs and reducing the amount of breakage, spoilage, and theft. Most overseas shipments are placed in standard carrier containers. Check with the appropriate carriers for the exact dimensions and weight limits so that you can determine how many cartons will fit in a container. When either the freight forwarder or the airline gives you a price per pound or kilogram, be sure to base your calculations on both weight and volume. The airline will charge you the higher of the two. Ocean freight rates are obtained from the shipping line or your freight forwarder. Again, these are based on weight or cube, whichever is higher.

Terms of Sale

Understanding the terms of an international business transaction can spell the difference between profit and loss on a particular sale. American companies often turn down profitable business because they misunderstand the terms. A complete list of important terms and their definitions is contained in *Incoterms 1980,* a booklet issued by ICC Publishing Corporation, Inc., 801 Second Avenue, New York 10017. ICC also publishes a *Guide to Incoterms.*

The following are a few of the more common terms:

• *CIF* (Cost, Insurance, Freight). Under this term, the seller quotes a price for goods including insurance, all transportation, and miscellaneous charges to the point of debarkation from the vessel or aircraft. If noted by proper code, certain transportation agents' commissions would be included.

• *C and F* (Cost and Freight named port of shipment). Under this term, the seller quotes a price for the goods that includes all transportation to the named point of debarkation. Transportation and insurance costs after that point are the buyer's responsibility.

• *FAS* (Free alongside a ship at named U.S. port of export). The seller assumes freight and insurance costs to dockside, including unloading and wharfing, but the buyer handles loading, ocean transportation, and insurance.

• *FOB* (Free on Board named port of shipment). The seller is responsible only for loading the goods onto a transportation vessel (ship, plane, truck) at a named point. The buyer is responsible for all other subsequent expenses. FOB can also be named inland point of origin, and port of exportation.

• *EX Works* (named point of origin, for example, your factory or warehouse). The buyer pays all freight and insurance costs. The seller provides the product packaged for export but has no cost obligations beyond this point.

Whenever possible, quote CIF because this meets the importer's need to know the cost delivered to a foreign port.

Exchange Rates

As the owner or manager of a small business, you will prefer payment in dollars, but this may not meet your customers' needs. When it is necessary to accept payment in a foreign currency, consult an international bank's foreign exchange department about hedging the currency risks through a financial contract. The bank sells the anticipated foreign receipts at the planned date of payment to offset any loss or gain in the exchange rate. The bank will quote you the cost of this service, which should be included in your price.

Pro Forma Invoices

Another way for smaller businesses to reduce export risks is by using pro forma invoices. Type the invoice on your letterhead or regular invoice form but clearly state that this is a pro forma.

Pro forma invoices (and, for that matter, quotations) should include: the customer's name and address; the customer's reference number and date of inquiry; a detailed description of the products or services involved, including model numbers, price of each item, gross and net shipping weights, cubic volume and dimensions packed for export; trade discounts; delivery point; terms of payment; insuring and shipping costs; total charges to be paid by the customer; and estimated shipping date and date of arrival at the overseas port. If a quotation, state that prices are subject to change without notice or that prices are good for a certain time period. The buyer receives and agrees to the pro forma invoice before you ship. This reduces the risk of errors and disagreement. If you export a service, the pro forma invoice becomes your service agreement.

Managing Export Risks

Many smaller companies neglect export markets because of the credit and transit risks involved. Often they are neglecting profitable business because they do not understand the techniques for controlling these risks. Accurate and timely credit reports along with export insurance and letters of credit help reduce these risks. If you export through an ETC/EMC or other third party, they accept these risks.

Use the same credit standards and sources for overseas customers as you do for domestic accounts. Check with the account's bank, call or write the other suppliers, ask for current financial statements, and run credit reports. The *World Trade Data Reports* (WTDR), prepared by DOC commercial offices abroad, contain information on a company's business activities, standing in the local business community, and credit worthiness. Dun and Bradstreet's international division provides credit reports on overseas companies similar to its domestic reports. FCIB-NACM, a trade association located at 520 Eighth Avenue, New York, provides special international credit reports and offers excellent seminars on international credit and collection.

Most nations have credit rating services like D & B. The largest in Europe is Graydon, which has an American subsidiary, Graydon America, at 71 West 23rd Street in New York. The FCIA publishes a guide to *Agencies Providing Foreign Credit Information.*

Accounts receivable due from overseas companies can and should be insured against loss by the Foreign Credit Insurance Association (FCIA), a service of the Export-Import Bank (Eximbank). Your bank may have a master policy, which can be used along with letters of credit. Most often you will have to buy this insurance. FCIA offers special policies for small and new exporters. The cost varies with the risk but averages 1 percent of the account receivable. You can purchase umbrella and customer-specific policies insuring 90 percent of the commercial risk (insolvency or default) and 100 percent of the political risk through your freight forwarder, state export agency, bank, or insurance agent, or direct from regional FCIA offices. This export insurance allows you to be more competitive with terms and to obtain less expensive bank financing for your export accounts receivable.

Open cargo policies insure all transit risks warehouse to warehouse, door to door. You can purchase such policies from an agent, but most small companies use their freight forwarder's policy.

Financing the Sale, Getting Paid

Just as with domestic sales, you are going to want your money in a hurry when your company sells overseas. However, customers prefer to delay payment as a means of financing for their business and look at payment terms as a competitive issue. If you export through a third party, they assume the collection responsibility, and they become your account receivable like any other domestic account. Financing overseas receivables and the mechanisms for collection can be expensive and should be included in costing a transaction.

Smaller companies whose export business is limited find it difficult to obtain financing. Look for a bank with an international department capable of profitably serving a company your size. There are only several hundred U.S. banks with international departments. Consider banks in other cities and states. If you have a choice, consider whether the bank has foreign branches or correspondents. Also compare charges for letters of credit, processing drafts, credit reports, and collecting payments. Find out what experience the bank has with U.S. and state government financing programs that support small business export transactions.

The Export-Import Bank (Eximbank) offers a small business credit program through your local bank on direct loans for capital and quasi-capital goods exports. The bank lends up to 85 percent of the export contract at a fixed interest rate on terms ranging from one to five years. Available dollars are limited and paperwork can prove overwhelming. The Small Business Administration also makes revolving line of credit loans on exports. This limited program is now being expanded and the paperwork burden reduced.

Through the Overseas Private Investment Corporation (OPIC), the federal government facilitates U.S. private investment in less developed nations. The Private Export Funding Corporation (PEFCO) lends to borrowers in foreign countries for the purchase of U.S. goods and services. The Foreign Agricultural Service (FAS) of the U.S. Department of Agriculture provides financing for agricultural exports through the Food for Peace program and the Commodity Credit Corporation.

The economic development agencies of most states provide loan and loan guarantee programs to small business exporters and their banks. Sometimes the state agency acts as an agent for an Eximbank program; at other times the programs are state-funded. The California Export Finance Office offers 85 percent loan guarantees to exporters and can process loans in fifteen days. XPORT, run by the New York/New Jersey Port Authority Trading Company, provides export loans and advice.

Methods of Payment

As in any domestic sale, cash in advance would be wonderful, but, except for sample purchases, seldom occurs. The next safest payment term is an irrevocable letter of credit, under which payment is guaranteed by one or several banks. If you cannot negotiate an irrevocable letter of credit, consider documentary collection.

Documentary collection against payment or acceptance is the international equivalent of COD. Under these terms (sight drafts), payment is after shipment but before the buyer receives the goods. Title does not pass to the buyer and the buyer does not receive the documents until payment is made to the collecting bank. Sometimes payment is made by a time draft collectible in thirty, sixty, or ninety days, which is financable. In either case, the cargo cannot be released until the original bill of lading or airway bill is properly endorsed by the buyer and surrendered to the carrier. Buyers still have the right to refuse shipment. Banks charge 1/4 percent to 1/2 percent of the receivable value for this service.

Documentary drafts and letters of credit involve banks acting as intermediaries to assure each party that the other has met its obligations. The banks check shipping and insurance forms to make sure that the conditions of sale have been met. One bank is located in the exporter's country, the other in the importer's country.

With letters of credit, you present documents to a U.S. bank proving that goods have been shipped in agreement with the purchase order terms. Based on this proof, the bank either pays you immediately or guarantees payment based on agreed-upon terms (thirty, sixty, ninety days). Letters of credit are similar to drafts but more secure. With an irrevocable letter of credit, the bank must pay even if your customer defaults. However, the bank will not pay an amount exceeding what the letter of credit states and will not pay if some term, the shipment date, for example, was not met. Carefully review letters of credit to make sure that you can exactly meet the conditions and that the terms are correctly stated. Documents that are not accurately signed or not dated properly can delay payments. Shipment of damaged goods also nullify letters of credit. It is to the exporter's advantage to keep the terms simple and without reference to other documents such as purchase orders, quotations, or pro formas.

A letter of credit containing requirements you cannot meet is worthless because extending it after expiration or amending terms is at the option of your customer. Some letters of credit allow for partial shipments; some give maximum and minimum quantities; and some give first and last dates for shipment. You want a letter of credit that is transferable so that you can sell it or borrow against it. Other common errors in dealing with letters of credit include the exporter presenting documents late, not having them legalized, not obtaining completed on-board bills of lading, not obtaining insurance coverage soon enough, or making a partial shipment.

As you can see, letters of credit are issued by a bank at the buyer's request but favor the seller. The issuing bank promises to pay a specified amount of money upon receipt of documents showing that the terms of sale, shipping date, insurance coverage, and so on have been met. Depending on the risk, banks charge 1/4 percent to 1/2 percent of a receivable for providing letters of credit.

Normally, bank fees for collection services are charged to the buyer and should be stated as such in your quotations or drafts. If you absorb the cost, add it to your price. As an exporter, you ask your customers to have their bank provide a letter of credit through your U.S. bank. The U.S. bank provides you with a copy of the letter of credit along with its letter of confirmation.

Letters of credit come in various forms: revocable versus irrevocable, confirmed versus advised, straight versus negotiated credit, signed versus usance. You want an irrevocable letter of credit, usually confirmed by an

American bank. This means that if the terms are met the American bank agrees to pay even if the buyer's foreign bank defaults. A straight letter of credit can be paid only by the issuing bank, whereas a negotiated letter can be presented at any bank. Signed letters of credit require immediate payment when conditions have been met; usance allows previously agreed to extended terms such as thirty, sixty, or ninety days.

With well-established overseas customers who have a good credit rating you might ship on open account, as you would domestically. With a new account that has a good credit rating, you might ask for a 50 percent payment up front on the first few shipments.

Revolving letters of credit are helpful for export customers to whom you ship regularly. After each shipment the buyer replenishes the letter of credit up to a specified level. Standing letters of credit are used as backup for customers you ship to on open account. Should the customer not pay under the terms of your invoice, the letter of credit takes effect and the bank pays you. This is a form of credit insurance or performance bond and does not require all the detailed paperwork of an operating letter of credit.

Packing, Labeling and Documentation

Export shipping crates must take into account weight and the possibility of breakage, damage by moisture, and pilferage. Export shipments are often loaded in nets by cranes or down chutes, spend time near or on salt water, and are subject to stealing. Crates can come into violent contact with each other on the dock or in the ship's hole. Cargo may be loaded or unloaded in the rain. Use heavy enough moisture-resistant packing material and make sure that weight is evenly distributed. If possible, use pallets and consider strapping, seals, and shrink wrapping to prevent theft. Air shipments do not require as much protection as ocean shipments.

Specific markings and labels are used on export packages to meet shipping regulations, assure proper handling, conceal the identity of the contents, and help receivers identify shipments. You need to include the following markings on export shipments: shipper's mark, country of origin, weight, number of packages and size of case, handling marks, cautionary marks, port of entry, and whether the shipment contains hazardous materials. All appropriate marks should be given in pounds and kilograms, inches and centimeters, English and the language of the country of destination.

Many small companies decide against exporting directly because of

the documentation required. If you use an ETC/EMC or other intermediary, they do the documentation for you. If you export directly, use a
freight forwarder to help with documentation.

The accuracy and conformity of the shipping documents can determine whether you get paid on time and whether shipments clear customs
on arrival. The requirements for shipping documents vary depending on
the country of destination and the goods being shipped.

A shipper's export declaration (SED) is necessary for any shipment
requiring a validated export license or an export shipment valued in excess
of $500. The SED states the general or specific license involved, the quan-
tities shipped, the FOB value, and the destination. Except for U.S. territories, possessions, and Canada, all export items require a license. Many
items are automatically covered under a general license that you need not
apply for. However, for reasons of national security, short supply, or foreign policy compliance, certain goods require a license for each transaction.

A commercial invoice for export requires more information than a
domestic invoice does and is essential for customs clearance at destination.
It can be used by a foreign government to determine the true value of
goods for custom duty assessment. Like its domestic counterpart, the export invoice includes "sold to" and "shipped to" headings, order date,
purchase order number, shipping date, payment terms, description of the
goods, units, and total price. Unlike its domestic counterpart, the export
invoice must also include method of shipment, terms of sale, letter of
credit number, air waybill or steamship line voyage number, bill of lading, and container and seal number. The invoice must be free of errors
and corrections. The invoice must be signed below a statement similar to
"we certify that the above merchandise is in accordance with the buyer's
order, that it is of United States America origin and manufacture, and that
the invoice is true and correct in all particulars."

Export packing lists require more detail than domestic ones because
they are used by the shipper, forwarding agent, and customs officials to
verify weight, volume, and correct cargo. Include the packing list inside
the export carton or outside in a waterproof envelope marked "packing
list enclosed." The export packing list itemizes the material in each individual package, indicates the type of package, shows the weights and measurements of each package, and notes shipping marks, port city, shipper's
and customer's reference numbers, and letter of credit number.

Ocean bills of lading and air waybills are contracts between the owner
of the goods and the carrier. They are used as proof that the goods were
received by the carrier and, if marked clear on board, indicate that the

carrier has taken no exception to their condition. Some bills of lading are negotiable and can be used to transfer title.

If the terms of sale are CIF, you must provide an insurance certificate. Other documents occasionally required include a consular invoice, certificate of origin, inspection certificate, dock or warehouse receipt, and destination statement.

For a small company starting direct exporting, a good freight forwarder serves as an essential part of your staff. A freight forwarder acts as your agent in moving cargo overseas, consolidating shipments, and advising you on freight costs, port charges, consulor fees, documentation, insurance, licenses, price quotations, letters of credit, type of packing, commercial invoices, and packing lists. They insure that everything is in order for an export shipment and can reserve the necessary space for you on ocean vessels or airplanes. These agents are familiar with import and export rules and regulations, methods of shipping, and the documentation necessary for foreign trade. Virtually all export shippers depend on forwarders in varying degree

Freight forwarders receive a commission from the carriers they book and charge you for the services they perform. You should always check the freight rates quoted by the forwarder against what the competition charges.

Pick a freight forwarder with expertise in your particular areas of need, type of merchandise, and country of distribution. Check references from other small companies that use the forwarder. Some forwarders specialize in import work, others in consolidations and storage control. Check with the Federal Maritime Commission for a list of freight forwarders in your area.

Other Considerations

This chapter has provided you with an overview of exporting. Entire reference books with more detail have been written on this subject. These books include lists of useful government agencies with telephone numbers and addresses. You definitely need *A Basic Guide To Exporting* published by the U.S. Department of Commerce and you should consider purchasing *Exporting From Start to Finance*, published by Liberty House.

You will benefit internationally and domestically by also exploring certain broader strategic issues, such as matching your competitive advantages to market opportunities, developing proprietory means of creating value for customers, using information as a competitive advantage, think-

ing globally about products and markets yet understanding regional differences, sourcing globally, and knowing how to overcome the barriers to
domestic and international growth.

We live in a borderless, shrinking world with interlinked economies.
As a small business person you can benefit by understanding this new
order where performance standards for products/services reflect customer
needs in a global, rather than a domestic, marketplace.

Index